S0-BCO-073

THE MAKING OF THE MODERN CHILD

THE MAKING OF THE MODERN CHILD

CHILDREN'S LITERATURE AND CHILDHOOD IN THE LATE EIGHTEENTH CENTURY

ANDREW O'MALLEY

Routledge

New York   London

Published in 2003 by
Routledge
29 West 35th Street
New York, NY 10001
www.routledge-ny.com

Published in Great Britain by
Routledge
11 New Fetter Lane
London EC4P 4EE
www.routledge.co.uk

Routledge is an imprint of the Taylor & Francis Group.

Copyright © 2003 by Taylor & Francis Books, Inc.

Printed in the United States of America on acid-free paper.
10 9 8 7 6 5 4 3 2

All rights reserved. No part of this book may be reprinted or reproduced or utilized in any form or by any electronic, mechanical or other means, now known or hereafter invented, including photocopying and recording or in any information storage or retrieval system, without permission in writing from the publisher.

Library of Congress Cataloging-in-Publication Data

O'Malley, Andrew, 1968–
      The making of the modern child : children's literature
and childhood in the late eighteenth century / by Andrew O'Malley.
         p.   cm.—(Children's literature and culture : 28)
      Includes bibliographical references and index.
      ISBN 0-415-94299-3 (alk. paper)
      1. Children's literature, English—History and criticism.   2. English
literature—18th century—History and criticism.   3. Children—Books and
reading—Great Britain—History—18th century.   4. Children—Great
Britain—History—18th century.   I. Title.   II. Series.

PR990.043   2003
820.8′09282′09033—dc21   2003006065

Contents

Acknowledgments

I have received help and support from a number of sources, and would like to express my gratitude to: Jo-Ann Wallace and Isobel Grundy for all their guidance and assistance; Leslie Cormack, Patricia Demers, Gary Kelly, David Miall, and Anne Shteir for their insights and comments on my work; Leslie McGrath and the kind people at the Osborne Collection of Early Children's Books in Toronto for their help in locating materials over the years and for the photographs used in this book; Clive Hunt and the Special Collections staff at the Bodleian Library for helping me find my way around the Opie and John Johnson Collections; the staff of the University of Toronto Thomas Fisher Rare Book Library for assistance and photographic services; David Connor for his assistance in preparing the manuscript. I thank my parents, Brian and Anneliese, and my sister Nadine for their continued love and support. Most importantly, I thank Nima Naghibi for all the love she has given me, for her patience, and for her thoughtful criticism of my work.

Series Editor's Foreword

JACK ZIPES

Dedicated to furthering original research in children's literature and culture, the Children's Literature and Culture series includes monographs on individual authors and illustrators, historical examinations of different periods, literary analyses of genres, and comparative studies on literature and the mass media. The series is international in scope and is intended to encourage innovative research in children's literature with a focus on interdisciplinary methodology.

Children's literature and culture are understood in the broadest sense of the term children to encompass the period of childhood up through adolescence. Owing to the fact that the notion of childhood has changed so much since the origination of children's literature, this Routledge series is particularly concerned with transformations in children's culture and how they have affected the representation and socialization of children. While the emphasis of the series is on children's literature, all types of studies that deal with children's radio, film, television, and art are included in an endeavor to grasp the aesthetics and values of children's culture. Not only have there been momentous changes in children's culture in the last fifty years, but there have been radical shifts in the scholarship that deals with these changes. In this regard, the goal of the Children's Literature and Culture series is to enhance research in this field and, at the same time, point to new directions that bring together the best scholarly work throughout the world.

Introduction

The English Middle Classes of the Late Eighteenth Century and the Impetus for Pedagogical Reform

A market for a variety of literatures specifically designed to cater to the pedagogical needs of children emerged in the second half of the eighteenth century out of a complex nexus of historical, economic, social and cultural factors unique to this period in England. The onset of the industrial revolution, the democratic revolutions in America and France, and the rationalization of the sciences and of medical practices ushered in radical changes to class relations and led to the formation of new subject categories, among them the modern child. Instrumental in these developments were the middle classes who generated the vast majority of the pedagogical and pediatric literature, as well as the children's books proper, which defined the child-subject and situated it within a changing set of discourses.

The category "middle class" can mean quite different things to different people. Because it is a term that is central to the arguments that follow, it is worth making, at this point, a few preliminary clarifications and qualifications (more will follow later). I am seeking to describe the middle classes as they stood and understood themselves in the late eighteenth century. The origins of a middle-class culture lie, as is widely accepted, in the merchant classes of the sixteenth and seventeenth centuries. Asa Briggs, for example, remarks: "the merchant classes may have been particularly inclined towards the adoption of Puritan values, to 'inveigling against idleness,' for instance, and to believing in their occupations as divine 'callings,' and some, at least, of them had long shown that they had little patience for hierarchy in Church or in State."[1] Merchants of the sixteenth and seventeenth centuries, however, cannot truly be accorded the status of a "class" in the same sense as the middling ranks of the late eighteenth century. Their numbers were small, and while they occupied an economic position in between the minute aristocracy and the vast plebeian orders, they were still, at this stage, not an ideologically distinct group. It is the

1

alignment along ideological lines of the often not obviously connected groups of people in the middle of the class structure that constitutes, in my mind, a true middle class. The middling sorts of merchants, prosperous farmers, professionals, and so on, of the late seventeenth and earlier eighteenth centuries still fit, albeit with increasing difficulty, into the traditional hierarchy and patronage arrangements against which the middle classes of the late eighteenth century sought to define themselves.

In order to understand how and why the middle classes shaped the category of childhood in the late eighteenth century, some comments on who this highly diverse and stratified group was and what it was trying, more broadly, to accomplish in English society are necessary. Within the middle ranks of English society in this period there are arguably more points of difference and opposition than of similarity. The middle classes included members of both rural and urban communities, Whigs and Tories, radical Dissenters and conservative adherents to the Church of England, and people who earned their living as professionals, as merchants and as farmers.

Mitzi Myers has very usefully remarked, however, that to focus on the divisions within the ranks of the middle classes on such points of political contention as the French Revolution is to draw attention away from their ideological cohesion and shared view of a reformed society: "[t]o downplay political hostilities and connect middle-class groups seldom considered together is to illuminate the pervasiveness and the ideological significance of reformist ethic as an agent of the class redistribution of moral authority necessary for fundamental social change."[2] The middle classes were unified by a desire to differentiate themselves from the classes above them (the upper classes, gentry, and aristocracy who subsisted by virtue of unearned privilege) and below them (the plebeian wage earners and agrarian laborers who subsisted day to day), and by a desire to reform what they saw as an increasingly corrupted society and political order. Ludmilla Jordanova rightly observes that defining itself against the classes above and below shaped not only middle-class identity, but child-rearing practices as well: "What justifies the term 'middle-class' is the way in which a position vis-à-vis children is defined in opposition to the rich on one hand and the poor on the other. Hostility to the overindulgence of the wealthy and the neglect and deprivation of the poor serves to clear a middle ground for the moderate, rational treatment of children."[3] How this "middle ground" was constructed and demarcated in the children's literature of the late eighteenth century is explored at greater length in chapter 2.

The desire for social reform reached across political divisions and was shared, not only by the antimonarchical republicans, but even by conservatives who favored the monarchy: "Many of those who deplored aristocratic vice and demanded a moral regeneration of society often retained quite conservative notions of how society should be organized, notions that stressed the appropriate reciprocities between ranks and the need for Christian stewardship, whether aristocratic or bourgeois."[4]

Reform sentiments were widespread in the middle classes; the extent of the reform envisioned was a matter of degree. Even Joseph Priestley, whose republican politics led "Church and King" mobs to destroy his house and laboratory in 1791, saw himself as ideologically aligned with the rest of the English middle classes. Jacobins, in Priestley's mind, were not "intimating a desire of any thing more than such an improvement of our own constitution, as all sober citizens, of every persuasion, have longed for."[5]

To some extent, middle-class culture in late eighteenth-century England can be described as an oppositional culture. Part of the cohesion that existed within the middle classes stems from a shared recognition of difference from the upper and lower classes, and the awareness that they did not fit into the traditional patrician-plebeian patronage arrangements that bound the upper and lower orders together. This view of the middle classes is not, however, universally held by historians of the eighteenth century. J. C. D. Clarke, for example, dismisses as misleading humanist (his term) historical accounts of a growing, distinct middle class defining itself against a traditional elite in the eighteenth century. He argues that the period did indeed see a broadening of economic opportunity, but that those who prospered from it were more prone to emulating the class behavior of the old elite than to forming a new class identity: "[i]f the landed and mercantile elites were specialized and distanced by function, they were still united in deferring to a common code of manners and values: that of the traditional elite."[6]

Emulation of the fashions and practices of one's class superiors was indeed widespread in eighteenth-century English society, as J. M. Golby and A. W. Perdue have shown.[7] The number of children's books warning their middle-class readers against emulation of the elite, while attacking the vices engendered by overindulgence and luxury, suggests, however, a growing discontent with the inherited privilege enjoyed by the upper classes. While the practice of deference may have lingered, representations in children's texts and elsewhere were pointing to an emerging, oppositional middle-class ideology.[8]

Isaac Kramnick has identified one of the defining ideological concerns of the middle classes (in this case the radical dissenting middle class) as a change in what he calls "the structuring metaphor of society."[9] The traditional system of patronage and deference with its stable hierarchy of linked social stations came under attack in the late eighteenth century from a radical bourgeoisie who envisioned life as a race in which success was determined not by inherited privilege but by ingenuity, application, and effort. Republican bourgeois ideology posited an egalitarian and individualistic society in which the person with the most talent and drive succeeded, and this success was aided by a diligent observation of such virtues as thrift, self-denial, industry, and, of course, education.

The discourse of democracy and egalitarian society espoused by eighteenth-century dissenters was, according to Kramnick, in part motivated by self-interest:

> The ideal of equality of opportunity and its rendition in the metaphor of life as a fairly run race was at its origins in the eighteenth century an effort to reduce inequality and perpetuate it. It was egalitarian at its birth because it lashed out at the exclusiveness of aristocratic privilege, but it sought to replace an aristocratic elite with a new elite albeit one based more broadly on talent and merit. Equality of opportunity is a theory not really of equality but of justified and morally acceptable inequality. What can legitimate a system in which some have more than others? Only that all have an equal opportunity to get more. (*Republican*, 14–15)

Gary Kelly has also pointed out the contradictions of middle-class egalitarian discourse and the theory of upward socioeconomic mobility through merit: "this economy of money and merit legitimized both social inequality and the social and hegemonic claims of the middle classes."[10] While the redress of the injustices of traditional privilege for the good of all of British society (including the aristocracy, decaying under the influence of its own luxury and vice) motivated egalitarian philosophy and the spirit of reform, it clearly favored those already subscribing to a middle-class ideology.[11]

In this period in England, political power was still monopolized by the aristocracy, and the beliefs and views of the middle classes, while spreading, were still only held by a minority of the population: "[t]hese were the views of people who knew that their values were not shared by the majority. Until such cultural patterns became more widely accepted, [they] thought of themselves as Christian warriors."[12] These beliefs and views, while not yet dominant or hegemonic, were still ideological, as they unified a group with similar class interests, despite the numerous and important differences, conflicts, and fractures within that group. They also legitimated the middle class's bid to become the dominant, central class in English society by stressing their perceived moral superiority, greater productivity, and progressiveness over the classes above and below them.

The concerted and widespread focus on education, religion, and the family at the heart of the middle classes' efforts to distinguish themselves from other classes was an ideological project; as Raymond Williams observes, "[t]he educational institutions are usually the main agencies of transmission of an effective dominant culture."[13] The middle classes may not have been dominant in the late eighteenth century—they would become so in the nineteenth century—but they recognized the importance of education, and more specifically of children, in the mobilization of their class goals.

John Locke's notion of the child's mind as *tabula rasa,* proposed in *Some Thoughts Concerning Education* (1693), was, even more so than Rousseau's concept of the child as uncorrupted product of nature, at the core of pedagogical discourse in the late eighteenth century. This model served as more than a philosophical and psychological observation on the state of the infant brain and the mechanisms of knowledge acquisition; it helped underpin the ideology of equal opportunity. The mind of the child was similar to the "man in his natural state," described by Locke in his *Two Treatises of Government,* before hereditary privilege and monarchy had made the playing field uneven: "being furnished with like Faculties, sharing all in one Community of Nature, there cannot be supposed any *Subordination* among us."[14] Starting from a position of equality, unhindered by obstacles to their development, and, by the same token, unaided by unfair hereditary privilege and hierarchy, the children who would naturally succeed would be those who had received the best education and who, by dint of industrious application, had acquired the most useful skills and knowledge.[15] This conception of the infant mind as the site on which the aspirations of republican middle-class ideology could be realized explains in large part the dissenters' enormous focus on education. Dissenters from all walks of life participated in the development of a middle-class pedagogy—not only such professional pedagogues as Maria and Richard Lovell Edgeworth, but also such leading dissenting scientists as Joseph Priestley and Erasmus Darwin, and such dissenting industrialists as Josiah Wedgwood.

The concern for acquiring useful knowledge was, of course, not only manifested in the proliferation of educational works for children. Dissenters of the day organized themselves into countless scientific societies dedicated to the advancement of such fields as chemistry, agriculture, and industrial technology and to the publication of new scientific findings. Joseph Johnson, the prominent publisher and radical, published *The Analytical Review, or History of Literature, Domestic and Foreign, on an Enlarged Plan* from 1788 to 1798, a series that, perhaps more than any other, captured the spirit of human perfectibility of late Enlightenment thought. This truly encyclopedic journal, which boasted such celebrated contributors as Mary Wollstonecraft and William Godwin, was designed to catalog and critique the new scientific and literary knowledge of contemporary England.[16] Its mission was to cast an enlightened, rational, and objective light on all fields of human knowledge, in the process establishing itself as a social and cultural authority for a new age.

Rather than dictate taste and knowledge to the public "from above"— from a position of privilege—as other learned journals and critics did, *The Analytical Review* sought to provide the public with the tools to make an informed choice of reading materials. In his address "To the Public" at the beginning of the first volume, Johnson couches his condemnation of traditional literary critics in the rather charged language of despotism: "In many cases they have entirely lost sight of that modesty, which ought always to accompany him, who being a private individual, presumes to speak to the public at large, and have set themselves up as a kind of oracles, and distributing from their dark thrones, decisions to regulate the ideas and sentiments of the literary world."[17]

The monopoly of knowledge by a small, privileged community is as arbitrary and irrational as the archaic system of political authority founded on oracles and thrones to which Johnson alludes. While challenging a system of privilege at the level of textual authority and the dissemination of information, *The Analytical Review* also espoused dissenting republican political philosophy.[18]

As Kramnick observes, radical dissenters only made up around seven percent of the population of England in the late eighteenth century.[19] The explosion of interest in childhood, and especially in how best to instruct, manage, and improve children, was spread across the middle classes regardless of political or religious affiliation, and attracted the attention of members of both the upper and lower classes as well. J. H. Plumb's article "The New World of Children in Eighteenth-Century England" provides a useful index of the forms of educational and diversionary activities indicative of this new and widespread emphasis on children and their upbringing. Plumb argues that the virtues radical dissenters espoused to promote social reform and individual improvement—"sobriety, obedience, industry, thrift, benevolence and compassion"—were almost universally sought by middle-class parents by 1770, as they were ubiquitously touted in advertisements for both children's books and schools.[20] Further, the interest in industry and science, so prevalent in dissenting academies and societies, spread rapidly in the "new world of children." Children's toys (especially those designed for boys) reflected this: "there were complex mechanical toys—water mills, looms, miniature printing presses and so on, which could be assembled and made to work" (309–10). Indeed, Plumb asserts that middle-class parents were increasingly directing their children's play toward productive ends: "through most . . . amusements ran the theme of self-improvement and self-education" (308).

As Ludmilla Jordanova has pointed out, Plumb's essentially liberal humanist and progressivist historiography of childhood in the eighteenth century has some failings. Plumb's gloss of class and gender differences, and his implicit assertion that the changing attitudes toward childhood in the period constituted, by definition, improvements, are at the center of Jordanova's critique. Plumb paints a picture of eighteenth-century childhood that ignores, for example, "the ubiquity of child labour in the period," and "often generalizes on the basis of male experience, which encourages us to think about children and childhood as naturally unified categories."[21] In "Conceptualizing Childhood in the Eighteenth Century: The Problem of Child Labour," Jordanova suggests how such issues come to be glossed by historians: "that which is simply taken for granted, no matter how common, is least likely to be commented on by contemporaries, especially if it contributes to their well-being"(Jordanova, 1987a, 190). The history of childhood is, like that of any other subject, necessarily fragmented along such lines as class, gender, and race, even though the historical record overwhelmingly documents the experiences of privileged boys.

Plumb's desire to represent a unified history of progress and improvement in the lives of eighteenth-century children is perhaps informed by his own identification with the middle-class ideology characteristic of the age. His assertion that Locke's program of enlightened education in *Some Thoughts Concerning Education* marks a distinct improvement in "the lot of children in the eighteenth century" coincides with the very same humanistic and optimistic faith in perfectibility that characterizes enlightenment philosophy. In other words, it is not surprising that he finds "Locke's attitude to child-rearing . . . modern" (Jordanova, 1990, 67, 68). These attitudes stem from the very humanistic myth of progress to which Plumb himself subscribes: the rationalization of thought through reason leads to progress, which is by definition good.

Despite such difficulties with Plumb's research, he still presents persuasive evidence that changes were occurring in the ways in which parents from the middling ranks perceived their children and in the expectations they had of their young. Middle-class and lower middle-class parents recognized the opportunities industrial and commercial expansion offered, and sought in unprecedented numbers to secure a practical education for their sons.[22] Further, the fact that the virtues and values Kramnick associates with the radical middle classes were being espoused by evangelical and politically conservative pedagogues and children's writers suggests an ideological agreement at the level of how children should be raised that managed to supersede religious and political differences.[23]

In *Family Fortunes,* Leonore Davidoff and Catherine Hall suggest a number of points of agreement that helped provide some unity within the middle classes. In large part, the middle classes emerged in reaction to aristocratic excesses in the eighteenth century: "In particular, aristocratic disdain for sordid money matters, their casual attitude to debt and addiction to gambling, which had amounted to a mania in some late eighteenth-century circles, were anathema to the middling ranks whose very existence depended on the establishment of creditworthiness and avoidance of financial embarrassment" (Davidoff and Hall, 21).

Joseph Priestley was one of many to observe that those in the upper classes who were lax in their repayment of debt were shirking both their fiscal and moral responsibilities to the hard-working middle classes: "Another thing to be particularly attended to in the education of persons of large fortunes is the moral obligation, as well as the personal advantage, of the *punctual and timely payment of all debts,* particularly those that may be due to tradesmen, who, being really honest, and therefore not making an exhorbitant [sic] profit, cannot afford to give long credit."[24]

The mother in Mary Wiseman's *A Letter from a Lady to her Daughter, on the Manner of Passing Sunday Rationally and Agreeably* emphasizes to her daughter "how very necessary speedy payment is to the good of society in general."[25] Late payment of the milliner can throw the whole economic system off kilter: "they do not consider that till *they* pay *her* she cannot pay for the materials she is to make up; *her* tradesman waits for her money to pay a second; he is unable to pay a third; till at last the wretched weaver wants that bread for himself and children" (20, her emphasis).

Asa Briggs adds to this a shared grievance over the unequal degree of taxation endured by the middle classes, especially in the distribution of the burdens of the Napoleonic wars in the early nineteenth century. This recognition of common grievance led to an understanding of the middle ranks as the most productive classes, and of "the special role of the middle classes in society as a strategic and 'progressive' group."[26] The necessity of avoiding the vices of the privileged classes, and in turn of inculcating the virtues of industry, thrift, sobriety, and so on, were shared by the middle classes not only because they helped bring economic success in the changing marketplace of the industrial revolution, but because they could also help assure economic survival. The middle classes often lived in a world "of uncertainty, arising not only from shifting economic fortunes but also from the depredations of illness and accident" against which the development of regular work habits and the avoidance of vice provided a strong defense (Davidoff and Hall, 22). Plebeians certainly endured even greater uncertainty, and had much different means of coping with it. Hans Blumenberg describes the plebeian awareness that any day could bring such potentially fatal catastrophes as famine, drought, war, or disease as living with a constant sense of the "absolutism of reality." In response to this lack of control over their circumstances, many plebeians adopted what the middle classes bemoaned as profligate attitudes to work, domestic economy, and consumption, what Gary Kelly has called a "lottery mentality." This was the mechanism by which many plebeians traditionally rationalized, accepted, and endured the hardships and misfortunes of an uncertain economic future.[27] For the middle classes, the mentality of investment in the future through hard work and self-denial became a more rational and desirable defense (in their minds and experience) against possible misfortune.

Equally important to the evolution of a middle-class identity in the period was a shared perception of cultural, and in many cases moral, difference from the classes below. The most visible expression of this difference came in the form of middle-class efforts to reform plebeian work habits and prodigality—such cultural practices as the celebration of traditional feast days, as well as the customary and state sponsored mechanisms of charity—which helped, in their view, to perpetuate plebeian vices. Reform came from various segments of the middle classes, including such radicals as Joseph Priestley and such conservatives as Sarah Trimmer. Priestley, for example, described a plebeian class both plagued by and paradoxically rewarded for idleness by the current poor laws: "the prodigious number of the ignorant, the profligate, and the profane parts of the lower orders of the community, whom the impolicy of our poor laws chiefly, has rendered utterly averse to labour and economy, to a degree far below that of any of the brute creation" (cited in Kramnick 1990, 59). He, along with such dissenting industrialists as Josiah Wedgwood and Matthew Boulton, opposed a state-sponsored charity that relied on tax revenues garnered chiefly from the middle classes. Instead, charity and the relief of the poor should be left in the hands of the (presumably middle-class) individual: "the deserving poor should, if need be, be taken care of by 'the charity of the well disposed'" (Kramnick, 1990, 55). Although her political conservatism would prevent her from advocating the dismantling of the state's charitable apparatus, Sarah Trimmer's participation in the Sunday School program represents an important development in middle-class, privately-sponsored charity. In *The Œconomy of Charity* (1787), she celebrates the prospect of a reform of plebeian ignorance and vice through the union of publicly- and privately-funded charity schools: "[b]ut thanks to divine Providence! a *happy revolution* has begun among us; and we may now hope to see public charity going hand in hand with private benefice."[28] In both cases reform of the lower orders had similar objectives: "to civilize, domesticate and edify the working man,"[29] and to provide "modest, discreet, trusty," and productive servants and workers (Trimmer, *Œconomy,* 28). On the subject of plebeian reform, the middle-class ideologies of utility and moral improvement shared a common ground.

Part of the agenda for reform focused on an inculcation in the lower orders of a modified, or diminished, version of the domestic ideology at the heart of middle-class identity. Middle- (along with some upper-) class reformers sought (with dubious success) to prohibit, or at least disrupt, the essentially communal feast-day activities, sports, and pastimes in which the lower classes participated, and which the gentry not only condoned but patronized. The alehouse, with its attendant communal activities, not to mention its association with drunken and licentious behavior, became vilified by the middle classes who promoted a quieter, more moral and domestic form of recreation: "they elevated the home as the place of family affection, quiet pleasures and domestic leisure" (Belcham, 55).

The degree to which middle-class attempts at such reforms succeeded in altering the attitudes, beliefs, and practices of the lower classes is debatable. The economic, social, and cultural group which I have been attempting to define as middle-class was far from homogenous, and the same can be said of the lower class: "[w]ithin the working class there were many contesting cultural groupings—'respectable' and 'rough,' chapel and pub, autodidact and illiterate" (Belcham, 59). While "improvement minded" lower-class families may have pursued the ideology of self-improvement, advancement, and respectability through the literacy, sobriety, and domesticity espoused by the middle classes, many others resisted the intrusion.

Nonetheless, the middle-class proponents of these virtues persevered. The middle classes of the late eighteenth century fostered a division between the public and domestic spheres, and the family, especially children, became the focus of greater attention. The predominantly masculine public sphere came to be viewed by the middle classes as something of a necessary evil in the securing of a comfortable and separate domestic life: "[t]he goal of all the bustle of the market place was to provide a proper moral and religious life for the family" (Davidoff and Hall, 21). Of course, this separation of spheres was motivated by more than the desire for a new form of comfort; for the middle classes, the home became the seedbed for the social reforms they sought. Hannah More, for example, whose Cheap Repository Tracts were designed to persuade the lower classes to adopt the burgeoning domestic ideology, saw this connection clearly: "[s]he argued that politics were not for women but asserted that politics began at home; the only way to save the nation was to reform from the bottom up and a truly religious home provided the only sure foundation" (Davidoff and Hall, 171). This was a view that spanned the entire spectrum of middle-class positions; reform through a moral home life and a greater attention to the raising of children "was the voice of the middle class uniting Anglican and Dissenting audiences. Uniting, furthermore, Radicals, Liberals and Tories from all strata of the occupational spectrum" (Davidoff and Hall, 179).[30]

Religion was another factor that, paradoxically, given middle-class affiliations with a variety of Protestant churches, provided some ideological cohesion to the middle ranks. As Priestley observed in *An Essay on the First Principles of Government* (1768), the variety of religious (and political) sects existing in the English society of his time survived all manner of internal disagreement: "the greatest enemy of popery may see something he dislikes in the conduct of the first reformers, the warmest zeal against episcopacy is consistent with the just sense of the faults of the puritans, and much more an enemy of Charles the first, be an enemy of Cromwell."[31] The only implied agreement here is at the level of a shared opposition to Roman Catholicism, and this did not require any particular unity within or between the branches of the Anglican and Dissenting faiths.

The most active churchgoers were from the middle classes, and being seriously committed to Christianity became a sign of social status across the different churches. Unitarians and Evangelicals differed, as Davidoff and Hall remark, in their philosophies as well as their religious doctrines: "unlike evangelicals, Unitarians were intellectual in their orientation, influenced by science and philosophy . . . [T]he rationalist tradition to which they belonged brought Unitarians close to Utilitarians" (96). They shared, however, a commitment to their faith and their right to practice it: "[s]erious Christians or committed believers of whatever denominational persuasion agreed that whether their beliefs stemmed from faith or reason they were right to have the courage of their convictions" (Davidoff and Hall, 106).

Perhaps the most important point of agreement, for my argument, between disparate religious groups within the middle classes came at the level of child-rearing and education: "Evangelical and Enlightenment traditions, despite their differences, focused on children's character as the basis for reforming society" (Davidoff and Hall, 343). Mary Wollstonecraft, a rationalist, republican Jacobin, and advocate of women's equality, and Sarah Trimmer, a conservative Evangelical and monarchist, may have had little in common politically, yet their children's writings contain many striking similarities.[32] Wollstonecraft's *Original Stories from Real Life* and Trimmer's *Fabulous Histories* (also published as *History of the Robins*), for example, both teach charity, obedience, kindness to animals, and an appreciation of the natural world.[33] As Alan Richardson observes, radicals and conservatives may have had different ideas about the nature of civil society, but they viewed education in very similar ways: "reformist writers and activists—from conservatives wishing to shore up the status quo to 'Jacobins' wishing to overturn it—saw education as a, if not the, key locus for promoting social stability or engineering social revolution."[34] According to Davidoff and Hall, such lessons translated into real life experience for the middle-class family of the late eighteenth century: "[i]n the course of a family walk, a Utilitarian parent gave practical lessons on botany while the evangelical called attention to God's handiwork" (343). Despite deeply held differences in religious belief, the material practices of the extremely varied middle classes were often the same.

Children's literature became one of the crucial mechanisms for disseminating and consolidating middle-class ideology. For children to participate successfully in the new ideological project of the period, they had to be rendered into subjects whose energies could be controlled and effectively harnessed. The child as a differentiated subject category—an "other"—arises out of the same reformulations of power and ways of knowing that altered the practices and forms of such varying fields as the natural sciences and medicine, and the mechanisms of discipline and punition. The child as "other" becomes in this period the subject of all these discourses; writers for and about children in the late eighteenth century agreed that reason was the guiding principle of human activity, and that children, by definition and by the very nature of their *tabula rasa* minds (susceptible to every form of impression), were deficient in this essential and normalizing faculty. Christianity was, of course, also the guiding principle of the age. However, as the Methodists demonstrated, a faith in Christianity need not be incompatible with the improving and perfecting power of reason. Indeed, reason was viewed as a God-given gift separating humanity from the rest of creation. Sensibility, which emerged as a corrective to cool rationality, still served, by its opposition, to underscore the primacy of reason. If the ideal figure of the age was the productive, moral, self-disciplined, healthy, male adult governed by the faculty of reason, the child came to be viewed in many regards as its opposite: the subject interpellated through absence and difference.[35]

The child-as-other, as subject in need of reason, then, became the object of study, description, and categorization; in order for the child to be made whole and rational, its otherness must be contained and controlled within various discourses. This shift in approach to children parallels the change in how such "others" as the mentally or physically ill and the criminal were viewed and treated; indeed, the child was often compared to such figures within the pedagogical and pediatric literatures of the period.[36] Foucault describes this unprecedented focus of the medical gaze on the state of childhood as a fundamentally qualitative shift: "The problem of 'children' (that is, of their number at birth and the relation of their births to mortalities) is now joined by the problem of 'childhood' (that is of survival to adulthood . . .). It is no longer just a matter of producing an optimum number of children, but one of the correct management of this age of life."[37]

Medical practice, the management of children, and the good of society intersect for the first time in the eighteenth century, and the family—the domestic microcosm of society—becomes the center for the articulation of these concerns: "The family is assigned a linking role between general objectives regarding the good health of the social body and individuals' desire or need for care. This enables a private ethic of good health as the reciprocal duty of parents and children to be articulated on a collective system of hygiene and scientific technique of cure made available . . . by a professional corps of doctors" (Foucault 1980, 174).

The reform of society through the family—"from the ground up" to use Davidoff's and Hall's terms—envisioned by the middle-class domestic ideologues coincides here with the changing face of medical discourse and practice. Middle-class parents were not only interested in the education and reading habits of their children; along with the blossoming market for works of pedagogical theory and for children's books came a growing trade in pediatric texts intended for domestic use.

One feature common to both the medical and pedagogical discourses of childhood in this period is the use of the individual case study, which, as Foucault indicates in *The Birth of the Clinic,* became the norm in medical discourse in the late eighteenth century.[38] Pediatric texts such as William Buchan's *Advice to Mothers* and works of educational theory such as the Edgeworth's *Practical Education* present the reader with "real life" biographical accounts of children's passions, illnesses, distempers, and miscarriages in behavior, enumerating the "symptoms" and describing the processes through which cures were discovered.[39] Even the children's books themselves often followed a similar pattern. Mary Pilkington published, in 1799, a series of biographical accounts of the "real" lives, fortunes, and misfortunes of a number of girls, entitled *Biography for Girls; or, Moral and*

Instructive Examples, for Young Ladies, which was followed the next year by a similarly-conceived work for boys: *Biography for Boys; or, Characteristic Histories.* Mary Wollstonecraft's *Original Stories from Real Life* is a pseudo-biographical account—a sort of extended case study—of the education and progressive improvement of two young girls under the watchful eye of their governess, Mrs. Mason.

The sheer quantity of the writing for and about children using this "real-life" biographical style suggests a new technology of control in the raising and management of children, one that parallels the development of discourses around various categories of the "other": "the child, the patient, the madman, the prisoner, were to become, with increasing ease from the eighteenth century . . . the object of individual descriptions and biographical accounts. This turning of real lives into writing . . . functions as a procedure of objectification and subjection."[40] Why the individual case study saw such widespread acceptance in medical and pedagogical discourse is a complicated question. It replaced such earlier genres as the illness-focused medical account and the allegorical account for purposes of instruction. Instead of applying the specifics of a medical condition, or of an instance of childhood misbehavior, to patients or children in general, the case study focused on the symptoms and particulars as they manifested themselves in a specific individual. This seems a logical and necessary evolution of enlightenment scientific discourse, which was founded on the discovery or production of general principles based on individual and empirically reproducible experiments and phenomena. In the science of the late Enlightenment, the aggregate of observations generated by these individual experiments supplied the basis for generalization. This movement in discursive practice—from general principle applied downwards to individual cases, to general principles established through the classifying and categorizing of an aggregate of individual cases—represents a shift in episteme, in technologies and ways of knowing.[41]

The individual case study replaces, to some extent, allegory in works of instruction for children in the late eighteenth century in response to changing categories of subjecthood.[42] Allegory provides a general model of social conduct or behavior within an integrated, hierarchical, and stable class structure (a feudal system, for example); it depicts the shared experience of a community.[43] The centrality of the individual and discourses of equality and individual liberty and responsibility were at the heart of the growing middle-class ideology of the period. The accompanying shift in focus away from the community, and, in the definition of social order, away from "the great chain of being" to a focus on the individual and the individual within society, necessitated a new form of narrative that reflected this ideological change: the individual case study in both its medical and pedagogical forms.[44]

In *Discipline and Punish,* Foucault describes the operations of power and the classification of the criminal as a subject within the changing discourse of punishment and incarceration in the late eighteenth century. The irrational behavior of criminals, like that of children, came to be seen less as a result of sinfulness or intentional malice, and more as the product of a mind deficient in reason. Consequently, the logic of punition moved from one informed by a desire for retribution (against an individual body offending or violating the body politic) to one directed at reform: "[w]e punish, but this is a way of saying that we wish to obtain a cure" (Foucault 1977, 22).

In the late seventeenth century, Locke was already advising parents against whipping and other forms of physical correction when dealing with a child's miscarriages in behavior. Instead, he recommended the more subtle approach of critiquing children and instilling a sense of shame of their irrationality. In *Some Thoughts Concerning Education,* Locke suggests that "*Esteem* and *Disgrace* are, of all others, the most powerful incentives to the Mind. . . . If you can once get into Children a love of Credit, and an apprehension of Shame and Disgrace, you have put into them the true Principle, which will constantly work, and incline them to the right" (116). An adherence to virtue and reason should be rewarded, while deviation should be met with shame: "by these Means you can come once to shame them of their Faults . . . and make them in love with the Pleasure of being well thought on, [and] you may turn them as you please" (117).[45] Locke invokes here the power of normalization, the desire in the subject to have difference erased and to be accepted as same, rather than demarcated as other, as the guiding principle in correction and discipline. As Foucault observes, "[s]hameful punishments are effective because they are based on the vanity that was at the root of the crime" (Foucault 1977, 107). Eighteenth-century pedagogues believed, similarly, that the child's miscarriages in behavior (disobedience, obstinacy, love of finery, abuse of lesser beasts and lower orders, etc.) stemmed more often than not from an irrational sense of pride or self-worth. The fear of having one's irrational sense of vanity exposed is what makes shame work within this formula.

Shame as a mechanism for regulating the behavior of children, in Lockean pedagogy, operates in much the same way as the panopticism Foucault describes in his analysis of inmate surveillance: through the internalization of the gaze. Panopticism works because of the subject's belief (or fear) that he or she is under the constant scrutiny of a regulating authority. In the case of the child subject, the risk of shame, or more accurately the detection of behavior considered by the parental authority as shameful, is internalized by the child, and becomes a self-regulating mechanism: "[t]his would teach them Modesty and Shame; and they would quickly come to have a *natural* Abhorrence for that, which, they found, made them slighted and neglected by every Body" (Locke, *Some Thoughts,* 117; emphasis mine). While the "Pain of Whipping" may provide a temporary counteraction to undesirable behavior in children, it cannot match the long-lasting benefits of internalizing the naturalized, self-regulatory effects of shame: "[i]ngenious *Shame,* and the Apprehension of Displeasure, are the only true Restraint: These alone ought to hold the Reins, and keep the Child in order" (Locke *Some Thoughts,* 118).[46] The panoptic gaze of authority, which was intended not only to regulate the behavior of inmates but to effect a cure for their irrational criminality, is here envisioned as having ultimately the same effect on the child subjected to the scrutiny of parental authority: "a Look or Nod only ought to correct them, when they do amiss" (Locke, *Some Thoughts,* 138).

To what extent parents acted on this advice in the eighteenth century is questionable, but it was widely taken up by such educational writers as the Edgeworths, and representations of children being beaten in the children's books of the age are fairly uncommon. If Locke's suggested method of correction did not take hold in general practice, it still signaled an important shift in thinking about not only how children should be punished, but what caused childhood miscarriages in behavior, and how children could be brought to regulate their own behavior.[47]

Necessary to such a change in proposed methods of punition was a reevaluation of the concept of childhood, and more importantly, a recategorization of the child as a subject deficient in reason. The scientific "thaw" of the eighteenth century opened up a new "power of normalization" which "individualizes by making it possible to measure gaps, to determine levels, to fix specialities and to render the differences useful by fitting them one to the other" (Foucault 1977, 184). This process of normalization required a continuous and thorough examination and observation of the subject "that maintains the disciplined individual in his subjection" (Foucault 1977, 187). The remarkable increase in attention paid to children and the subject of childhood in the late eighteenth century can, I believe, be viewed in the light of this normalizing power affecting such related discourses as the treatment of the ill, the management of the mad, and the correction of the criminal, alongside all of whom the child subject was regularly categorized. For the middle classes, concerned not only with the advancement of their individual children, but more broadly with the perpetuation of their ideology and the consolidation of their class position in future generations, the mechanisms of control and normalization embedded in the various discourses of childhood were essential tools.

The social and cultural environment in which such epistemic changes could occur must be considered in terms of a class culture and its material practices. This is not to say that the changing discourses of childhood are mere superstructural reflections of the determining economic base of early capitalism. As Raymond Williams has demonstrated in his application of the Frankfurt School concept of homologous structures, the relationship is much more complex than earlier Marxist formulations allowed: "there may be no direct or easily apparent similarity, and certainly nothing like reflection or reproduction, between the superstructural process and the reality of the base, but in which there is an essential homology or correspondence of structures which can be discovered by analysis" (Williams 1980, 33).

If the base necessarily precedes the superstructure, if cultural and intellectual activities are merely reflections of preexisting economic realities, how could the middle classes have used such cultural products as children's literature to *enable* a new economy based on industrial capitalism?[48] The realms of art and ideas cannot be viewed in isolation from productive practices, or as mere reflections of these practices. They are "real practices, elements of a whole material social process" which define a system of production as much "as 'production,' as 'the base,' or as the 'self-subsistent world.'"[49] The pedagogical, pediatric, and children's literatures of the late eighteenth century, which depicted the types of individual virtues and social practices upon which the embryonic system of industrial capitalism would eventually depend for its continuation, helped *create* that very system.

Chapter 1

The Coach and Six: Chapbook Residue in Late Eighteenth-Century Children's Literature

The trend towards a predominantly didactic form of children's book character-istic of the rational and evangelical writing movements of the late eighteenth century did not, of course, leap out onto the market fully formed.[1] Predating, and, indeed, eventually coexisting with, the rational diversions and evangel-ical children's books by such authors as Maria Edgeworth, Thomas Day, Sarah Trimmer, and Dorothy Kilner that flooded the English market in the last two decades of the eighteenth century were scores of what can be called "transitional" books. These books, while acknowledging the trend toward in-culcating middle-class values and ideology in young readers, still employed earlier chapbook forms and themes. The survival of such chapbook elements in a middle-class pedagogical environment growing increasingly hostile to plebeian influences raises issues of class relations and the cultural production of class. This chapter will survey not only such well-known early children's books as *A Little Pretty Pocket Book* (1744) and *The History of Little Goody Two-Shoes* (1766), but also lesser-known works such as *The Friends; or the History of Billy Freeman and Tommy Truelove* (c. 1787), and *Nurse Dan-dlem's Little Repository of Great Instruction* (c. 1784), so as to demonstrate the ubiquity of these transitional books in the late-eighteenth century.[2]

From 1801 to 1805, Sarah Trimmer published *The Guardian of Education*, a compendium of her views on education, anti-jacobin essays, and reviews of contemporary pedagogical theories and children's books. Her reviews, es-pecially, provide an index of the changing attitudes toward what constituted acceptable children's reading in the late eighteenth and early nineteenth cen-turies. While her evangelical agenda in reforming children's literature led her to dismiss such enormously influential works as Rousseau's *Emile* as ir-religious, she still found much to praise in the Rousseau-inspired rational diversions for children of such writers as Maria Edgeworth and Thomas Day. The middle-class values of utility, industry, and book-learning were becoming increasingly prevalent in children's books, and while Trimmer insisted that these be tempered with an education in the scriptures, she welcomed this change. One of the main points on which she and the rationalist children's writers fully concurred was the need to rid the nursery of the vicious and potentially subversive influences of the chapbooks and fairy tales that had perennially stocked its shelves. Such fairy tales as "Cinderella," "Blue Beard," and "Little Red Riding Hood," "which were in circulation when those who are now grandmothers, were themselves children," had by Trimmer's time become potential sites of "danger" and "impropriety."[3] Trimmer argued, for example, that such chapbook favorites as "Valentine and Orson," threatened to make the susceptible minds of children "acquainted with the lascivious vices of mankind" (*Guardian,* 75). She was certainly not the first to condemn children's consumption of such texts. J. Hamilton Moore, for example, using Lockean sensationalist terms, warned some twenty years earlier against the dangerous impact of fantasy on the young: "we generally see youth suffered to read romances, which impress on their minds such notions of Fairies, Goblins, &c. that exist only in the imagination, and being strongly imbibed, take much time to erradicate, and very often baffle all power of philosophy."[4] Unlike Trimmer's critique, however, such earlier condemnations of fairy tales were rarely as laden with ideological and class concerns.

Trimmer's opinions of chapbooks were echoed by her more secular and politically radical contemporaries. When advising parents on suitable reading for their children, Catharine Macaulay dismisses such tales as "Tom Thumb, Jack Hickathrift, Jack the Giant Killer . . . as mere negatives as to their effects on the mind."[5] Other chapbooks and fairy tales, according to Macaulay, pose a much greater danger to the child's moral and intellectual development: "Those tales which endeavour to recommend virtue, not from its intrinsic value; not from that tranquility of soul, which ever attends it; not from that mental enjoyment, which God has annexed to the practice and cultivation of the benign affections; but from some carnal advantage with which its votaries are to be constantly rewarded, ought to be exploded from every system of education" (53).

Carnality, however, is not the most injurious effect of chapbooks. Plebeian projections and fantasies of social advancement "hold out an imaginary bribe," which gives children "an erroneous idea of the ways of Providence" (Macaulay, 53). Chapbooks subvert the realities of class and social structures, conflating random chance with the divine providence God bestows on the deserving and industrious.

Victor Neuburg's and Harry B. Weiss's histories of English chapbooks provide some useful insights into this once ubiquitous form of literature. Neuburg defines chapbooks loosely as cheap "paper-covered books offered for sale by pedlars, hawkers and other itinerant merchants who were generally known as chapmen."[6] Chapbooks, Neuburg says, consisted primarily of tales of romance and chivalry, fantastic voyages and supernatural creatures, which, although certainly not an exhaustive list of chapbook literary themes, accounts for many of the most popular and widely-circulating varieties of the form. It should be noted that Neuburg focuses on fantasy-oriented chapbooks, as opposed to, for example, such popular narratives as accounts of famous criminal trials, because he analyzes these texts principally as children's books. His goal is to call attention to a previously overlooked form of children's literature, and his study takes the form of a nostalgic appreciation of forgotten classics. Although he does acknowledge that chapbooks were "[i]ntended in the first instance for adults" (mostly of the "poorer classes"), his main concern is with children's consumption of these texts: "the content and convenient size of these books had made an immediate appeal to young readers" (Neuberg, 75).

Weiss's study of chapbooks is detailed and especially helpful in its account of chapbook publishers and distributors. He recognizes a very broad spectrum of themes and narratives in his account of chapbook contents: "[d]evils, and angels, scoundrels and heroes, love and hate, murders, deathbed statements, witchcraft, riddles, tragedy, romance, song, jests, fairy tales, religion, shipwrecks, confessions, fables, hymns, speeches, executions, and all that goes to make up life, real and unreal, are reflected in the ephemeral chapbooks that once circulated so freely and are now so scarce."[7]

Weiss's study is aimed primarily at the book collector and antiquarian, and is not concerned with the ideological content of chapbooks or with their role in the development of class consciousness. His assertion that "[t]he term chapbook may include anything from a broadside to a good-sized book," and that they were sold at prices ranging from "a few farthings to a shilling" (1), may be accurate if we consider a chapbook as any form of printed material sold by itinerant vendors. However, such a broad definition draws attention away from the chapbook as an expression of plebeian popular culture, and as the primary form of literary consumption for the lower classes. It was, after all, the chapbook's projections of plebeian fantasies of miraculous social advancement, its subversions of the social order, and its unrepentant portrayals of drunken ribaldry and even criminal activity that middle-class pedagogues of the late eighteenth century considered so potentially vicious an influence on their young. It is the at times uneasy coexistence of the residue of this plebeian moral economy with the values of the growing middle classes, in what I shall dub the "transitional," or "hybrid" works of such children's book publishers as John Newbery and John Marshall, that make them such intriguing studies in the formation of class and class identity.

Mary Jackson's study of English children's books up to 1839, *Engines of Instruction, Mischief, and Magic,* contains a thorough treatment of the transitional books of the mid and late eighteenth century. Her work takes into account the importance of middle-class virtues and propriety in the development of children's literature in the eighteenth century (especially in its last two decades). In fact, she also uses the term "transitional" to describe the works of Marshall and the Newbery house (after the death of John). Her usage of the term, however, refers more to the transition from what she describes as a relatively liberal to a more conservative political climate in the years 1768 to 1788, than to a transition from plebeian, chapbook-based children's literature to a middle-class moral and didactic form of children's texts. Jackson's argument concerning the ideological work performed by children's literature is much more inclusive than my own. Where this study distinguishes the middle classes (admittedly a very diverse and stratified group itself) as the primary source of the ideological content of children's literature in its early years, Jackson's terms are far more general: "Children's books were largely propagandistic in nature. They were tools for social, moral, religious and political conditioning. They represented the enormously powerful collusive efforts of parents, producers of books, *and indeed most adults—in a word of society—*to program the young, to engineer conformity to the prevailing cultural values."[8] The observation that children's literature performs the ideological work of social conditioning is an important one, but Jackson's inclusion of virtually all adults, even society in general, in such an ideological project overlooks the divisions and differences within a given society. Children's literature reflects not only a society's desire to modify the behavior of children, but the class and ideological conflicts within that society as well: especially, as in the case of late eighteenth-century England, one undergoing a dramatic class restructuring.

While avoiding a strict progress model to describe the history of children's books, Jackson's work does operate under some of the assumptions characteristic of earlier historians in the field. She does not assume that the history of children's literature is a simple linear progression from sorry beginnings to the Victorian ideal of Edward Lear-styled nonsense and Lewis Carroll-styled fantasy. However, like F. J. Harvey Darton, Percy Muir, and Geoffrey Summerfield before her, Jackson tends to view the changing attitudes towards what has historically constituted appropriate children's reading as a battle between the stern-faced forces of conservatism and didacticism, and the fun-loving forces of fantasy and levity. Such binaries—didacticism versus fun, rigidity versus liberality—tend to draw attention away from the material conditions in which children's books were (and continue to be) produced, and from the class dynamics at work in the dissemination of children's books in the period. Jackson is not as blatantly prejudiced against the didactic efforts of late eighteenth-century writers as is Percy Muir, who lumps them all together under the rubric of "A Monstrous Regiment," and who views their work as an unfortunate stepping stone toward the inevitable "Triumph of Nonsense." Nonetheless, she does envision a progression from the work of reformers and Rousseau-inspired writers to a more ideal pre- and early-Victorian time when children regained "The Right to Laugh, the Right to Dream" they had lost when chapbooks, and then transitional books, were all but removed from the nursery in the last decades of the eighteenth century.[9]

Transitional books can also be thought of as hybrids, alloying often seemingly incongruous elements from various sources and discourses. Their physical characteristics often suggest their hybrid content. In the main, they retained much of the traditional appearance and format of chapbooks. They were generally duodecimo volumes printed on cheap paper containing woodcuts often quite obviously recycled from other publications; unlike traditional chapbooks, however, they were often bound (albeit usually in inexpensive paper floral boards) and priced above the 1d. norm for most chapbooks. The binding and increase in price over chapbooks also distinguishes these texts as products less geared towards plebeian readers and more towards the lower middle classes, who in many instances would have only recently left the ranks of the laboring classes. Another feature identifying the chapbook origins of these works is that they commonly do not list an identifiable author. These books give the impression, as do chapbooks, of having evolved more out of a collective oral tradition than out of the individual imagination of a middle-class writer. Individual authorship and ascribing original ideas to specific individual sources were not major concerns for either chapbook readers or publishers. These stories were quite often printed forms of ancient, orally-transmitted stories of indeterminate authorship. By contrast, the more modern didactic children's stories of the late eighteenth century were generally ascribed to a specific author (often writing under a pseudonym), which suggests not only the middle-class novelistic form that most of these authors were trying to emulate, but more broadly the emphasis on individual thought, action, responsibility, and property at the heart of middle-class ideology. The printing presses of John Marshall and the Newberys constituted the largest sources of such works in London, but similar texts emerged from the houses of provincial publishers like John Pytt of Gloucester, T. Wilson of York, and S. Hodgson of Newcastle.

Among the earliest examples of this hybridization of plebeian chapbook elements and middle-class pedagogy are the works of John Newbery, which, while combining "instruction with delight," also negotiate what would later become the more disputed and treacherous territory between fairy tales and rational diversions for children. *A Little Pretty Pocket-Book* (1744), considered by many to be the first modern children's book,[10] opens with a preface directed at parents that essentially paraphrases the pedagogical advice found in John Locke's *Some Thoughts Concerning Education:* "[s]ubdue therefore your Children's Passions; curb their Tempers, and make them subservient to the Rules of Reason" (12). This preface is followed by two letters to the reader from Jack the Giant-Killer, whom Newbery has greatly reformed from his chapbook days. He now espouses the importance of reading and obedience for children who wish to become happy and successful adults, rather than the virtues of robbing and killing giants. This work also contains, to my knowledge, the first instance of the "coach-and-six" reward system, which I discuss at greater length below. The reformed Jack the Giant-Killer here describes the material success enjoyed by a particularly studious boy of his acquaintance: "There was in my Country a little Boy who learned his Book to that surprising Degree, that his Master could scarce teach him fast enough, for he had his Lesson almost as soon as it was pointed out to him; which raised the Attention of every Body. . . . His Learning and Behaviour purchased him the Esteem of the greatest People, and raised him from a mean State of Life to a Coach and Six, in which he rides to this day" (*Pretty,* 74). As we shall see, this became the standard device for demonstrating and promoting the value of book learning until the last years of the century.

A brief look at the seventeenth- and eighteenth-century chapbook *The History of Jack and the Giants, The First Part* reveals the sanitization Jack has undergone by the time he reaches the pages of *A Little Pretty Pocket-Book.* In the chapbook bearing his name, Jack is recognized as a remarkable figure from a very early age, not (as we shall see in the case of Goody Two-Shoes) for his obedience, kindness, and devotion to literacy, but for his subversive capacity for trickery and mischief: "the very Learned many times he baffled, by his cunning and sharp ready Inventions."[11] In fact, it is his very ability—at the tender age of seven—to outwit the local Vicar (arguably the most literate and educated man in any seventeenth-century rural community) that sets him apart. The Vicar, no doubt out of an honest concern for young Jack's spiritual well-being, inquires into his catechistic knowledge: "*How many Commandments are there? Jack* told him *There are Nine.* The Parson replied, *There are Ten. Nay,* quoth *Jack,* Mr. Parson, *you are out* [;] *it's true there were Ten, but you broke one with your Maid* Margery. The Parson replied, *Thou art an arch Wag, Jack*" (*Giants,* 6).

As an adult, Jack uses his inherent cunning to destroy a series of giants in increasingly gruesome fashion (for example, he manages to trick a Welsh giant into disemboweling himself: "he ript his own Belly from the Bottom to the Top, and out dropt his Tripes and Trolly-bubs" (*Giants,* 16)). His final accomplishment sees him exorcising evil spirits from a Lady and decapitating Lucifer himself with the help of various magical items won from another giant: a coat of invisibility, a cap of knowledge, a sword of sharpness, and shoes of extraordinary swiftness (*Giants,* 20). It is worth noting here that these items come from Jack's *uncle* the giant: "a huge and monstrous Giant with three Heads, he'll fight five hundred Men in Armour, and make them flee before him" (*Giants,* 18). It is perhaps by virtue of his supernatural lineage that Jack possesses inherent advantages over regular folk. For saving both the Lady and King Arthur's son, who sought her hand in marriage, Jack is rewarded with an

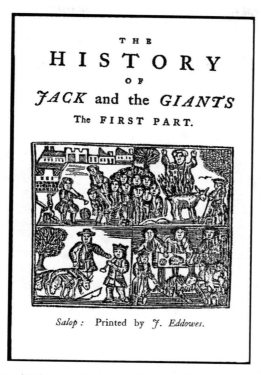

Fig. 1 *The History of Jack and the Giants, The First Part.* N.P.: J. Eddoes, n.d. Courtesy of the Bruce Peel Special Collections Library, University of Alberta

unparalleled advance in social status: "Jack for his good Service, was made one of the Knights of the Round Table" (*Giants,* 23).

This at once extraordinary and fairly typical chapbook hero, who relies on such traditional plebeian virtues as cunning and wit (often a very bawdy wit at that), luck, and supernatural assistance to help secure wealth and social advancement, becomes, in response to the shifting moral economy of Newbery's middle-class readership, a champion of industry, obedience, and book-learning as the keys to success in life. At the same time, however, his mere presence in the text—even stripped of his attributes and magical items—points to a residual chapbook influence in these early middle-class children's books.

The History of Little Goody Two-Shoes was by far the most successful of Newbery's early titles. It has received a fair bit of (often unfavorable) critical attention, more than has usually been accorded individual children's books of the period. Some of this attention has been fueled by the mystery of the book's authorship, and early speculation that Oliver Goldsmith might have penned it. Percy Muir dismisses the text because of its stylistic flaws: "of a rather inferior order, not very well constructed" (Muir, 68). Almost fifty years later, Geoffrey Summerfield would echo this aesthetic critique: "the novel is so confused . . . the tone is so inconsistent and uncertain that it is continuously difficult to know whether to take it seriously."[12] The bulk of Summerfield's discussion is dedicated to proving Goldsmith's authorship of the work. Patricia Demers and Gordon Moyles recognize the audience to whom the account of Goody's virtues was primarily directed: "middle-class children who said their prayers, sought their parents' blessing, learned their lessons, and bestowed charity,"[13] while Isaac Kramnick was perhaps the first to analyze closely the bourgeois ideological work the text performs: "[s]elf-denial is the cornerstone of capitalism, and this is in fact the final message of the book" ("Children's Literature," 25).

The story takes this idea of advancement through such middle-class virtues as developing reading skills, industrious application, and self-denial as its central theme. In the first volume, we find Margery (soon to be Goody) and her brother Tommy orphaned and reduced to the most miserable poverty by the greed of the local squire. They are so badly off, in fact, that Margery goes about with only one shoe until the benevolent clergyman, Mr. Smith, takes her in and buys a match for her single shoe. She is so excited with her pair of shoes that she shows them off proudly to all in the village, who thus name her Goody Two-Shoes. At an early age, she develops a remarkable skill for reading, and devotes herself to the education of the poor in her neighborhood. The second volume of their novel documents her continued service as educator, her opening of a village school, her marriage to a rich husband, and her eventual rise to the status of local hero and legend. Goody comes, by virtue of her kindness and devotion to literacy, eventually to realize the remarkable advancement in class and status promised on the book's title page: "Who from a State of Rags and Care,/ And having Shoes but Half a Pair;/ Their Fortune and their Fame would fix,/ And Gallop in a Coach and Six." Possessed as if from birth of an almost supernatural capacity for learning and kindness, she passes through the narrative comforting the poor, teaching them how to read, and dispensing such gems of wisdom as: "Industry is Fortune's right Hand, and Frugality her left./ Make much of Three-pence, or you ne'er will be worth a Groat" (*Goody*, 41).

Despite this fairly clear alignment of Two-Shoes with middle-class virtues (she also advises the poor to be content with their class position, to avoid finery, debauchery, and other aristocratic excesses), the text takes conflicting class positions throughout. It rails against the cruelty of the landed gentry classes, whose enclosure of common farm lands in the eighteenth century threatened to "reduce the common People to a State of Vassalage, worse than that of the Barons of old" (*Goody*, 12). Goody's parents themselves are victimized by Sir Timothy Gripe, who, in collusion with Farmer Graspall and an unjust system of enclosure, achieves "sole Dominion over the Poor, whom he depressed and abused in a manner too horrible to mention" (*Goody*, 8). While the narrator is ostensibly calling for a reform of the squirarchy's exploitative treatment of the poor, Goody exhorts the poor to habits of early rising and daily industry for their own improvement: "He that will thrive,/ Must rise at Five./ He that hath thriv'n,/ May rise at Seven" (*Goody*, 39). The text, while certainly sympathetic to the plight of the victimized "common People," still condemns their ignorant superstitions. After a funeral, all the townsfolk become convinced that the chapel is haunted. Goody lectures them on the irrationality of their superstitious folk beliefs, and the narrator in turn lectures the reader: "I hope you will not believe any foolish Stories that ignorant, weak, or designing People may tell you about Ghosts; for Tales of Ghosts, Witches, and Fairies, are the Frolicks of a distempered Brain" (*Goody*, 56).

It is not unusual to find this combination of anti-aristocratic sentiment and suspicion of plebeian culture in the rational, enlightened children's books of the end of the century, as the next chapter will illustrate more fully. Their authors came predominantly from the urban middle classes, who regularly defined themselves against the vices and prejudices of the classes below and above them. What is unusual here is the seemingly peaceful cohabitation of these middle-class sentiments in the same text with episodes of a decidedly fantastic, fairy-tale quality. In the second part of her story, we find Goody working in a school where she teaches a number of birds how to read, and one of them—a rook—how to speak as well. Talking animals have been used for didactic purposes in children's stories since the time of Aesop, and were used in the late eighteenth century by such moralists as Trimmer (*History of the Robins*) and Dorothy Kilner (*The Rational Brutes*).[14] While Goody's menagerie acts mostly as an entertaining fantasy element, Trimmer and Kilner use theirs as symbolic examples of the lower orders expressing contentment with their lot in life, or as objects upon whom children can practice their budding virtue of charity.

Goody's menagerie expands to include a sky-lark, a lamb, and a dog, and she trains them to perform various functions around the school. Her powers of instruction have by now reached supernatural proportions, and her magical empathy towards animals coincides much more closely with popular chap-book constructions of reality than with either those of novelistic realism, of the level-headed, practical, middle-class figure Goody originally embodied.[15] Goody, by the end of her story, has become a hero of almost mythical proportions to the underprivileged of her community, receiving the sort of adoration reserved for such chapbook figures as Robin Hood or King Arthur. Before her death she is revered as "a Mother to the Poor, a Physician to the Sick, and a Friend to all who were in Distress;" so beloved is she that after her death, a monument is erected in the churchyard in her honor, "over which the Poor as they pass weep continually, so that the Stone is ever bathed in Tears" (*Goody*, 140). This bears some resemblance to the endings of many *Robin Hood* chapbooks and garlands. Robin's enemy, the Prioress, despite her animosity toward him, erects a stone with an epitaph so that his fame will continue: "His epitaph, as records tell,/ within these hundred years/ By many was discerned well."[16]

This sort of residue of plebeian culture in books intended mostly for children of the middle classes is perhaps not so surprising in the early Newbery works of the mid-eighteenth century. Newbery astutely observed that a new market for children's books tailored to more modern middle-class sensibilities was flourishing, and the most readily available models for this new children's literature were chapbooks. To make these ancient characters more palatable to the parents of his target audience, he reformed them somewhat and had them espouse the kinds of virtues and ideology middle-class parents were increasingly wanting to hear.

In his study of this enormously influential publisher, *John Newbery and his Books: Trade and Plum-Cakes for ever, Huzza!,* John Rowe Townsend indicates *that* Newbery was of modest farming stock: "an eighteenth-century farm boy from a small village in Berkshire, who went to London and prospered."[17] His own early reading, and his apprenticeship to a provincial publisher in Reading, would surely have made him very familiar with chapbook literature. This, combined with his eventual rise into the upper middle classes through the production and dissemination of texts (not to mention a thriving business in patent medicines) may go some way in explaining his formula of combining plebeian chapbook characters and narrative elements with the middle-class values that furthered his own success. However, the fact that such stories continued to be popular and widely published in the last two decades of the century, when the dangers of fantasy, chapbooks, and fairy tales to the impressionable minds of middle-class youth were almost universally acknowledged by the leading pedagogues and children's writers of the day, suggests a more complex cultural dynamic.[18]

Raymond Williams, in *Marxism and Literature,* warns against an epochal view of cultural history, which tends to describe the cultural activity of a given period more or less exclusively in terms of its dominant class culture and overlooks the conflicts operating within that structure: "In authentic historical analysis it is necessary at every point to recognize the complex interrelations between movements and tendencies both within and beyond a specific and effective dominance. It is necessary to examine how these relate to the whole cultural process rather than to the selected and abstracted dominant system" (121). He further makes a useful distinction between the *archaic*—a cultural element that present culture recognizes as existing exclusively in the past or as a bygone tradition that may occasionally, but quite deliberately, be revived— and the *residual,* which "has been effectively formed in the past, but . . . is still active in the cultural process, not only and often not at all as an element of the past, but as an effective element of the present" (*Marxism,* 122). This idea of residual cultural influence, I believe, helps a great deal in understanding the presence of plebeian chapbook elements in a children's literature dominated by middle-class ideology in the late eighteenth century. It also helps explain how the dominant middle-class ideology and pedagogy successfully defuse potentially subversive plebeian qualities and manage to co-opt and appropriate them.

Although Sarah Trimmer may have railed violently against the lottery mentality espousing social advancement through the arbitrary workings of chance (Primrose's climb up the social ladder because of her remarkable beauty in *The History of Primrose Prettyface* was particularly noxious to Trimmer), or objected to the portrayal of unjust treatment of the poor in *Goody Two-Shoes,* such stories still performed the middle-class ideological work she believed so necessary to proper children's books.[19] They managed successfully to convey the essential middle-class virtues of hard work, self-denial, industry, and education because their chapbook elements were very often effectively subordinated to, or overshadowed by, a middle-class ideology. As Alan Richardson has observed, "the relationship of the didactic writers to the fairy tale might better be described as one of appropriation than one of censorship."[20] This appropriation put plebeian characters and narratives to work for middle-class ideological ends but never fully muted the forces that generated them. These elements are residual in that they are not part of an effective dominance; because they are actively in conflict with the class culture seeking to appropriate them, they cannot be understood as archaic.

By the end of the century, the Newbery house had diversified considerably and was responding to the demands of the middle classes for rational and useful diversions for their young. While old Newbery favorites such as *A Little Pretty Pocket Book* and *Goody Two Shoes* remained popular and widely in print, later Newbery offerings included books of natural history, botany, and zoology.[21] Story books were still the staples in the Newbery publishing diet, but these too, as the eighteenth century drew to a close, took on an increasingly moral, didactic, and rational flavor.[22]

This trend in children's publishing in the last two decades of the eighteenth century was by no means universal, as the popularity and ubiquity of certain of John Marshall's children's books will attest.[23] Marshall was something of a literary scavenger. Many of his books were blatant plagiarisms of earlier Newbery titles (*The Entertaining History of Little Goody Goosecap* (c. 1790) being perhaps the most obvious of his Newbery pilferings). He did publish many books appealing more strictly to the rational sensibilities of the middle classes. For example, he published Mary Ann Kilner's *The Adventures of a Whipping-Top* (178?), and her *Memoirs of a Peg-Top* (c. 1785)—both perennial favorites in the didactic genre in which an inanimate object teaches young readers valuable lessons of charity and contentment with one's place—as well as Lady Eleanor Fenn's *The Art of Teaching in Sport* (1785). Perhaps most surprisingly, he published imitations of the Cheap Repository Tracts, Hannah

More's project to replace traditional chapbooks with stories of devotion for the poor, such as *The Servant Man Turned Soldier; or, The Fair Weather Christian.* His stock-in-trade, however, remained the rational tale/chapbook hybrid.[24]

Marshall employed some fairly crafty tactics in the hawking of his wares. Although cheaply made and sold, his books often had gilt edging, and were generally bound, which gave them an air of middle-class respectability. Furthermore, he was quick to pick up on the catchwords and phrases of the didactic trend in children's writing; many of his titles advertised "moral" or "rational" works for "the Improvement of Young Minds," while the pages inside contained fairly unaltered chapbook tales of kings and queens, sorcerers and giants. *Nurse Dandlem's Little Repository of Great Instruction for all who Would be Good and Noble* is one of the more unabashed examples of Marshall's dubious advertising practices.[25] The title is obviously designed to attract the eye of conscientious parents seeking moral tales for their young, with its references to instruction, goodness, and nobility, but the contents are thinly veiled (if veiled at all) chapbook and fairy-tale stories. To the more vigilant middle-class parental eye, the fact that the source of this "repository of great instruction" is a nurse should have triggered alarm bells. By this time, educational writers such as Maria Edgeworth and Mary Wollstonecraft were warning parents to keep their children away from nurses, maids, and other potentially vicious plebeian influences, as they tended to fill children's heads with tales of ghosts and goblins (Wollstonecraft, for example, observes in *Thoughts on the Education of Daughters,* that nurses "are of course ignorant," and that their influence on children is generally pernicious).[26] As we shall see in chapter 3 as well, such "unsanctioned" female medical practitioners as the nurse and midwife were coming increasingly under fire. The book opens at a school run by the venerable Nurse Dandlem, who, we are informed, is to be greatly respected as she is 100 years old. This reference to her miraculous age places the story immediately in the realm of chapbooks and the supernatural, and the story she tells her students continues in that vein.

Ostensibly a tale designed to coerce children into minding their book, *Nurse Dandlem's Little Repository* quickly veers off into fantasy-inspired adventure. While playing truant from school one day, the protagonist, Wake Wilful, is kidnapped into naval service by a press gang. He is later captured by pirates, who find him too bad a boy even for their liking and strand him on an enchanted island near the Caribbean. The island is ruled by a sorcerer-giant, Grumbolumbo, who has amongst his minions hobgoblins and a dragon, and who traps Wake in a cave for safe keeping until his wedding day when the poor lad will be served up as an entrée at the feast. The good Fairy Starbright takes pity on Wake, and helps him escape by poisoning the giant, but not before securing his promise that he will be a good, studious, and obedient boy (a promise he of course keeps). Nurse Dandlem tacks on a moral at the end, and warns her students against falling victim to poor Wake's misadventures: "[t]he way therefore to avoid his troubles, is to be obedient to your parents, submissive to your teachers, and respectful to every one; to take care to learn your lesson, and not fight and quarrel with your school-fellows" (*Nurse*, 29). The moral, while paying lip service to the middle-class virtues of obedience and literacy, is clearly an afterthought appended to what is essentially a chapbook tale of exotic travel, strange monsters, and success through the medium of supernatural assistance. The middle-class message is merely a veneer, while the substance of the tale is rooted firmly in a plebeian moral economy.

Most Marshall books are not such obvious glosses of fairy tales and chapbooks; they usually negotiate much more subtly the border between the chapbook tales children were supposed, regrettably, to love and the middle-class pedagogical requirements their parents sought.[27] In *The Friends; or, the History of Billy Freeman and Tommy Truelove* (c. 1790), the virtues of "learning and industry" are lauded on the first page, as Billy's father "acquired a very great fortune by them" (*Friends*, 7). When we first encounter Billy, he has a run-in with the dog of a neighboring farmer, and is subsequently swarmed by angry turkeys. A passing gentleman rescues him and sits him down to read from "Marshall's Universal Battledores." When he discovers Billy cannot read, the gentleman exclaims: "I am sure both the dog and the turkies are good-natured to all Boys and Girls who learn their Book, and are dutiful to their Parents" (*Friends*, 9). By demonstrating how literacy imparts a quasi-magical ability to pacify beasts, and how animals recognize the innate superiority of the literate, Marshall books manage to yoke (an often begrudgingly acknowledged) desire for fantasy with the advantages to be gained from literacy.

The most common technique in Marshall books for convincing the child of the desirability of learning one's book is the regular connection they make between literacy and remarkable (if not wholly unrealistic) social advancement. It was a commonplace in the moral and rational children's books of the day that children, being less rational and, by extension, more plebeian in their tastes, were attracted to flashy displays of finery. Indeed the countless books advocating plain and modest dress, preaching utility over prettiness, and warning of the evils, both physical and psychological, attendant on children exposed to the niceties of aristocratic living make this attraction abundantly clear.[28] Whereas most of Marshall's middle-class contemporaries tried to root out the child's magpie tendencies, he capitalized on them. In *The Friends*, the passing gentleman makes a deal with Billy: "When you can tell your letters, come to my house, and I will...present you with many of my friend Mr. Marshall's gilt Books" (*Friends*, 11). This sort of barefaced hucksterism was quite common in children's books of the period, but Marshall also plays on the child's widely assumed love of pretty, shiny things: Billy "wanted the book for the sake of the gold cover" (*Friends*, 11).[29]

Literacy was not the only virtue rewarded in Marshall books; industry, obedience, charity, tidiness and all the other qualities expected of the middle-class child received credit as well, and the rewards were almost always the same. However, in many Marshall books, all other virtues seem to stem from literacy, and the reward scheme for its mastery is perhaps best summed up in a short verse from *The Friends*: "He who learns this book throughout,/ Shall have a horse to ride about:/ And she who learns her letters fair,/ Shall have a coach to take the air" (*Friends,* 11). The promise of immediate gratification of desires is one of the traits such moralists and pedagogues as Sarah Trimmer found most contemptible in fairytales and chapbooks because it presented young readers with an unrealistic model of class advancement. Trimmer's radical contemporary Catharine Macaulay argued that such promises can only breed dissatisfaction in children: "They will put a sudden period to their happiness, by telling them, that if they are very good and learn their book, &c. &c. they shall have a very fine baby, a fine coach the horses [sic], or some other toy equally adapted to inflame their imagination; and by the help of comparison, to make them quite disgusted with what before had filled their minds with satisfaction" (Macaulay, 77–78). In the moral economy of middle-class ideology the acquisition of knowledge was either sufficient reward in itself, or a long-term investment whose dividends only became obvious after great diligence and application. In the moral economy of the Marshall book, the child receives both immediate reward for learning his book (more of Mr. Marshall's gilt-edged books in *The Friends,* or even a dog and a pony in *The History of Master Billy Friendly, and his Sister, Miss Polly Friendly*), as well as the promise of extraordinary wealth in the future, often taking the form of the "coach-and-six."

By the mid eighteenth century, most travel was done by hired or mail coaches, and owning any sort of carriage, coach, or chaise was an indication of a fair degree of wealth. A coach-and-six, however, given its initial price, the upkeep of the horses, and the servants required for its maintenance, would have been reserved principally for the aristocracy or the wealthiest members of the mercantile middle classes. George III's royal state coach, built in 1761, was drawn by eight horses, and coaches drawn by six horses were often used in royal processions to carry high nobles and court dignitaries.[30] The social advancement Marshall is proposing by mentioning the "coach-and-six" is, therefore, of the most extraordinary magnitude. Marshall's use of dramatic social advancement and its material trappings as a reward for virtue, was, as I have suggested with the case of *Goody Two-Shoes,* a popular device in early Newbery books as well. Miss Sally Silence in *The Twelfth Day-Gift,* for example, is similarly rewarded for "her great Love of Truth and her vast Dislike of Noise and Nonsense."[31] She is raised from poverty by a duke who recognizes her virtue and decides to marry her; as a wedding gift, "he bought her a fine Gilt Coach, on which were painted two Doves, with an

Olive-branch, to represent their Peace and conjugal Affection; and she was drawn by six Milk-white Horses" (25).

The History of Master Billy Friendly, and his Sister, Miss Polly Friendly follows this model of socioeconomic advancement through literacy and good behavior, while introducing a more pronounced gender division in terms of both rewards and expected behavior. After a childhood marked by obedience, churchgoing, tidiness, studiousness, and so forth, Billy is rewarded with a rise to remarkable economic and political prominence: "you see he is a parliament-man ... and rides in a fancy chariot, and yet is not proud and puffed up, and above speaking to a poor body ... and yet he knows how to behave and speak to any body, and can talk to a judge, aye, and the King too, for ought I know."[32] Polly's similarly model observation of the appropriate virtues lands her the Lord-Mayor for a husband and a "grand-gilt coach, drawn by fine prancing horses" (*Billy,* 35).

At one level both Billy and Polly fulfill the chapbook fantasy of incredible social advancement coming to characters of humble origins, and this rise in class position is again rendered in the form most tangible to the child reader: the "fine chariot," or "grand-gilt coach." Both Billy and Polly achieve their new stations through diligent study of their book and the practice of essentially the same middle-class virtues; but we also begin to see here an acknowledgment of a middle-class domestic ideology and a differentiation of social virtues by gender. For example, while the obedience they show their parents is celebrated in both children, it is more emphasized in Polly's case; she shows "a becoming respect and good manners to her superiors *and equals*" (*Billy,* 25; italics mine). Where Billy is expected to keep good company and avoid fighting with his playfellows, Polly is expected to be "ready to and willing to do as she was bid" (*Billy,* 26). The more pronounced emphasis on Polly's obedience and subservience implies that these qualities are expected more from girls than from boys.

Similarly, Polly's charitable activities receive greater attention than those of her brother. Billy's acts of charity are either of a fairly muscular variety (he helps save a poor family from a fire), or take the form of a generous but perfunctory condescension to those less fortunate (giving a penny to a poor child). Polly, meanwhile, is equipped with a veritable charity radar: "she was from a child charitable to the poor, and used often to point out poor distressed objects to her papa and mamma. Or if she saw any little girl when she was walking out, who *appeared* in distress, she would give her money" (*Billy,* 25; italics mine). Two features differentiate her charity from that of her brother: her charity is often mediated by her parents—she locates the needy, but her parents perform the actual administration of relief—indicating her continued obedience and subservience to her elders; furthermore, she is so sensitive to the needs of others that even the *appearance* of distress elicits her sympathy. As Polly reaches adulthood, the trend continues: "[a]s she grew up, she made it her business to visit the poor, and to make everybody happy in her neighbourhood" (*Billy*, 33). While Billy's qualities eventually suit him to a life of public service (he becomes a "parliament-man"), Polly is being groomed for service at a more domestic level (the poor in her immediate neighborhood). This is a trend discussed at greater length in chapter 5.

Presumably in response to criticism of the pedagogical strategies of some Marshall books, the preface to his *The Wisdom of Crop the Conjuror* offers some rationalization for the "coach-and-six" reward system: "coaches, horses, &c. are the only things which most engage the attention of children; they are the only blessings their infant understandings are capable of comprehending; and if it is an evil to promise these, it can only be a partial evil, which wears away as the judgment becomes better informed" (*Wisdom,* vi). Perhaps more surprising is the writer's assertion—one that goes directly against the conventional middle-class didactic wisdom of the day—that even the universally vilified effects of fairy tales on the child's mind will eventually be outgrown: "[b]ut that which seems more injurious (the representing of hobgoblins, monsters, &c.) is as soon confuted as the other, (not ill-meant) but ill-judged opinion" (*Wisdom,* vi). True to form, this Marshall work negotiates a space between middle-class ideology and plebeian cultural tradition. Crop, a fortune-teller and the grandson of the illustrious Nurse Dandlem, prophesies social advancement and its concomitant material rewards for young Billy Learnwell: "[y]ou will be a great man, for you learn your book, you shall have horses and coaches plenty, and every thing you wish for" (*Wisdom,* 13). Performing a function very similar to that of Newbery's reformed Jack-the-Giant-Killer in *A Little Pretty Pocket Book,* the traditional folk figure of the fortune-teller here praises the middle-class virtues of studiousness and book-learning, and predicts rewards designed to appeal to the child's supposed desires for the trappings of wealth and status.

The implicit comparison between the minds and desires of children and plebeians was common to many children's writers of the late eighteenth century. However, while Marshall seems to regard this as a passing phase, most moral and didactic writers viewed this tendency in children with much greater suspicion, and warned constantly against exciting both unrealistic hopes of wealth and status and irrational notions of supernatural agents: "[a] moment's consideration will surely be sufficient to convince people of the least reflection, of the danger, as well as the impropriety, of putting such books as these [fairy tales] into the hands of little children, whose minds are susceptible of every impression; and who from the liveliness of their imaginations are apt to convert into realities whatever forcibly strikes their fancy" (Trimmer, *Guardian,* 4:75). Trimmer, it appears, understood chapbook residue in children's literature to constitute a more serious challenge to the developing middle-class morality and ideology she championed.

The Wisdom of Crop the Conjuror is not only unusual for its open statement of pedagogical intent in the preface, but for its representation of class mobility in both directions. It contains the tale of Tom Trot, who, like Goody Two-Shoes, is poor but diligent in his reading. He is hired to teach Jack, a gentleman's son, to read, but has no success because Jack proves such a hopeless dolt. With a frankness surprising in a social inferior, Tom tells Jack's father that it would be best to apprentice his son as a chimney sweep: "[i]f Jack will not climb up the Hill of Learning, he may get up a chimney well enough; and though he will not burthen his head with sense, he may carry a good load of soot on his back" (*Wisdom,* 41). This potential descent from gentleman's son to the lowest station of manual labor is presented as a logical progression, or regression: "[t]his is the reward of idleness, and every one that will not mind his book, should be served so if I was King" (*Wisdom,* 42). The story ends with this remarkable twist: "Jack's father now took Tom as his son, and bought him all the books in the world" (*Wisdom,* 42).

Marshall was by no means the only publisher producing these sorts of hybrid children's books in the late eighteenth century. As I mentioned earlier, the Newbery house continued to reprint its perennial favorites, and W. Tringham of London's *Entertaining Memoirs of Little Personages, or, Moral Amusements for Young Gentlemen* (1788) and its companion volume for young ladies provide examples of how hybrid books mix comic and ribald tales and tales of miraculous social advancement with admonishments to mind one's book.

This format appears to have enjoyed success among more provincial publishers as well, where the product often leaned much further to the side of the chapbook than the middle-class tale of moral instruction. John Feather, in *The Provincial Book Trade in Eighteenth-Century England,* remarks that although London was the principal center for chapbook publication—as it was for all books—the bulk of the provincial book trade was in chapbooks: "[t]he ubiquity of chapbooks and ballads is apparent everywhere in the country trade. They were by far the most common form of printed matter throughout provincial England."[33] This may help account for the more pronounced chapbook flavor of these works. *The History of Tommy Sugar Plumb, and his Golden Book,* published by John Pytt of Gloucester around 1773, has the crude recycled woodcuts, cheap paper, and random collection of stories, battledores, and so on, of the traditional chapbook, while still containing the seeds of a middle-class ideology. The hero of the main story, Tommy Sugar Plumb, reaps the typical rewards for his youthful good nature and attentiveness to reading, and goes on to become a beneficiary to his community by spreading literacy to others: "Tommy came at last to be a great Man, and to ride in his Coach, and had great Heaps of Money; with some of which he bought more golden Books to give away."[34]

This formula is decidedly not present in *Mother Shipton's Legacy* (1797), published in York by Wilson, Spence, and Mawman. Like Mother Bunch, Mother Shipton was a famous chapbook figure, whose stories are here collected and marketed as a children's book. The title page of this work suggests its bricolage quality and plebeian orientation: "A Favourite Fortune-Book, in which is Given, a Pleasing Interpretation of Dreams: and a Collection of Prophetic Verses, Moral and Entertaining."[35] Mixed in with such barely edifying tales as that of the boy who asks to have his fortune told only to find out he will be whipped for being naughty, are a calendar of the various "Dog Days" or unlucky days of the year, and a chapter on the interpretation of moles: "[a] mole on the tip of the right ear: A mole thus rising on the ear,/ Of drowning you stand much in fear" (*Shipton*, 11).[36] Were it not for the oddly moralizing alphabet (which follows a chapter on dream interpretation), I would be tempted to consider this a chapbook outright: "A: Industrious, yet honest, you'll acquire/ All blessings which true wisdom dares desire" (*Shipton*, 72).

Mother Chit-Chat's Curious Tales and Puzzles; or, Master and Miss's Entertaining Companion, published in Newcastle by S. Hodgson, provides a similar mixture of stories, puzzles, games, and moral instruction. The bulk of the moral instruction takes the form of a fifteen page account of "the Creation, the Fall of Man, the Deluge; and the Nativity, Life and Death of our SAVIOUR." This is followed by such folk-tale favorites as "Little Red Riding-Hood," "The King and the Woodman," and "The Story of Reynard the Fox," at the end of each of which is appended a moral (under the heading "Moral"). These are obviously recent additions to the ancient chapbook tales designed to accommodate the trend toward moral instruction of the age; but the fact that they are separate from the tales themselves allows the reader easily to skip over them, and they do not interfere with the integrity of the works they are meant to moralize. These and other more provincial children's publications have the same format as such early Newbery books as *A Little Pretty Pocketbook* (a collection of verses, alphabets, stories, games, etc.), but do not go to the same lengths to reform their chapbook elements and characters for more middle-class consumption. While they do make mention of the importance of literacy, industry, and other virtues central to the middle-class instructional works of the same period, their plebeian roots are much more deeply entrenched.[37]

I have suggested that the chapbook elements in the hybrid books of the late eighteenth century can be viewed more as a survival of residual plebeian culture within an increasingly dominant middle-class ideology than as a successful appropriation of lower-class culture. This cannot be said for the Cheap Repository Tracts, which, while adopting the traditional look and format of chapbooks, constitute a very deliberate attempt to reform plebeian moral economy. The Cheap Repository Tracts were not the only texts to appropriate plebeian forms for middle-class ideological ends, although they were the most systematic. *Father Gander's Tales,* for example, promises, by its title, stories in the vein of the popular Mother Goose fairy tales, but instead delivers a series of highly didactic accounts of children displaying obedience to parents, honesty, and contentment with their class position. As the narrator explains, "those stupid Tales of Little Red Riding Hood, Blue Beard, &c." abound "with lies and improbabilities, entirely unfit to amuse, much more to instruct the minds of youth."[38] Mitzi Myers argues that La Comtesse de Genlis's famous *Tales of the Castle* (1784) is a similar middle-class appropriation of plebeian culture: "as the French title (*Les Veillées du Château*) indicates, she transforms the old peasant custom of the *veillée,* the evening fireside entertainment that preserved the old wives' tales of popular culture to be passed on by servants and nannies to the children of the elite."[39] *The Analytical Review,* the more radical voice of middle-class reform, celebrated the Cheap Repository Tracts' ingenious appropriation of traditional plebeian literary forms and their attempts to replace chapbooks and broadsheet songs and ballads with more salutary reading material for the poor: "[s]ome are written in verse, as ballads and songs, intended to supplant the mischievous which is everywhere in circulation under these names" (*The AR,* 25: 93).

As Gary Kelly has indicated, these "pseudo-popular chapbooks" were conceived of by Hannah More in 1795 in response to the threat Jacobinism posed to the established order of English society and the widespread dissemination of Thomas Paine's *Rights of Man* in abridged chapbook form (Kelly 1987, 147–148). More was not only concerned to counteract the vicious influence of republican thinking in the lower orders, but was more broadly intent on reforming the customs, beliefs, and behaviors reflected in traditional chapbooks, and transforming the plebeian household into a "diminished version of middle-class . . . virtues" (Kelly 1987, 152).

> Cheap Repository's pseudo-popular chapbooks consistently argue that the poverty and misery of the labouring poor are caused not by "things as they are" but by their own idleness, folly, bad management, and mistaken attempts to emulate their betters—their attitude of *carpe diem,* their interest in luck and fortune-telling, their fatalism and improvidence, their toleration of petty crime on the grounds of need, their habits of deceiving their masters, and their imitation of the upper-class amorous culture of gallantry, seduction, and betrayal. (Kelly 1987, 151)

The tracts follow a very simple didactic formula to point out the evils attendant on these plebeian traits: "Most begin by describing a single central character, usually poor, who is put to some kind of trial. The character either responds well and is moderately rewarded or goes downhill and dies repenting."[40]

The success of this type of appropriation of plebeian literary forms to further middle-class ideological ends was dubious at best, despite production and distribution levels of the Tracts in the millions.[41] Gary Kelly has pointed out that there is little evidence More's Tracts were actually bought by the laboring poor for whom they were intended: "The tracts were sold in bulk, to the gentry and middle classes, and distributed free to the labouring classes" (Kelly 1987, 154).[42] Although they were primarily intended to teach adults such virtues as sobriety, frugality, and contentment with one's lot in life, the Cheap Repository Tracts were printed by such children's book publishers as Marshall and Hazard and distributed in Sunday Schools and charity schools; their simple moral tales also lent themselves to a child audience.[43]

Given that a good deal has been written on the Tracts already, and that their content is quite uniform, a brief glimpse at the type of lower-class family they envisage will suffice here. *The Cottager's Saturday Night; A Poem,*[44] portrays a family spending its one free night of the week not in excess and ribaldry, or in games and storytelling, but in a wholesome repast followed by prayer and Bible reading:

> But now the Supper crowns their simple board,
> The oatmeal porridge cheap and wholesome food,
> The milk their only Cow does well afford, [. . .]
> The cheerful Supper done, with serious face,
> They round the embers form a circle wide;
> The Sire turns o'er with Patriarchal grace,
> The huge big Bible, once his father's pride,
> His hat is reverently laid aside,
> His hoary locks growing so thin and bare;
> From strains that once did sweet in Zion glide,
> He takes a portion with judicious care;
> And, "Let us worship GOD!" he says with
>   solemn air.

The ideal lower-class family is content with the simple fare suitable to their station; their fireside reading is strictly devotional, and the overall proceedings are sober and solemn. As Kelly remarks, the regulation of plebeian eating habits was a recurring concern of the Tracts: "[e]ven the popular 'moral economy' of food, of the right to poach and steal from the gentry, and the right to such occasional 'luxuries' as tea, sugar, and meat is attacked in favour of [. . .] self-denial, planning ahead, and the virtues of the potato and cooking leftovers" (Kelly 1987, 151–152).

Such dietary proscriptions echo Benjamin Franklin's injunctions to domestic frugality to the poor in his endlessly republished *Franklin's Way to Wealth; or, Poor Richard Improved* ("Buy what thou hast no need of, and ere long thou shalt sell thy necessaries").[45] In many editions of this work, including that of 1814, which I cite here, Franklin's maxims, designed to inculcate an investment mentality in the poor, are combined with an essay on domestic economy entitled "How to Make a Little, Earnestly addressed to the Industrious Poor." Here, the pseudonymous Bob Short recommends a diet of onions and leeks, as they provide cheap nutrition, and the making of broth from meat, as opposed to more wasteful methods of preparation such as roasting and broiling. Not surprisingly, he rails against the habit of gin drinking in the poor, as well as the habit of tea drinking: "[s]ugar and tea were never used until the eighteenth century; since the poor have been tea-drinkers, half of them have been beggard and starved" (*Franklin's*, 18). Tea time for the poor amounts not only to a wasteful expenditure, but also to a dangerous class transgression and undesirable emulation of one's class betters. As Poor Richard remarks, "it is truly a folly for the poor to ape the rich, as for the frog to swell in order to equal the ox" (*Franklin's*, 10).

Given their very deliberate emulation of the traditional chapbook format (unbound, 24 pages, crude woodcuts, etc.), their replacement of Jack-the-Giant-Killer with Mary Wood the Housemaid or John the Penitent Robber, and their highly systematic methods of distribution, it is difficult to view the Cheap Repository project as anything other than appropriation and an attempt to regulate and control the behavior of the potentially revolutionary lower orders. The hybrid books for children posit very tangible and substantial rewards for their lower-class protagonists who adopt middle-class virtues; in the Cheap Repository Tracts, the poor are expected to reform their ways in exchange for the prospect of spiritual rewards in the next life. Hannah More's concerns over potential disruption of the social order fueled the Cheap Repository project; the upward class mobility enjoyed by such characters as Tommy Truelove and Polly Friendly would have been anathema to her.

With their "coach-and-six" reward schemes and their dedication to literacy as the key to success, the hybrid books of Newbery and Marshall can be seen as appealing to lower middle-class and improvement-minded lower-class aspirations for social advancement. In a period of increasing industrialization and changing business practices, the need for literate clerks made class advancement through reading and writing skills a more legitimate proposition than ever before. Indeed, John Newbery, perhaps the leading proponent of success through minding one's book, experienced firsthand a meteoric rise in station from son of a small farmer to wealthy and respected publisher who "got to own his own coach" (Townsend, xi).[46]

Mary Jackson describes the period of 1768 to 1788 (the period in which the hybrid books were in greatest abundance) as a time when chapbook elements in children's stories enjoyed a relatively high degree of tolerance. The conservative backlash created by the onset of the French Revolution, she argues, spurred the removal of plebeian influences from children's books, and ushered in the age of the respectable middle-class pedagogues. By 1789, "the vested interests of the higher orders" had forced "tradesmen [to abandon] what their betters contemned and [to adopt], at least ostensibly or temporarily, what they sanctioned" (Jackson, 105). The model of extraordinary social mobility through literacy espoused by Marshall, the Newberys, and others would still have appealed to lower middle-class and working poor parents, but not to the rational moralists and evangelical writers who would come to dominate the children's book trade in the final decade of the eighteenth century "when fears of Jacobin [. . .] influences on the poor and even the artisans of the lower middle-class both widened and intensified class conservatism" (Jackson, 55). These writers would come to envision a mostly fixed class structure, with the middle classes occupying its moral and economic center, in which the advancement of the lower orders was viewed as, at best, unrealistic, and, at worst, threatening or subversive.

Gillian Avery has also noted a shift in the values and virtues espoused in children's books in the last two decades of the eighteenth century. In *Childhood's Pattern,* she argues that children's books of the mid-century, such as *A Little Pretty Pocket-Book,* made little or no class distinction in their readership, and espoused morals "of a very obvious and materialistic sort."[47] The uncertain changing social climate ushered in by the American and, later, the French Revolutions made such crude values unacceptable: "Be punctual and diligent, obedient and dutiful, do not lie or thieve or blow up your sister, beware of mad dogs and gaming, and you will live to be a successful sugar planter and to give your rivals a handsome funeral. This in essence seems to be the uncomplicated and cheerful message of the old-styled late Georgian book. It was a message that various schools of thought found lacking" (Avery, 24).

Replacing this type of narrative was "the cult of the informed child," in the development of which both evangelicals and rationalists participated. To suggest, however, that "old-style" children's books were uninformed by notions of class, or to classify books like *A Little Pretty Pocket Book* as "simple" chapbooks, is to ignore both the ideological work these texts performed and the tensions between middle-class and plebeian cultures they expressed.

Children's books combining middle-class values with elements of chapbook narratives and plebeian fantasies of social advancement did, however, persist, albeit in diminished numbers, and in the face of increasing opposition, in the turbulent 1790s. Furthermore, the moral and didactic tales of such writers as Trimmer and Edgeworth, which characterize this decade, had numerous predecessors in the previous two decades, Anna Barbauld and the Kilners, for example, were producing rational and morally edifying books for children by the 1770s. The French Revolution may indeed, as Jackson suggests, have precipitated the reform of children's reading, but the middle-class ideological groundwork for this change had been laid well in advance.

Chapter 2
Class Relations in Middle-Class Children's Literature: Interacting with and Representing the Poor and the Rich

The development of a class consciousness and ideology in the English middle classes of the late eighteenth century relied heavily on its self-representation as the moral and productive center of English society, and on its self-differentiation from the classes above and below. This concern manifested itself repeatedly in the children's literature of the period, which presented young middle-class readers with countless representations of the poor and the rich, and with narratives depicting how they should (and should not) interact with each. Children were taught by example to avoid the potential hazards of excessive contact with the lower orders (particularly the servant class), to resist the temptation of emulating the profligate vices of the gentry and upper classes, and to be charitable and respectful to the industrious and deserving laboring poor.

By the Augustan period, most middle-class families had at least one live-in servant, and this was true throughout the eighteenth century: "The employment of domestic servants was virtually universal amongst the middle class and indeed went down into the fairly lowly strata of the artisan population of Augustan London."[1] Bridget Hill also observes that "[s]ervants were ubiquitous in eighteenth-century England," but suggests that the term servant included a much broader variety of occupations than domestic service.[2] Josiah Wedgwood included even the employees in his pottery works under the rubric of servant, and this broadening of the category beyond its currently understood usage was not uncommon: "Contemporaries made no such distinction between living-in servants and day-labourers who lived in their own homes and came in to work for an employer on a part-time and casual basis. Similarly charwomen and washer-women employed on a casual basis are frequently included under the label of 'servants' " (Hill, 13). Hill accounts for this change in the category of service to include various types of labor by pointing to the move from prior paternalistic class relations, based on duty and obligation, to wage-based contractual relations over the course of the eighteenth century (Hill, 17). The vices of domestic servants against which children's writers and pedagogues of the late eighteenth century repeatedly warned applied, therefore, not only to the live-in maid, but to her economic class more generally.

Hill's expansion of the category of servant raises the question of the position of the governess in the middle-class home. While still an employee in the domestic sphere, the governess was often represented as a legitimate educator and surrogate parent, and often as a heroic ideal of virtue and reason (cf. Mrs. Mason in Wollstonecraft's *Original Stories*). The status of the governess was ill-defined and constantly renegotiated in the eighteenth and nineteenth centuries (see, for example, Nancy Armstrong, *Desire and Domestic Fiction*, 78–79), but Maria Edgeworth describes her position in the late eighteenth century in *Practical Education:* "A governess is no longer treated as an upper servant, or as an intermediate between a servant and a gentlewoman: she is now treated as the friend and companion of the family" (cited in Myers 1989, 59).

Since Locke's time, parents had been advised by pedagogues about the potential danger to children this plebeian presence represented in the middle- and upper-class home: "They frequently learn from unbred or debauched Servants such Language, untowardly Tricks and Vices, as otherwise they possibly would be ignorant of all their Lives" (Locke, *Some Thoughts,* 127).[3] The vices, prejudices, ignorance, and superstitions of the lower classes were seen by many middle-class parents and pedagogues as corrupting influences on the impressionable, unformed mind of the child; allowing the child unsupervised contact with servants threatened to undermine the moral and rational education the middle classes sought to promote.[4] As the prolific and influential children's writer Lady Eleanor Fenn observed in *The Art of Teaching in Sport* (1785): "I would as soon abandon the direction of the subterraneous parts of a palace to a mason's labourer, as trust the first seven or eight years of a child to the government of a servant without education, and without view."[5] The education of children constitutes not only the foundation for their own future happiness and usefulness, but for that of society as well; to leave it in the hands of the servant or laborer and not the master was to court disaster. Although the work of educating the young may appear lowly and "subterraneous"—not as glamorous or visible as writing for the fully-formed adult mind—it constitutes the foundation for a larger architecture of society.

Locke, whose treatise on education was originally intended for a more or less elite mercantile and moneyed "gentlemanly" class, and Lady Eleanor Fenn, who inhabited the more conservative end of the upper middle classes, espouse a not altogether surprising suspicion of the domestic servant. However, this suspicion of the plebeian vices servants threatened to introduce into the domestic sphere was shared by even the most radical middle-class pedagogues. Despite his progressive opposition to servitude and his outrage at the injustices suffered by the poor, even such a radical writer as William Godwin expressed his concerns over the malignant effects servants had on children in no uncertain terms; he considered the domestic servant "a species of being in whom we apprehend the most sordid of defects. If they are not in an emphatical degree criminal, at least their ignorance makes them dangerous, and their subjection makes them narrow."[6] Godwin even goes so far as to suggest that leaving one's house, let alone one's children, in the care of servants is tantamount to letting the animals run the zoo: "If we were told of a man who appropriated a considerable portion of his house to the habitation of rats, and pole-cats, and serpents, and wolves, we certainly should not applaud either his taste or his judgment" (Godwin, 204). Egalitarian philosophy and republican sympathies did not override a ubiquitous middle-class suspicion of, and hostility toward, the plebeian classes and plebeian class culture.[7]

Godwin's use of animal metaphor to describe the danger posed by servants, and his implication that they constitute an altogether different "species" of humanity is quite revealing. Children themselves were considered to be, in both pedagogical and pediatric discourses of the period, a completely different category, or "species," of humanity as well, and were often warned in stories that their miscarriages in behavior and reason lowered them to the level of animals.[8] While pedagogues and writers for children may have aligned servants with children, at the level of superstition, appetite for fantastic narratives or world views, and lack of reason, they recognized that this condition, given the proper education, would only be temporary in children. However, as Mary Wollstonecraft observes in *Thoughts on the Education of Daughters,* this is not the case with servants: "[w]e cannot make our servants wise or good" (39). Because they grew to adulthood without the benefit of a moral and rational education, the irrationality of servants had been ingrained, and this plebeian intractability and resistance to improvement made them singularly unfit to raise the middle-class child envisioned by such pedagogues. As the Edgeworths put it in *Practical Education,* servants are of a class "who have never studied the human mind, who have little motive for study" (123). Wollstonecraft's and Edgeworth's assertions on the unimprovable nature of servants are, in one sense, confirmed by Bridget Hill's study of eighteenth-century service. While entering service may once have provided a possible route to upward class mobility (by learning and eventually applying the skills and cultural practices of one's employer), this prospect became increasingly unlikely for the eighteenth-century servant: "The servant, whether called servant in husbandry or domestic servant, who entered the household of an employer with the intention that when he or she left it would be to become a master or mistress employing his or her own servants, was an increasing rarity" (14–15).

The lack of opportunity afforded servants may account more for their perceived intractability than any innate incapacity for learning.[9] Regardless of the reasons for this perception, the impressionable minds of children were now understood to require the regular influence and constant supervision of an adult, presumably of the middle class, who had enjoyed the benefits of a rational education.

Although such attitudes towards servants were commonplace in pedagogical writings of the period, there were some exceptions. The reviewer of *Practical Education* for *The Analytical Review,* for example, objects to the Edgeworths' advice to keep servants and children totally separated:

> that two sets of human beings should live under one roof, and the one under so degraded a state, as not to be thought worthy of holding any communication with the other; that the domestics should move about like mutes in an eastern seraglio, forbidden, on pain of expulsion, to speak to the child . . . we suppose must produce a pride and suspicion on one side, and an indignant hatred on the other, much more hurtful to the mind, than almost any habits, which, with common care in the choice of servants, a child could acquire from a freer communication with them. (*The AR,* 28.637)

Mitzi Myers has indicated that Maria Edgeworth's attitudes towards servants were not so entirely negative as such criticism would imply; indeed, in *Practical Education* she recognized the need for educated servants within the middle-class home and the desire of servants to improve themselves and their station. Myers cites *Practical Education* to demonstrate that, for Edgeworth at least, the democratic notion of perfectibility extended to the servant class as well: "Their vices and their ignorance arise from the same causes, the want of education. They are not a separate cast in society doomed to ignorance, or degraded by inherent vice; they are capable, they are desirous of education. Let them be well educated" (cited in Myers 1989, 59). The servants of the future could, perhaps, be made rational and virtuous, even if those in the present generally were not.

The dangers of consorting with servants were not remarked upon solely in works of pedagogical theory; they naturally found their way into the literature for children as well. In *Scenes for Children* (c. 1790), Mrs. Denby, a devoted middle-class mother, sees her efforts at providing her two children, Edward and Maria, with a sound Lockean education undermined when they spend a single evening alone with the servants. She has performed her maternal duty admirably, using shame and reward to instill a sense of reason in her children: "[t]he tenderness mixed with her reproofs, seldom failed to success: she opened their understandings, she appealed to their hearts, and they rectified their conduct themselves."[10] One evening, however, she goes out to dine at a friend's house—a rare occurrence indeed for this paragon of maternal devotion—only to find, on her return, her children overcome by fits. When she asks them what is wrong, Maria replies: "Mamma, after you went out, we drank our tea in the kitchen with the maids. . . . Jenny says there are such things [as ghosts] . . . and we begged her to tell us about them to-night, before we went to bed, and she did, and I am sure there is one in the house" (*Scenes,* 67). The price of ensuring the success of a rational education in one's children is eternal vigilance, not only because the plebeian culture of servants is fraught with irrational superstitions of ghosts and goblins, but because children, who are by definition themselves subjects lacking reason, have a natural affinity for such forms of irrationality; it was the children who *begged* Jenny to tell them about ghosts.

According to David Williams, author of a pedagogical system entitled *Lectures on Education,* the danger in child-servant contact lies in the combination of childhood inquisitiveness and plebeian ignorance: "The general occupation of infancy is to *enquire.* . . . But their direction is usually committed to nurses and servants; who either check curiosity by sullenness and severity; or by giving false answers, and referring appearances to wrong causes, disappoint this important faculty in its first exertions; and fix habits of credulity and superstition, which are never to be corrected" (I:55).

Ghost stories told to children by servants were a particularly popular object of criticism for middle-class pedagogues because they demonstrated most clearly the influence on the young of the irrational superstitions of this class. Wollstonecraft, for example, warned parents in *Thoughts on the Education of Daughters* about the "improbable tales, and superstitious accounts of invisible beings" servants relate to children, "which breed strange prejudices and vain fears in their minds" (10). The narrator of Richard Johnson's *The Adventures of a Silver Penny* associates this plebeian practice with mental illness: "[t]hose who pretend to have seen them are either fools or madmen, whose minds must be very weak, or whose senses are much disordered" (40).

Maria Edgeworth's books for children suggest a more subtle undermining of the development of the child's reason resulting from excessive contact with servants. The peevish, disobedient, or temperamental child in Edgeworth's children's stories is very often the child whose upbringing has been left largely to its maid or nurse. In "The Birthday Present," the spoiled Little Bell's regular tantrums and displays of selfishness are forms of behavior directly attributable to the contact she has had with the domestics. She has grown "idle, fretful, and selfish, so that nothing could make her happy," in large part because it was her "maid who educated her."[11] Further, "she had learned from her maid a total disregard of truth," as well as "habits of tyranny, meanness and falsehood" (II:24).

In *Practical Education,* the Edgeworths warned parents of the devious practices of servants when left to care for a child: "[they] seek to ingratiate themselves into a child's affections through flattery" (122). This model of behavior plays itself out in Little Bell's story; her maid is always telling her that everything she owns is "fit for a queen" (18). In the logic of late eighteenth-century middle-class pedagogy, a servant's flattery of privileged children threatened to excite both the inherent vanity of the child, and the characteristically plebeian vice of irrationally admiring and desiring the trappings of wealth. Edgeworth's representation of Little Bell and the impact her maid has had on her character underscores the perceived double threat embodied in the domestic servant. As Mitzi Myers remarks, the vices of servants were those of both the upper and lower classes: "[d]omestics symbolized not only the unenlightened ignorance of the old wife, but also upper-class artifice" (Myers 1989, 57).

Middle-class writers generally acknowledged children's fascination with the trappings of wealth and status, and thought that it fostered a potentially dangerous affinity with the decadent luxuries of the gentry and aristocratic classes. In *Original Stories,* Wollstonecraft's Mrs. Mason makes the connection between the child's and the servant's love of ostentatious displays of wealth "[t]he lower class of mankind, and children, are fond of finery; gaudy dazzling appearances catch their attention" (390). The plebeian desire for greater status, and more specifically for its outward signifiers (beautiful clothing, carriages, finery in general), highlighted another important reason to keep middle-class children away from servants. Servants have been raised in a chapbook culture in which wealth, and more importantly, the outward appearance of wealth, was equated with happiness and social status. As Wollstonecraft's Mrs. Mason tries to show her pupils, "[s]ervants, and those women whose minds have had a very limited range, place all their happiness in ornaments" (*Original,* 410). Middle-class writers wanted children to associate happiness with morality and social utility instead.

The desire of the domestic servant to advance herself through flattery, as well as her desire to emulate her class betters, is the product, paradoxically, of her proximity to the middle-class subject—the very subject parents and pedagogues sought to distance and differentiate from the servant class: "servants, from their situation, from all that they see of the society of their superiors, and from the early prejudices of their own education, learn to admire the wealth and rank to which they are bound to pay homage" (Edgeworth and Edgeworth, 121).[12] In a middle-class pedagogy intended to produce industrious, self-sufficient subjects free from the awe and deference traditionally accorded to the upper classes and aristocracy, this characteristically servile brand of "homage" is necessarily viewed as both irrational and destructive.[13]

In Maria Edgeworth's "The Birthday Present," it is precisely this sort of reverence accorded by Bell's maid and the house's footman to upper-class finery that is at the source of her misconduct and ultimate unhappiness. The servants in Bell's household have, by virtue of their proximity to their class superiors, and presumably by virtue of the laxity of their employers, acquired a false notion of their own class superiority. They equate money with upper-class privilege, and translate their proximity with a moneyed family into the right to mistreat those whom they deem their social inferiors. The footman, for example, feels that his "livery laced in silver" grants him the right to ruin the bobbins and thread of an honest, industrious, young lace weaver who comes to the door selling her wares (8). When the girl returns to seek reparation for her broken tools and ruined lace, Bell's maid chastises her as a "little, idle, good-for-nothing thing;" when she is gone, the maid disparagingly refers to her (and presumably any other honest, poor laborer) as "these folk" (*Parents,* 23, 24).

The result of such influences on young Bell is predictable. She receives from Rosamond, the protagonist of Edgeworth's most famous story, "The Purple Jar," a delicately constructed filigreed basket, which at first pleases her because of its beauty, but—as it is a frivolous rather than a useful item—ultimately disappoints her when she destroys it through her carelessness. Bell's misguided love of useless finery is represented by the fleeting pleasure she derives from the filigree basket she receives on her birthday. Not only is the gift extravagant and of little practical use, it lacks durability and its beauty is ruined almost immediately. The ideal middle-class child appreciates things (and indeed people) not for their outward, gaudy appearance—their aristocratic pretentions as it were—but for their utility, durability and serviceability.[14] Part of the danger in allowing servants to fuel the child's vanity and love of luxury and ornament lies in their implicit reinscription of the upper-class vice and wastefulness that the middle classes found so contemptible. The plebeian tendency to emulate their betters, as well as the chapbook and folk tale "Cinderella" fantasies that underpinned this tendency, were seen as counterproductive to an ideology that defined itself against aristocratic-style excess.

Maria Edgeworth divided her stories for children along class lines in *The Parent's Assistant*; as she observes in her preface to this work, the different classes "have few ideas, few habits, in common, their peculiar vices and virtues do not arise from the same causes, and their ambition is to be directed to different objects" (II:vii). Stories like "The Purple Jar" and "The Birthday Present" were designed to instruct and improve children of the middle classes, while a narrative like "The Basket Woman" was directed more at the reform and education of the plebeian reader. Of course, given that the readership of Edgeworth's stories would have come principally from the middle classes, one can assume that her tales depicting the poor (both honest and dishonest) were also intended to present the middle-class child with models of proper and improper behavior in their class inferiors.

"The Basket Woman" tells the tale of a poor old woman who takes in two orphaned children. She is exemplary in her kindness to the children and in her industry: "[s]he worked hard at her spinning-wheel, and at her knitting to support herself and them. She earned money also in another way; she used to follow all the carriages . . . and when the horses stopped to take breath . . . she put stones behind the carriage-wheels to prevent them from rolling backwards down the slippery hill" (2). She has also taken care to instill the virtues of the poor but respectable laborer in her two charges: "she explained to them what it meant by telling the truth, and what it is to be honest; she taught them to dislike idleness, and to wish that they could be useful" (3). The children, seeing how hard their grandmother (as they refer to her) works to sustain them, offer to take over the job of "scotching" the carriage wheels, thus allowing the industrious old woman the freedom "to sit still at her wheel all day" (5–6). The boy exhibits an admirable work ethic in his new job, and even develops an ingenious new system to make his efforts more efficient; he invents a "scotcher"—a wedge of wood fitted to the end of a broken crutch handle—that "answered the purpose perfectly" (9). The children are already exhibiting the kind of industrious application and internalization of middle-class ideology (writ small) that such reform efforts as the Cheap Repository Tract Society were trying to promote in the poor.[15]

Luck brings the children a substantial fortune, when "a bright golden guinea" is, presumably by accident, thrown into their cap by a carriage passenger along with the halfpennies they usually receive for their services (13). Their initial temptation is to gorge themselves on the "two hundred and fifty-two dozen" plums the guinea could purchase; despite internalizing the virtue of industry, the lottery mentality of their class (and of their age)—the desire to waste their windfall frivolously—comes briefly to the surface (15). They quickly reconsider this initial expression of desire for frivolous luxury, opting instead for a blanket their elderly benefactor sorely needs: "we might buy something for my grandmother, that would be *very useful* to her indeed, with this guinea; something that would *last a great while*" (15, italics mine). The blanket, unlike the plums, is an investment whose benefits would be felt over the long term.

As exemplary as is this display of the middle-class investment mentality in the poor, honesty and respect for rightful ownership emerge as the more important virtues to observe. The children consult their grandmother about whether the money is legitimately theirs; since they did not earn it by their labor, she advises them that "it is not honestly ours; those who threw it to you, gave it by mistake" (20). The only honest way of amassing a fortune is through hard work; such chance windfalls (by which the chapbook hero often improves his lot) necessarily come at the expense of another, and the grandmother, therefore, insists that the children return the guinea to its rightful owner.[16]

The children manage to locate the carriage out of which the guinea was accidentally thrown, and discover the inn at which the gentleman in question and his family are staying. When they try to return the guinea, they are swindled by the family's servant who promises to return it to his master but instead proceeds to spend it in the most extravagant fashion at the inn: "[p]ray, Mrs. Landlady, please to let me have roasted larks for my supper . . . I make it a rule to taste the best of everything, wherever I go; and waiter, let me have a bottle of claret" (28). The servant here acts as a virtual catalog of what the middle classes viewed as the perennial plebeian vices: he steals; he is dishonest; he puts on airs and emulates his betters; he squanders his ill-gotten wealth on luxury and drink. In short, he is everything the honest and industrious poor are not and should make sure to avoid.

Fortunately, all is set right by an honest basket weaver who happens to be selling her goods at the inn, and who observes the servant's dishonesty. The guinea is eventually returned to the gentleman, and the reward he gives the children is twofold: he buys the needed blanket for the grandmother and pays the basket woman to teach the children her trade, thereby allowing them to provide for themselves through their own industry (no plums for the children, sadly). While at one level a noble gesture on the gentleman's part, his charity is of the sort that guarantees the children will remain poor (albeit respectably so). It grants them the opportunity to pursue a menial occupation suited to their station and sufficient to provide for their humble needs; it does not grant them the opportunity at an education that could afford them any real chance at class advancement.

Such portraits for young readers of the industrious poor—those who had absorbed many of the key middle-class virtues while remaining satisfied with their humble stations in life—focused most often on the figure of the agricultural laborer, who was thought to be far removed from the vices of the domestic servant. Peter Coveney, in *The Image of Childhood,* refers to this literary phenomenon of the nobly impoverished worker as the "cult of poverty": "[t]he poor are very honest; and the greater their poverty the nobler they prove" (49). Rousseau's *Emile,* which espoused the benefits of honest labor and a simple rustic existence as the means to forming healthy children and eventually useful members of society, contributed to the idealized representations of the poor but contented rural laborer typical of this "cult." Rousseau goes so far as to argue, in fact, that the agrarian poor, by virtue of the perfect simplicity of their lifestyle and their innate contentedness, require no education: "the poor may come to manhood without our help" (*Emile,* 49).

This middle-class fantasy of the poor worker who desires nothing more than to toil honestly and subsist modestly served a number of didactic and ideological purposes. In Anna Barbauld and John Aikin's *New Christmas Tales* (the second part of *Evenings at Home*), for example, the story "Humble Life" sings the praises of peasant simplicity while correcting a young boy's inclination to despise poverty. While out on an instructive walk through the country, young Charles and his father pass by a humble cottage. Charles observes that he could never endure the abject misery that surely must be the fate of its inhabitants. His father remarks that "if they are healthy and contented, I don't know that we have anything to boast of. I believe the man is able to procure wholesome food for his family, and clothes and firing to keep them from suffering from cold, and nature wants little more."[17] Since, as all good eighteenth-century pedagogues and children's writers knew, children learn better from example than from precept,[18] Charles's father takes him into the cottage to prove his assertion, and Poor Jacob, the simple farmer who lives there, happily obliges them. Jacob shows his guests the model of humble industry that is his home, pointing out that even his young children are engaged in productive work: "[i]t is but poor employment, but better than being idle. The first lesson is that their hands were made to get their bread with" (Aiken and Barbauld, 453). He also assures young Charles that his only desire is for he and his family to keep their health so that they may all remain productive. Charles's father heartily approves: "[k]eep such a contented mind, my friend, and you will have few to envy" (Aiken and Barbauld, 456).

The contented laborer became, in late eighteenth-century children's literature, a stock figure. An almost identical character appears in C. G. Salzmann's *Elements of Morality* (translated from the German by Mary Wollstonecraft) in the form of a gardener: "health is dearer to me than a whole sack-full of gold: as long as I have health I can work hard" (22). Thomas Day's Little Jack, a pastoral, rustic ideal of health who was suckled by a goat in his infancy, is raised by an old hermit who, from his deathbed, imparts to Jack the same message: "I have lived, said the old man, a great many years in poverty, but I do not know that I have been worse off than had I been rich" (34). Such happy examples of honest laborers teach middle-class children like young Charles not only that the poor are not to be despised, but also that they have no desire ever to become rich.[19] Further, by advancing such representations of a plebeian class that has gladly adopted a diminished form of middle-class ideology and has no intention of moving up the class ladder, these texts support the middle classes' view of themselves as rightful heirs to the role of economic center and social benefactors of English society.[20]

Idealized plebeian characters in middle-class children's books of the period were sometimes so content with their station as to reject actively any chance opportunity to take on even the appearance of class advancement. The Trueman family in *The Entertaining and Instructive History of John Trueman* (c. 1800) is a model of lower-class frugality, propriety, and industry: "[t]heir money did not go to the grocer's for tea, sugar, and butter. . . . If a neighbor came in, Betty still continued her work. She had no time for gossiping and tea-drinking."[21] Betty, Mrs. Trueman, not only ensures that her family's behavior and morality conform to the Cheap Repository Tract model of proper plebeian frugality and humility, she acts as an instrument of reform amongst the members of her community as well.[22] When her neighbor proudly displays a scarlet coat for which she has paid the exorbitant price of fifteen shillings, Betty interrogates her on the relative prices of such cheaper (and, for their class, more appropriate) materials as brown linsey cloth and dowlas and then upbraids her for her extravagance: "If you had been as able as [the wealthy] Mrs. Ivyson, I should have thought it suitable, and should have said never a word: but with such families, Mary, and means, as you have, I should have been as much ashamed of going about the parish with a scarlet cloak, that cost me fifteen shillings, as I would have been of going about with three of my children's shirts pinned to my back" (*Entertaining*, 12). Betty is practically invoking the sumptuary laws of the sixteenth and seventeenth centuries here, which forbade people of lower stations to wear the fashions of their class superiors. However, as a member of the plebeian classes herself, her regulation of the propriety of her class equals reinforces the middle-class fantasy of the poor wanting to be and to look respectably poor: "such people as we ... have nothing to do with finery" (*Entertaining*, 15).[23]

Mary Ann Kilner's *The Adventures of a Pin-Cushion* (c. 1780) contains a similar instance of plebeian self-denial and rejection of improper extravagance in appearance. When a house mover discovers the pin cushion (the story's narrator) behind a bureau in a recently vacated house, he gives it to his friend, a maid, as a gift for her daughter Jenny, suggesting that "it will make her as fine as a lady" (II:6). Jenny's mother, acutely aware of what is proper to the class of both her and her daughter, flatly and rather indignantly rejects the gift: "as to making her fine ... indeed I do not desire it; and were you to present any thing to wear, she could not have it; for I think finery is not suitable for us" (6). In these narratives that depict to middle-class children the desires and aspirations of the poor, plebeians are so aware of and content with their class position that they reject even the smallest windfall that might suggest or enable some form of class advancement.

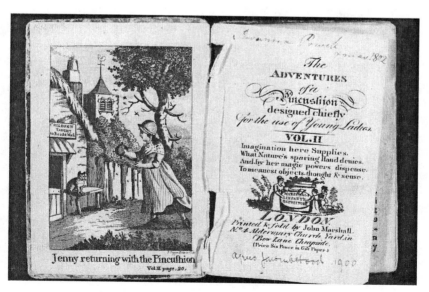

Fig. 2 Frontispiece and title page: Mary Ann Kilner, *The Adventures of a Pincushion Vol.2.* London: J. Marshall, c.1800. Courtesy of The Osborne Collection of Early Children's Books, Toronto Public Library

Of course, the poor were not always represented in such an idealized light; the Cheap Repository Tracts, for example, documented the vices of the plebeian classes exhaustively. While, more often than not, texts for middle-class children depict the poor (excluding the almost universally vilified servant class) as either content and hardworking or as humble, grateful objects of pity and charity, their lack of moral instruction does occasionally result in wickedness. The poem "Poor Children," in Jane and Ann Taylor's *Rhymes for the Nursery,* provides a model of plebeian behavior good middle-class children should seek to avoid:

> ... very often they are
> Quite naughty and wicked,—I never can bear
> To hear how they quarrel together, and swear.
>
> For often they use naughty words in their play,
> And I might have been quite as wicked as they,
> If I'd not been taught better, I heard mamma say.
>
> O, how very thankful I always should be,
> That I have kind parents to watch over me,
> Who teach me from wickedness ever to flee!
>
> And as mamma tells me, I certainly should,
> Mind all that is taught me, and be very good,
> For if those poor children knew better,—*they* would. (14–15)

Unlike the adult servant, in whom a variety of vices have taken root to the extent that he or she can no longer be improved by education, the poor child is seemingly still salvageable.

As such works as the Cheap Repository Tracts demonstrate, these representations of the poor—as either wicked or humble and industrious—were not meant solely for the consumption of the children of the middle classes. Sarah Trimmer managed quite ingeniously to incorporate her ideology of plebeian reform into the primers and spelling books used in Sunday charity schools. *The Charity School Spelling Book,* which had run to eleven editions by 1808, was widely used in the Sunday School program to teach poor children literacy skills.[24] While many of Trimmer's more conservative contemporaries were uncomfortable with the subversive possibilities of literate servants and laborers, the ideological content of these reading lessons would certainly have met with their approval. The first part of the book is an alphabet accompanied by memory drills in syllables; this is followed by a series of simple sentences fitted to the experiences of plebeian students: "[t]he Man digs well. The Boy plows well. The Girl sews fast. ... Good Girls make their own clothes. Good Boys take care of their shoes" (*Charity,* 16). The section on complex sentences includes such maxims as "Boys and Girls who will not work when they may, will go in rags all their lives" (17), as well as injunctions to the poor to be respectable in the eyes of their betters: "[t]hose who are poor, want friends, and friends can not be had, if folks will not be good" (18). The "friends" Trimmer has in mind are, of course, well-disposed social betters who would offer the deserving poor charitable assistance. The last section of this primer contains stories about poor children such as Jane Sparks, whom we find lamenting the fact that she has no money to buy clothes for her infant sister. Her sorrows are overheard by a "friend to the poor" who kindly takes her to the workhouse where she learns to "hem and sew, to spin and knit" (28). Through her own industry she is able to clothe her sister.[25] Jane's counterpart is the idle Becky Bond: "she was twelve years old, but she would not make a bed, or sweep a room, or scrub a shelf; though she was so big and strong that she might have kept a whole house clean with ease" (*Charity,* 29). Following the narrative logic of the Cheap Repository Tracts, Becky's laziness coincides with a moral laxitude that seals her fate: "[t]o romp with bad boys in the street was the great joy of Becky Bond's life, so she learnt of them to be bold, to swear, and call names, and at last to steal, and came to a bad end, you may be sure" (30).

Stories narrated by animals, and by such inanimate objects as pin cushions, whipping tops, and thimbles, also performed the didactic function of portraying the virtues of contentedness with one's lot in life and fortitude in the face of unforeseen adversity. Despite the breach with reality a horse or a silver penny telling its own story represented, the popularity of such figures in children's writing indicates that both moral and rational writers felt comfortable with introducing some fantasy elements into didactic narratives.[26] However, to ensure that the novelty of such improbabilities did not supplant their pedagogical ends in the child's mind, these narratives often opened with a caveat that they were imaginative fictions. Sarah Trimmer's *Fabulous Histories* (later republished as *The History of the Robins*) begins by informing the reader that it is only "by the force of the imagination" that animals can be "endued with the same faculties" as humans (x). Further, the stories contained within her work are not to be seen "as containing the real conversations of Birds, (for that it is impossible we should ever understand,) but as a series of FABLES, intended to convey moral instruction" (x–xi).[27] Similarly, Mrs. Benfield, the narrator of Dorothy Kilner's *The Rational Brutes,* warns her young audience to focus on the moral instruction in her tale of talking animals, without which her story would merely be "a very foolish one, for it supposed that birds and beasts, and fish, could talk and reason, which you know is quite impossible" (6). Such introductory appeals to the child's sense of perspective and of reality were necessary to middle-class authors seeking to reinforce the difference between their works and the dangerous plebeian fantasy contained in chapbooks and fairy tales.

The objective of *Fabulous Histories* is, as the title page indicates, to instruct children "respecting their treatment of animals," and this is true of countless other stories of anthropomorphized animals, such as Dorothy Kilner's *The Rational Brutes,* and the anonymously published *Memoirs of Dick the Little Pony.* Such works are informed by the later eighteenth century's spirit of sensibility with its exaggerated emphasis on the individual's capacity for feeling the sorrows of another. However, the close resemblance the representations of the animals in these stories bear to the idealized representations of the agrarian poor suggests that children are meant to derive lessons concerning their treatment of both the lower orders of society and of creation from these texts.

Trimmer's robin family is portrayed as industrious and respectably poor in much the same terms Aikin and Barbauld use to describe Poor Jacob and his family. The father exercises the "utmost industry and labour" to support his family, and advises them that, because they subsist on a tight budget and have many mouths to feed, they must "make use of every expedient for supplying our necessities" (*Fabulous,* 2). They are perfectly happy with the simple fare suited to their simple needs and, like Salzmann's gardener who prefers his rustic hardiness over luxury, actually prefer to drink water over wine: "that delightful element, more acceptable to them, than the most costly wine would have been" (*Fabulous,* 127). The virtues of cleanliness and propriety too—very much at the center of the Cheap Repository Tracts' agenda of reforming plebeian habits—are also preached by the mother robin to her young: "neatness was a very essential thing, being conducive to health, and also to render them agreeable in the eye of the world" (*Fabulous,* 28). Respectability in poverty can, according to the middle-class ideology of the age, be accomplished by abiding by the ideology without reaping its benefits. On the one hand, the poor must not emulate or aspire to the wealth and consumption patterns of their betters. On the other hand, they are expected to replicate the middle-class virtues of industry, self-denial, and propriety that make social advancement and its concomitant increase in wealth possible.[28]

Charity, which I will discuss at greater length later in this chapter, is the principal lesson Harriet and Frederick learn in their dealings with the robins. However, as the rational operation of the Wilson farm—to which the children pay a visit—demonstrates, the kind treatment of animals can have very practical and profitable benefits as well. The Wilsons treat their animals with the respect owed to those who labor, while still acknowledging that the dominion God has granted them over the animals is to be employed usefully and for the profit and improvement of all. For example, because the Wilsons "render their lives as happy as possible," their chickens repay them by supplying "great profit too; for they furnish us with a vast number of eggs...not only for our own use, but for the market also" (*Fabulous,* 148). Treating one's inferiors with kindness is not only a matter of Christian duty, it is a way of maximizing their utility and productivity, a lesson, of course, that can be applied with equal success to both human and animal labor.

The Wilsons increase their profits through ingenious as well as kind treatment of animals, as their innovation of beekeeping demonstrates. Rather than view bees as "little stinging creatures, whom it was dangerous to approach," as her neighbors do, Mrs. Wilson recognizes and exploits the value and utility of these creatures: "my neighbours laugh at me, and call me very whimsical and extravagant for indulging myself with them; but I find my account in keeping bees thus, even upon a principle of œconomy; for as I do not destroy them, I have greater numbers to work for me, and more money every year than the last" (*Fabulous*, 153). By looking past the annoyance and stings of the bees and recognizing their unexploited labor potential, the Wilson's demonstrate that profit and utility can be gained from even the lowest orders of creation.[29]

Treating animals with kindness leads not only to greater serviceability and productivity, but to an agreeable subservience in them as well; as Mr. Wilson observes of his livestock: "all the creatures belonging to us are very harmless and gentle, which is the natural consequence of kind treatment" (*Fabulous*, 173). A kindly approach to one's inferiors constitutes "authority in a proper manner," and allows the master to maintain his dominion over often stronger, more numerous, and potentially rebellious underlings (*Fabulous*, 174).

Mr. Wilson confides in Harriet and Frederick that the secret to his successful farm lies in "a principle of humanity as well as interest" (*Fabulous*, 184). He takes care not to let "any beast work beyond its strength and always [to] give them their food in due season" (*Fabulous*, 179). Apart from being very humane, this method of treating his animals "as my servants," demonstrates how kindness can serve as an investment in future profit (*Fabulous*, 179). The Wilsons' model farm conveys lessons, not only in kindness to animals, but also lessons that can be applied to labor relations; these will prove useful to middle-class children who will go on to become factory owners and leaders of industry, or who will one day manage the domestic servants in their own households. Further, in an age that had just witnessed numerous food riots as well as the Gordon Riots, and that would soon see the upheavals of the French Revolution, the capacity to avert the stings of bees, and to sustain and insure the docility of the lower orders was of particular import. In the political, social, and class turmoil of the 1790s, this message would become increasingly resonant.

In contrast to the humane yet rational and utilitarian model of animal management represented by the Wilson farm, *Fabulous Histories* provides two examples of the different poles of the abuse of animals: young Master Jenkins's cruelty to them, and Mrs. Addis's excessive affection for her pets. Edward Jenkins's litany of crimes against the animal kingdom includes such ingenious perversions as tying a dog and a cat together to watch them fight, and drowning puppies in front of their mother. Children's stories condemning young boys for bird nesting and other cruelties were very common in the age of sensibility. Some of Edward's abuses, however, suggest quite specific activities traditionally associated with certain plebeian cultural practices and feast-day celebrations. Edward describes how he and his friends go about torturing roosters: "we . . . got a Cock, whose legs we tied, and flung at him till he died. Then we set two others fighting, and fine sport we had; for one was pecked till his breast was laid open, and the other was blinded" (*Fabulous,* 63). Cockfighting was, along with such entertainments as bearbaiting, the subject of great controversy in the eighteenth century, and was often cited by upper- and middle-class moralists as an indication of the pressing need to reform traditional plebeian customs and manners.

John Brand, the late eighteenth-century antiquarian and author of *Observations on the Popular Antiquities of Great Britain,* described the popular plebeian sport of cockfighting as a "cruel and inhuman mode of diversion" and a "disgrace [to] human reason."[30] This "striking disgrace to the manly character of Britons" infected even the grandest of aristocrats: "[i]t has been by some called a royal diversion, and, as every one knows, the Cockpit at Whitehall was erected by a crowned head [Henry VIII], for the more magnificent celebration of the sport" (Brand, II:60, 62). The real danger in cockfighting, however, lay in its appeal to the laboring poor: "[i]t still continues to be a favourite sport of the colliers in the north of England. The clamorous wants of their families solicit them to go to work in vain, when a match is heard of" (II:63). Brand's critique of this particular plebeian cultural practice is twofold: first, its cruelty demeans the noble and masculine British spirit, and second, the gambling and drinking associated with the cockfight works counter to the middle-class model of domesticity reformers sought to inculcate in the laboring poor.

Trimmer's description of Edward's practice of tying one leg of a cock to a stake in the ground and then throwing stones and sticks at it until it died is certainly a direct reference to the game of "throwing at cocks," which was traditionally part of the plebeian Shrovetide festivities. The festival of Shrovetide (also known as Shrove Tuesday, or Pancake Tuesday, this was the Tuesday before the start of Lent) was itself viewed by middle-class reformers with a great deal of mistrust because of its popish origins and the lascivious behavior that accompanied it: "[t]he luxury and intemperance that usually prevailed at this season were vestiges of the Romish carnival" (Brand, I:64). The sport of "throwing at cocks," however, is singled out by Brand among the other traditional Shrovetide activities because of its unique degree of cruelty: "[t]his sport, now almost entirely forgotten among us, we wish to consign to eternal oblivion; an amusement fit only for the bloodiest savages, and not for humanised men, much less for Christians" (I:76–77).[31] Edward's mistreatment of animals is doubly vicious, as it both displays a lack of sensibility toward the feelings of lesser beings and links him to what middle-class reformers would have seen as the worst type of plebeian and, (as Brand's accounts point out) upper-class excess.[32]

While Edward Jenkins acts as an example to young readers of plebeian-style cruelty to animals, Mrs. Addis provides the Benson children with an example of upper-class overindulgence and pampering. She "has absolutely transferred the affection she ought to feel for her child" onto a menagerie of pampered pets (*Fabulous,* 107). This is not only a transgression of domestic and maternal duty, but of the natural hierarchy. Animals—who the text has demonstrated throughout are, like the agrarian poor, best suited to, and indeed prefer, honest work and a humble existence—suffer at the hands of Mrs. Addis the consequences of an unnatural advancement in status and of a luxurious and decadent lifestyle. As Mrs. Benson indicates to her children, the pampering to which these pets are subjected can only be detrimental to them: "[a]s for puss who lies in the cradle in all her splendor . . . she would pass her time pleasanter in a basket of clean straw. . . . The lap dog is, I am sure, a miserable object, full of diseases, the consequences of luxurious living" (*Fabulous,* 107–8). A life of excess is unhealthy to anyone—including, as we shall see, the upper classes—but especially to the lower orders of creation/society whom providence has fitted to a simpler mode of life.[33]

Trimmer's robins, having correctly recognized and accepted their humble station, desire none of the dangerous luxuries that have so weakened Mrs. Addis's pets. This type of contentedness with one's place in creation characterizes Dorothy Kilner's *Rational Brutes* as well. The animals in this book gather in a barn to exchange stories of the kinds of cruelty they have suffered at the hands of thoughtless boys.[34] While the text operates at one level as a plea by mistreated animals for increased sensibility, it also reinforces the notion that the lower orders, if treated well, will happily occupy their humble stations and labor for the benefit of their betters. As the hog remarks, "I think I may answer for all my dumb fellow creatures, that if we are treated gently, and used generously, there is not one of us, that would not be willing to do all that lay within our power to please and assist our masters" (*Rational,* 31–32). The assurances of farmer Wilson in *Fabulous Histories* that animals respond positively and with increased productivity to kind usage are confirmed here by the animals themselves.

The owl provides a cautionary tale from its own experience concerning the dangers of seeking to exceed one's providentially ordained station. Although its life was comfortable and all its needs provided for in the hayloft of its master's barn, the owl still sought the freedom to go where it pleased. As a result, its master clips its wings and cages it, a punishment the owl regards as warranted: "my impatience to improve my state, and enjoy still more liberty, reduced me to my present bondage" (*Rational,* 71). Having learned its proper place from this experience, it warns its fellow animals not to set their sights too high: "I would earnestly recommend you all to be satisfied with your condition" (*Rational,* 61). With its reference to liberty and bondage, the owl's story can be seen as more than a warning about the disappointment attendant on those of low station who aspire to social advancement; it warns about the

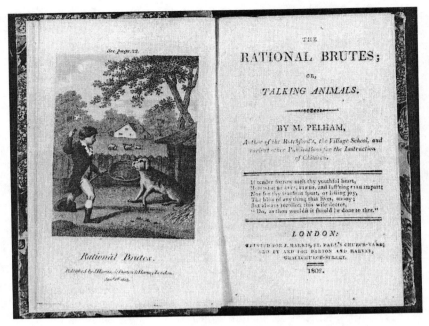

Fig. 3   Frontispiece and title page: Dorothy Kilner [M. Pelham], *The Rational Brutes; or,
Talking Animals.* London: J. Harris, 1803. Courtesy of The Osborne Collection of Early
Children's Books, Toronto Public Library

possible wages of rebellion and revolt against proper authority, an issue of
some pressing concern at the end of the eighteenth century.

The representation of animals as the symbolic equivalents to the lower
orders of society served not only to validate certain class structures and economic models, but to teach middle-class children their role within the class
structure as well. One of the most important and commonly represented social
functions children were meant to learn from their treatment of animals was
that of charity. The small-scale acts of charity children learn to bestow on the
lower orders of creation—collecting bread crumbs for the robins, or giving
a hungry dog a piece of a roll—serve as training for their eventual roles as
benefactors to society's poor. In *Fabulous Histories,* Harriet and Frederick
devise a scheme to provide for the needy robin family nesting in their garden without depriving "the many children who want bread" of their due: "I
will beg the cook to save all the crumbs in the breadpan, and desire John to
preserve all he makes when he cuts the loaf for dinner" (6). This admirable
display of ingenuity and frugality is accompanied by an important lesson in
the proper use of charity: concern for the relief of unfortunate animals must
never supersede the principal social objective of charity.

For some writers, such as Mary Wollstonecraft, the treatment of animals is the only proper venue for children's charitable activity: "[i]t is only to animals that children *can* do good; men are their superiors" (*Original,* 373).[35] Following Rousseau, Catharine Macaulay also disapproved of privileged children bestowing their spare change on the destitute. This sort of charity is ill-advised because children do not know the value of money and, more importantly, because it threatens to produce an unhealthy, aristocratic sense of class superiority: "[t]he parade with which children are commonly used to bestow alms, has a tendency to cherish the growth of pride, and a supercilious contempt for wretchedness" (117).[36] Nonetheless, while many children's writers celebrated examples of middle-class children giving their halfpennies away to the needy, they agreed with Wollstonecraft that brute creation was the proper site for the young to begin exercising the act of giving.

Children learned from stories their roles as providers to poor hungry dogs and birds from a very young age, as Anna Barbauld and Lady Eleanor Fenn's books for toddlers demonstrate. Barbauld was the first to devise texts for the very young, to use oversized print, and to restrict her writing to words of one or two syllables. Her first volume of *Lessons for Children* (1778), which follows the early adventures and education of its protagonist Charles, is designed for children two and three years old, certainly the youngest possible readership. One of the principal objectives of the text is to demonstrate to Charles his superiority over brute creation, indicated by his ability to speak and think, and ultimately by his ability to learn: "[i]f you do not learn, Charles, you are not good for half as much as Puss. You had better be drowned" (III:6–7). Once his proper place above the other animals is established, Charles goes about feeding the unfortunate creatures—always referred to as "poor" this or that—he encounters during his daily activities. From helping the poor animals he eventually makes a seamless transition to performing small acts of charity for the poor children he encounters.

Lady Eleanor Fenn's *Cobwebs to Catch Flies* was modeled after Barbauld's work but is addressed, according to the title page, to a slightly older readership, "Children from the age of Three to Eight Years."[37] In the chapter "The Dog," a young boy wins his mother's praise by sharing his cake with a hungry dog: "[y]ou are a good boy. We must be kind to all. We must give to them who want" (I:36). The following story, "The Farm-Yard," has the boy learning to be kind even to such filthy and malodorous a beast as the pig, when his natural instinct would be to despise it (39–43). Even the lowest orders of creation deserve the charity of the well disposed, and the sooner middle-class children learn not to despise such creatures as pigs for their squalor, the sooner they will learn not to despise the poverty of their social inferiors.

Transposing the lessons of kindness to animals onto the world of human society and class relations was the next logical step in the social and moral education of middle-class children, and narratives demonstrating to them the proper application of this particular virtue abounded in the late eighteenth century. Giving to the less fortunate was only part of the charity lesson these works sought to impart; the middle-class child needed to be able to identify the deserving object of her benevolence in order to ensure her efforts were put to good use. The proper recipients of charity had not only to be financially distressed, but humble, deferential, industrious, and impoverished by misfortune rather than by their own profligacy. Drunkards, spendthrifts, and those too lazy to work their way out of poverty did not warrant the charity of the well-disposed middle-class individual; such people came by their own intemperance to a fittingly miserable end.

The deserving poor are, for the most part, identified in middle-class children's books as honest working folk whom fate has dealt a hard blow. When out for a walk, Mrs. Mason and her two charges come across a family of migrant laborers seeking work. As they have no shelter, Mrs. Mason offers to let the weary travelers sleep in her barn. When the girls ask her why she offered them such assistance, Mrs. Mason replies: "the poor who are willing to work, [have] a right to the comforts of life" (*Original,* 393). Mrs. Benson and her children encounter a family of beggars in *Fabulous Histories,* and she gives them alms after the mother assures her that the family is begging only out of the most desperate need: "Oh! my good Lady, said the woman, we have not been used to beg, but to earn an honest livelihood by our industry: and never, till this sad day, have I known what it was to take charity" (111). Her reluctance and shame in taking money she has not earned marks her as a proper object of charity.

James Bisset's verse narrative *The Orphan Boy* provides a more complete example of how charity should ideally operate. Three sisters go out for a stroll—the standard mechanism for locating the deserving poor—and discover a destitute child. They inquire as to the particulars of his plight and he tells a miserable tale about the death of his parents and his subsequent reduction to poverty, without ever requesting their aid. So crucial to establishing his status as truly deserving of charity is his noble reluctance to ask for assistance that it is repeated twice in the story: "[he] ask'd no alms—but heav'd a sigh" (7); "[h]e ask'd no alms, nor begg'd relief" (9).[38] Each sister gives him a halfpenny from her purse, and with this money the boy is able, somewhat miraculously given the sum he receives, to feed himself back to health, to clothe himself properly, and to gain an apprenticeship to a trade. Once on his feet again, he never looks back: "An honest livelihood he gains,/ And strict integrity maintains" (14). This story encapsulates many middle-class concerns over charity in the period: the boy's relief comes from an act of individual charity rather than from state-sponsored charities which, in the eyes of many among the late eighteenth-century middle classes, only rewarded the lazy and profligate; it demonstrates that even the smallest of individual works of kindness can make substantial social differences; it shows that charity is primarily a means of affording the deserving poor the opportunity to help themselves rather than to subsist idly on the backs of taxpayers.[39]

In Mary Pilkington's story "The Fortunate Beggar; or, Inhumanity Reproved" from her *Tales of the Cottage,* the Harcourt children also come across, on an afternoon's outing, what appears to be a deserving candidate for relief in a young child begging for alms. Once they inform their father of the beggar's distress, he feels obliged to verify both the boy's story and the degree of his poverty before offering assistance: "[w]e must discover whether the child is really as distressed as he describes himself, and if so, do something to relieve him" (56–7).[40] The child's story checks out—his father has died, leaving the family without an income—and Mr. Harcourt offers the child's mother suitable employment on the family farm: "she might succeed a poor woman who used to have the care of the poultry and pigs, but who was lately dead, if she understood the management of them" (58). As in *The Orphan Boy* and Edgeworth's "The Basket Woman," charitable assistance takes the form of an opportunity for the poor to sustain themselves and their families with work suited to their station. The poor woman's reaction to Mr. Harcourt's act of generosity is a fairly typical representation of the effusive gratitude the poor show their benefactors in such narratives: "[t]he woman fell upon her knees, clasped her hands, and, with uplifted eyes, returned the Almighty thanks for the unexpected succour; then, turning to Mr. Harcourt, besought heaven to pour down its choicest blessings on his head" (58). This type of gratitude impresses on middle-class children the pleasure they themselves can derive from the act of charity. As Mrs. Bell informs her pupils in Dorothy Kilner's *The Village School:* "to give comfort and happiness to our fellow-creatures, is the surest way to have pleasure ourselves" (I:62). In order to sell children on the idea of charity, middle-class writers provided an incentive for their acts of generosity—the unequivocal praise and thanks the recipients of kindness heap on their benefactors.

E. P. Thompson has remarked that this sort of boundless gratitude in the poor for the assistance they receive from their social betters is essentially a middle-class fantasy. If anything, the plebeian classes of the eighteenth century in England took charity as their right, and held their class superiors hostage if it was not forthcoming: "[e]ven 'liberality' and 'charity' may be seen as calculated acts of class appeasement in times of dearth and calculated extortions (under threat of riot) by the crowd: what is (from above) an 'act of giving' is (from below) an 'act of getting'" ("Eighteenth-Century," 150). Despite this, middle-class children's books of the period uniformly depicted the poor as overwhelmed with gratitude at whatever minuscule kindness they were shown. Clearly, and not surprisingly, the reality of the "ingratious" plebeian takers-of-charity-as-their-due did not fit the idealized model of the humble yet contented poor whom children's writers touted as the proper recipients of middle-class beneficence.

The most common uses of the charity narrative in children's books of the period were to demonstrate how the destitute could improve their own condition with the merest of assistance, and how indebted to their benefactors and class superiors the recipients of aid would be. The implied role of charity in the broader middle-class social agenda of the period, as a potential mechanism for reforming the plebeian class and its cultural practices, receives a fuller articulation in *The Silver Thimble*. The narrator, the thimble of the title, winds up in the hands of Miss Steady, the young daughter of a model middle-class family. The chapter dedicated to the family's unique birthday celebrations, "Rational Birth-Day Pleasure," deserves some attention here. The Steady family utilizes the occasion of the birthday to promote the virtue of charity: "it was the custom with Mrs. Steady to celebrate the anniversary of her birth-day, by giving decent cloathing to six poor men and women, whose indigent circumstances and sobriety of conduct recommended them to her benevolence" (14). Two aspects of this celebration warrant further scrutiny: first, that the event is here referred to as a "custom," and later as a "festival," and second that it is a communal activity orchestrated by a middle-class family.

This sober communal festivity is meant to replace, with a middle-class alternative, such traditional plebeian celebrations as Shrovetide or Whitsuntide,

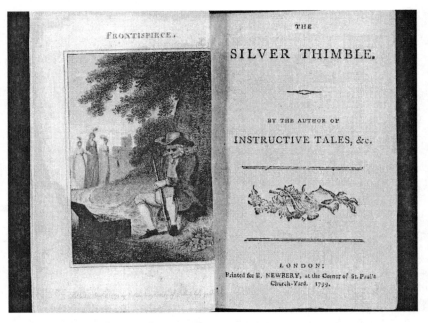

Fig. 4   Frontispiece and title page: [Sarah Trimmer], *The Silver Thimble*. London: E. Newbery, 1799. Courtesy of The Osborne Collection of Early Children's Books, Toronto Public Library

which many reformers reviled for their drunken excesses, fighting, and gaming. At the same time, it parallels, while eliminating the immoral excesses of, the royal custom of giving Maundy Money, as well as the traditional upper-class practice of dispensing hospitality on birthdays. The subversive, carnivalesque excesses of traditional plebeian feast days, and the upper class's tacit acceptance of and even participation in them, is here replaced by and rationalized into a ceremony reinscribing middle-class notions of individual Christian charity and lower-class gratitude. Mrs. Steady's rational "custom" also combines middle-class attempts to co-opt and rehabilitate traditional plebeian cultural activities with an important lesson in charity for both the reading audience and her own children, whose birthdays are celebrated in a similar fashion: "It was customary with this benevolent lady to make the birth-day of her children a day of jubilee among the poor, and that the young people on such occasions were permitted to display their liberality in giving away various kinds of useful linens to the surrounding peasantry, in the making of which they employed themselves during their leisure hours" (14–5).

Although certainly an honorable transformation of an occasion normally focused on receiving into one centered on giving, this "rationalization" of birthday celebrations also serves to inculcate in middle-class children the twin virtues of industry (they employ their time productively in the making of linens) and charity (the fruits of their labor benefit the needy). Further, it combines the child's experience of pleasure—the celebration of a birthday—with the social duties she will eventually perform as guardian and benefactor of the poor.

While middle-class children learned their duties to the lower orders and their proper relationship to the plebeian classes, they were also being taught to define themselves against the classes above them.[41] The republicanism, antiaristocratic and antimonarchical sentiments of the radical Dissenters were never explicitly articulated in their children's writing, but the regular representations of the lazy, indolent, ignorant, and often cruel gentry and upper classes in children's books served to warn middle-class children against the vices of their social betters and to suggest the kind of moral degeneracy that often accompanied inherited privilege.[42]

The upper classes owed their degenerate and weakened condition in large part to their absolute dependence on the lower orders for their survival. Epictetus, observes Catharine Macaulay, "describes the man of wealth in a state of almost equal dependence and humiliation to that of an infant" (66). The self-reliance, self-motivation, and industry promoted by middle-class writers were qualities that had become alien to the privileged classes who, after generations of reliance on the labor of others, were both unwilling and unable to fend for themselves.

To illustrate the utter helplessness of the upper classes, Macaulay tells an anecdote about the King of Spain, who, "finding himself greatly affected by the overheated air of his apartment, from the influence of too large a fire," called his servant "whose privilege it was to attend his majesty in this department" (67). The appropriate servant could not be found and none of the others were willing to overstep their prescribed duties, so "the monarch was almost suffocated before any one ventured to the province of the nobleman whose office it was to superintend his fire" (67). This anecdote highlights not only the king's inability to perform such simple and fundamental tasks as tending a fire, but the absurdly rigid and restrictive hierarchy that has rendered the monarchical form of government stagnant and ineffective.

The haughty but useless gentleman was a popular figure in the children's literature of the late eighteenth century, and variations on the "Gentleman and Basket-Maker" story appeared in numerous texts. John Marshall's *The Friends; or, the History of Billy Freeman and Tommy Truelove* contains a version of this reversal-of-fortunes story entitled "The Superiority of Worth, (not of Fortune,) makes the Gentleman." Set on a "savage and remote island," the tale describes the adventures of a man of idle privilege and a humble basketmaker who has long suffered the abuse of his social better, marooned together by an accident at sea. The natives revere the basketmaker for his useful skill, placing him in an exalted position in their tribe, and revile the gentleman for his uselessness, forcing him into the role of servant to the basketmaker. The Marshall version capitalizes on such chapbook elements as the exotic locale and woodcuts featuring half-naked dancing savages, but, in true hybrid fashion, turns the moral to middle-class ends with its critique of the parasitic upper classes: "[u]nnatural persons, who live as if they were born only for themselves, and set no other value on riches than as a means to indulge their passions, support their luxury, gratify their love of pleasures, a vain ostentation, or a restless curiosity; who are serviceable neither to their relations, their friends, nor their most ancient domestics; and who think themselves under no obligation by the ties of blood, gratitude, merit, or humanity" (34–5). Elements of Rousseau's celebration of "man in his natural state" and his condemnation of the refined culture that has made the privileged classes weak and unnatural combine here with the residual chapbook fantasy of miraculous advancement and subversion of class structures to produce a middle-class tale of utility and merit.[43]

Many of the vices of the rich, including wastefulness, drunkenness, idleness, and the irrational love of finery, were shared with the servants who sought to emulate them or with the agrarian poor with whom they often shared traditional social bonds. Priestley observes that, like the poor, the upper classes lack reason and self-restraint and tend to squander all they have: "[s]o long as the means of indulgence are in their power, they generally give a loose to their appetites and passions, and will not listen to the admonitions of reason and conscience" (*Miscellaneous,* 111). The difference between the vices of the rich and those of the poor is largely one of degree; the rich can, and do, indulge in debauchery more frequently and on a grander scale. The primary upper-class target in middle-class children's literature of the period was the rural English squire (the West-Indian plantation owner was another) and member of the landed gentry who spent lavishly while subsisting off the labor of his tenant farmers.[44] Implicitly included in this critique were, naturally, the nobility and aristocracy who shared, especially in the minds of the more revolutionary middle-class factions, the same profusion and tyrannical habits, but who were protected by their political power and influence.[45]

Squire Chase in Thomas Day's *The History of Sanford and Merton* serves as a typical model of the abuse of upper-class privilege in children's books of the period: "he rides among the people's corn, and breaks down their hedges, and shoots their poultry, and kills their dogs, and abuses the poor" (I:11).[46] This sort of utter disregard for the rights and property of others makes the squire a much more malignant and socially disruptive figure than even the most idle, dishonest, and profligate of the poor. At worst, the poor squander what they cannot afford to lose; the squire, however, squanders his own wealth (for which he has never had to labor) in debauch and then takes or destroys with impunity that of others.[47]

The spirit of Sensibility of the age and the established genre of children's narratives promoting the kind treatment of animals, along with an altogether warranted concern over the possibility of arrest for seditious publications, combined to make the children's animal "fable" (again, a misnomer for the types of animal stories being published at the time) a safe venue for the middle classes to espouse their objections to upper-class privilege. *The Memoirs of Dick the Little Pony* (1800) follows much the same lines as other animal/inanimate object-narrated tales. Dick begins his adventures as the property of the poor (here gypsies), whose vices are dutifully cataloged, finds himself under the ownership of a wealthy yet equally vicious family, and eventually discovers happiness with an ideal middle-class family.[48]

His experiences in a family enjoying the spoils of hereditary land ownership and title deserve particular scrutiny here. The father is a traditional English squire, cast from the same mold as Squire Western in Fielding's *Tom Jones,* whose great passions are hunting and drinking: "[he] kept his hounds and horses; and from long and intimate intercourse with them, seemed to partake of the nature of both. . . . he was what is called a good sort of country gentleman . . . whose knowledge is confined to his kennel and his stable; who has no idea of pastime beyond field sport, nor of pleasure in society, except in getting drunk. . . . and prides himself that his family has vegetated for some centuries upon the same estate . . . and neither improved nor wasted their income" (55–7). His wife is similarly dissolute: "[s]he had been brought up with care to qualify her for the station she filled; and in any other she would have been as much out of her element, as a jack-ass dancing a jig" (57).

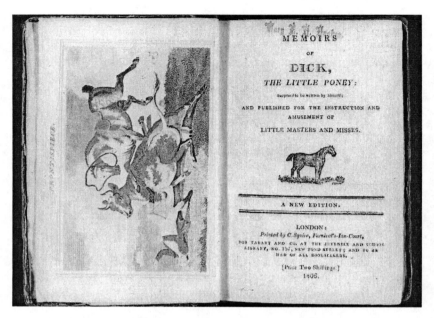

Fig. 5   Frontispiece and title page: *The Memoirs of Dick the Little Poney*. London: C. Squire, 1806. Courtesy of The Osborne Collection of Early Children's Books, Toronto Public Library

The squirarchy's love of hunting, especially fox hunting, came under regular attack in the late eighteenth century from advocates of the kind treatment of animals. The anonymously published *Mental Amusements* (1797) contains a fairly standard condemnation of this sport of the privileged: "The amusement of hunting has been called a remnant of gothic barbarity; and certainly it carries with it no traces of civilization. . . . It leads to the commission of petty trespasses without compunction; and the industrious farmer suffers in his property, and in his domestic peace, from the ravages of an equestrian cabal, who commit mischief out of sport, and outrage out of bravado" (115). Particularly noteworthy in this description is the reference to the injury suffered by the "industrious farmer" who would otherwise exist in "domestic peace," and the use of the term "cabal," with its overtones of ancient, pagan, and irrational superstition, and a secret closed society, to describe this upper-class cultural practice.

The squire purchases Dick from the gypsies as a gift for his son, who, given his parentage and lack of education, treats his new acquisition in an accordingly irrational and tyrannical manner: "he was ignorant, and evinced his power only in abuse" (46).[49] Through all his abuse, Dick is both philosophical and acquiescent of his position; he is, after all, only a horse, and, therefore, a normally mute subject at the lower end of nature's hierarchy. He does, however, offer a few words of wisdom, very similar to those of *Fabulous Histories'* Farmer Wilson and the titular animals in *Rational Brutes,* to those who have mastery over society's disempowered: "[w]ould superiority be loved or respected, it must use very gentle and conciliatory means to have even its lawful claims allowed, and cheerfully obeyed," for even "the most stupid animal is not insensible to kindness, but revolts from oppression" (46, 47). The middle-class child reading poor Dick's adventures in both the lower and upper strata of English society becomes sensitized to the indignities animals suffer at the hands of the lower classes. The text also warns how the irresponsibility and insensitivity toward society's disenfranchised, characteristic of those who have too long enjoyed the undeserved benefits of hereditary privilege, has the potential to provoke revolution.

Chapter 3
The Medical Management of the Late Eighteenth-Century Child

The new pedagogical methods and modes of writing for children in the late eighteenth century were predicated largely on John Locke's model of the infant mind as *tabula rasa,* David Hartley's theories of associationalism and psychological materialism, and the recognition within medical circles of the child as a separate and important medical category. While the influence of Lockean psychology on the children's literature of the period is widely recognized, Hartley's seminal *Observations on Man, his Frame, his Duty, and his Expectations* (1749) was central to the rational theories of psychology that would become paradigmatic by the end of the century.[1] This chapter will examine scientific writings about the mind and body of the child. It will consider how the directions for parents and guardians given by medical experts in advice books, as well as the medical writing about children intended for an expert audience, participated in the construction of the child as a modern subject.

In order to render Hartley's work accessible and available to a more general readership, Joseph Priestley offered a summary and explication of it to the public: "[i]t has long been the opinion of all admirers of Dr. Hartley among my acquaintances, as well as my own, that his *Observations on Man* could not have failed to have been more generally read, and his *theory of the human mind* to have prevailed, if it had been more intelligible."[2] Priestley's agenda for presenting a complex scientific theory of human thought in lay terms mirrors the mandate of Joseph Johnson's *Analytical Review,* discussed in the introduction to this text. His motivation for rendering a previously elite and exclusive form of knowledge in terms any reasonably educated person could comprehend is informed by his republican politics. In fact, when discussing certain specifics of Hartley's terminology (here "vibrantiuncles"), Priestley welcomes his readers to replace such complex scientific terms with whatever terms they choose, if it will help in their comprehension of the ideas at hand:

"[he] may, if he pleases, substitute for them the name of any other species of motion or impression, to which he may think the phenomena to be explained by them more exactly to correspond" (*Hartley's,* iv). It is this sort of democratization of once privileged scientific knowledge that allowed for the dissemination of the model of the human mind and its mechanisms of knowledge acquisition that underpinned much of the pedagogy and children's writing of the late eighteenth century.

It is worth discussing here the Hartleyan theory of mind, which would become widely accepted by the last quarter of the eighteenth century. Locke's description of the infant mind as *tabula rasa,* or as a soft piece of wax able to take any impression, helped define the pedagogical paradigm of the eighteenth century. Hartley refined Locke's ideas, suggesting a system of vibrations to describe more specifically how thoughts and memories (or impressions) were stored in the mind, and how they were translated into actions.[3] At the risk of oversimplifying Hartley's complex work, he hypothesized that the brain operated on mechanistic principles, that sensory input caused the particles of the brain to vibrate, and that these vibrations traveled through the body along minuscule fibers, motivating everything from memory, to speech, to physical action. His theory is founded on the materiality of the human mind, in opposition to earlier spiritual or immaterial models, and proposes a physical basis for the process of associating ideas. Priestley describes this psychological materialism as follows:

> This supposition of the particles of the brain retaining a disposition to vibrate as they have formerly vibrated, will be rendered more probable, from considering that all solid substances seem to retain a disposition to continue in any state before impressed. For this reason a bow of any kind that has been bent, does not restore itself to the same form that it had before, but leans a little to the other, in consequence of the spheres of attraction and repulsion belonging to the several particles having been altered by the change of their situation. Something similar to this may take place with respect to the brain. (*Hartley's,* xvi)

As John W. Yolton observes, in the materialist view of the mind, the repetition of these vibrations results in habitual patterns of thought and behavior: "[r]epeating vibrations establishes dispositions for those specific vibrations in the future."[4] The repetition of a certain stimulus to generate a given response, or vibration, in the materialist psychological model provides some possible insight into the highly formulaic nature of didactic children's literature in the second half of the eighteenth century. If associations are formed in the infant mind through the repetition of the same stimuli, the fact that late eighteenth-century middle-class children's narratives often follow similar patterns can be seen more as a pedagogical and psychological necessity than as an aesthetic failure or lack of originality in the genre.

Locke had argued in *Some Thoughts Concerning Education* that children should only be exposed to the best and most rational influences because of the impressionable nature of their minds, and late eighteenth-century psychological materialists also recognized the significance of their discoveries to the field of educating the young. James Long, in *An Enquiry into the Origins of the Human Appetites and Affections* (1757), theorized that "Perception X, for Instance," will, after sufficient repetition, always produce "the Motion Y" in the adult mind.[5] Long restates this point on repetition and mental conditioning in slightly different terms a little later in his text; if the brain is "impressed by the Objects F, G, it will acquire in time an Aptness and Disposition for forming the particular States F, G, and after more Repetitions, will actually have completed them" (33). This operation was precipitated in the unformed mind of the child, since "young and tender Minds can take in any Sort of Impressions" (16). Just as the first impressions received by a child's mind tended to become quickly and permanently fixed in Locke's model, the first patterns of vibration experienced by the particles of the child's mind would also be retained according to later materialist models.

Given that sense impressions caused vibrations, which in turn generated action and thought, the child's patterns of physical behavior could also be established from early sensory experiences. The science of eighteenth-century materialist psychology confirmed Locke's prior philosophical speculations on the importance of early childhood education. It also lent empirical scientific weight to the urgency and prominence the education industry would take on in the latter part of the century.

While the mind came to be seen in increasingly mechanical terms and as an organ like any other in the body, its disorders and the means of treating them were also being viewed in physical terms, as the work of late eighteenth-century medical experts demonstrates. Pierre Brouzet, Physician in Order to the French King (Louis XV), described the codependencies of mind and body, and of mental and physical health: "a mere physical cause may effectually dispose our organs to an habitual wrong judgement, and the mental disorders that are only a consequence of it."[6] Just as physical ailment could induce mental illness, the inverse was equally true.[7] As William Falconer, member of the Medical Society of London, observed in 1788: "at least half of the diseases, to which we are prone, originate from the influence of the passions on the human system."[8] Juvenal's maxim "a healthy mind in a healthy body" (*mens sana in corpore sano*) gained empirical proof in the rationalized medical discourse of the eighteenth century. It took on particular significance in the growing field of the medical management of children, whose minds and other organs, not being entirely formed, required a greater degree of attention and scrutiny in order to guarantee their proper development.

I have argued that such journals as *The Analytical Review* and such efforts as those of Joseph Priestley to convert complex scientific writing into forms more readily consumable by a general audience constitute a democratic dissemination of previously specialized and elitist knowledge. The late eighteenth century, however, was also the age of the scientific, in particular the medical, specialist. While greater numbers of people may have had access to forms of information that would once have been restricted to them, the rationalization of science during the Enlightenment bred an unprecedented number and variety of experts and fields of expertise. As a result, the number of nonexperts also grew, and advice books written by authorities in a given field for the use of the laity proliferated.

The growing number of medical advice books and experts generating these texts, on the one hand, signaled a greater availability of specialized knowledge in the public sphere. On the other, it represented a relatively organized effort to displace traditional forms of medicine and traditional medical practitioners. Just as pedagogical experts sought to remove the upbringing of the young from the hands of servants who lacked the benefits of a rational education, medical experts attempted to discredit any medical practice that was not informed by Enlightenment scientific methodologies. Brouzet, for example, pleads with his readers to take medical authority out of the hands of servants and nurses, and to "deliver the medicinal education of children to physicians" (xi). As medical advice became more available, this increased availability helped enforce a stricter medical orthodoxy by marginalizing practices that weren't approved by the enlightened experts.

In the eighteenth century, the traditionally female occupation of midwifery became one of the main sites of contestation over medical authority, and the struggle over this area of practice serves as a good example of efforts to create a medical orthodoxy. Alexander Hamilton, professor of midwifery at the University of Edinburgh, and member of the Royal College of Surgeons, was one of many enlightened physicians to argue that midwifery should be practiced only by rationally trained, male, medical specialists. In *A Treatise of Midwifery,* he bemoans the state of this vital branch of medical knowledge and practice: "[m]idwifery has participated in all the disadvantages which have contributed to retard the progress of medicine, and has also been subject to some peculiar misfortunes. For many ages it was entirely confined to women, who were either ignorant or inattentive."[9] Not only do female midwives lack the professional training (an approved, rational education in the sciences) needed to perform their function properly, they are seemingly unable to gain it because of their inattentiveness. Observation, keen attention, and the meticulous recording of data were at the root of the empirical methodologies upon which the rationalized sciences were predicated, and the implied absence of these qualities in women confirms them as unfit practitioners.

William Moss celebrates the timely intervention of men into this traditionally female occupation: "the interference of Men of sense, Fathers of Families, who ... have ventured beyond the limits formerly prescribed our sex ... to assert and defend the convictions of reason and truth against every force and assailment of prejudice and error."[10] William Cadogan's earlier opinion, in the influential *An Essay Upon Nursing,* about women's monopoly over this field of the medical management of children, follows along similar lines: "[i]n my Opinion, this Business has been too long fatally left to the Management of Women, who cannot be supposed to have proper Knowledge to fit them to such a Task, notwithstanding they look upon it to be their own Province."[11] Such gendered mistrust of midwives was widespread in Enlightenment medical discourse, and efforts to displace women from their traditional roles in facilitating labor go back at least to the midcentury.

Paradoxically, the blame for the woefully unprofessional state of midwifery was also placed on the very same enlightened medical community whose intervention in the field Hamilton and others deemed so necessary. John Leake, in *A Lecture Introductory to the Theory and Practice of Midwifery,* felt it necessary to make an earnest appeal to his peers on behalf of this overlooked but noble art: "Midwifery has indeed been degraded by the ignorance and unworthiness of many who practised it; and sometimes has been made the subject of levity by the licentious vulgar. Some of the medical profession there are, who, with more vanity than solid sense, think it below their dignity to exercise a manual art, or endeavour to save the life of their fellow creature by any other means than that of directing medicines or feeling the pulse."[12] William Dease, surgeon to the United Hospitals of St. Nicholas and St. Catherine's, shares Hamilton's prejudice against the traditional female midwife and Leake's concern over the state of the field in his *Observations in Midwifery.* However, he goes somewhat further than Leake in his critique of the established medical community's lack of participation in the field: "until this century, midwifry [sic] was generally practised by women; and recourse was had to the surgeon only in preternatural or difficult labours. This had the worst influence on the practice of surgeons; For, not having frequent opportunities of observing the gradual process of natural labours, they were at a loss in what manner they should assist women in preternatural or difficult case, which led them to imagine and adopt not only many absurd, but too often destructive, methods to accomplish delivery."[13] Dease's critique of the medical establishment's lack of interest in the field is less a subversion of contemporary orthodoxy than it is an alarm to take interest in a field that was escaping the reach of the Enlightenment's medical revolution.

Leake concludes his effort to dignify midwifery by citing Aristotle's praise of the art and by remarking that it was a noted interest of "the celebrated *Harvey,* physician to King Charles" (*Lecture,* 4). His efforts to persuade the professional medical community of the legitimacy of midwifery as a suitably scientific field of endeavor is two-pronged. First, it provides the impetus toward the further consolidation of medical orthodoxy by advocating the incorporation of a previously unregulated field of practice into the canon of enlightened medical knowledge. Second, it mirrors the middle-class suspicion of plebeian inclusion in domestic matters, articulated in contemporary pedagogical writing, by underscoring the dangers of allowing contact between the newborn infant and the degraded lower and uneducated orders. The ignorant midwife was no more suited to bringing children (especially those of middle-class families) into the world than the domestic servant was to managing their education and upbringing.[14]

Leake also participated in efforts to professionalize midwifery and bring it into the orthodox medical canon by offering an extensive course of lectures combined with hands-on practical training for (male) students in the discipline. His pamphlet *Syllabus or General Heads of a Course of Lectures on the Theory and Practice of Midwifery* (1787) outlines the main features of the course: lectures on the principles of the discipline, accompanied by anatomical models, descriptions of extraordinary cases, and first-hand experience with labors. Paying a bit more for "Privileges extraordinary," entitled the student to "a double share of Labours" and "to touch every patient at the time of admission into the Hospital during his residence there." Further, he would "see the treatment of Diseases incident to Lying-in Women" and "be permitted to examine the morbid appearance of bodies opened at the Hospital" (4–5). The student would thus gain, within a regulated institutional setting, privileged access to and knowledge of medical subjects (mother and newborn infant) who had very often been historically out of his reach.

The pamphlet for Thomas Pole's lecture series, *A Syllabus of a Course of Lectures on the Theory and Practice of Midwifery* (1797), describes a similar if somewhat more elaborate program of study at his medical theater. On top of the benefits of lectures, anatomical models, and practical experiences with labors, students were encouraged to join the school's "Philo-Medical Society," which met once a week for the purpose of "relating, and hearing related, the histories of interesting cases, which fall under their notice, during their attendance of the hospitals; of writing, in his turn, on medical subjects, for the purpose of discussion, and taking his part in the discussion of those written by others" (xv–xvi). The complex rules and hierarchies Pole proposes for governing this society and future societies (xix–xxx) indicate the efforts in the period to regulate midwifery and to exclude women from an authorized medical community of male midwives.

Dorothy and Roy Porter argue convincingly in *Patient's Progress: Doctors and Doctoring in Eighteenth-Century England* that the establishment of a medical orthodoxy did not proceed without resistance. Traditional forms of medicine and the medical fringe, what experts dismissed as quackery, remained resilient against the advance of Enlightenment medical theories and practices, and this was certainly true in the area of midwifery. Popular suspicion and skepticism of the efficacy of modern medicine remained widespread, and patients retained a great deal of agency in choosing their doctors and forms of treatment and medication.[15] In *Health for Sale,* Roy Porter describes late eighteenth-century quackery as "the capitalist mode of production in its medical face."[16] The nostrums and snake oils of unsanctioned practitioners remained, for a variety of reasons, popular despite attempts at centralizing medical orthodoxy: they often contained addictive ingredients such as opiates; they promised speedy "quick-fix" cures; perhaps most revealingly, they appealed to the growing consumer fetishism of the English middle classes and endorsed one of the grand myths of commercial capitalism: if something is expensive, it must be good.

Even within the ranks of medical experts there was a great deal of disagreement and dissent over how medicine should be practiced and who should practice it. In her article "Prescribing the Rules of Health: Self-Help and Advice in the Late Eighteenth Century," Ginnie Smith differentiates between the various gradations of medical expert in the period.[17] In descending order, these included members of the elite British Medical Academy, doctors, surgeons, apothecaries, and druggists, all of whom wrote medical advice books in this period. Within these different levels of medical authority, there was constant infighting and regular accusations of quackery. Opinions among the experts on what constituted legitimate, scientific medical practice were far from unanimous, and the medical community was by no means homogeneous.

One of the issues upon which medical writers disagreed most was that of nonexpert self-diagnosis and treatment: the validity of providing the untrained public with the tools for managing their own health and that of their families. Whereas some physicians, including William Buchan, believed that everyone should have access to at least some scientific medical knowledge and the basic tools to administer treatment, others sought to keep this information in the hands of the certified expert.

As Roy Porter remarks in "Spreading Medical Enlightenment: The Popularization of Medicine in Georgian England," Thomas Beddoes believed that "[i]n lay hands . . . medicine was a menace. Clinical treatment was an art so intricate, requiring such vast experience and refined judgment, that only the trained physician should tackle it."[18] In *A Guide for Self-Preservation, and Parental Affection,* Beddoes mocks the pseudonymous "Dr. Sleeklips," a "fashionable" doctor who shares specialized information with his patients (especially women) only to elevate himself in their eyes. As he patronizingly observes to his reader, this is not *his* way of practicing medicine: "[n]ow as you cannot understand any more of some of these things than my Lady, I shall confine myself to what lies in your power to observe and avoid."[19] His short pamphlet of medical advice for lay, domestic use takes the form of health-preserving regimens along with lists of foods, behaviors, and conditions to avoid, rather than descriptions of diseases and their symptoms and methods of treatment. On the opposite end of this debate were such radical popularizers as John Theobald, whose *Every Man His Own Physician* (1764) went through at least nine editions before 1770, and A. Hume's *Every Woman Her Own Physician,* which proposes "that every Woman of common understanding may have it in her power to prescribe proper remedies for herself or friends, without any other assistance."[20] Both of these texts, as well as numerous other domestic medical encyclopedias, gave the laity copious amounts of technical information, including instructions for mixing prescriptions at home.

Porter points to a shared middle-class radicalism among three of the period's leading physicians, William Buchan, Thomas Beddoes, and James Parkinson, as both a point of ideological unity within the discipline and as an opening up and democratization of medical knowledge: "All three railed against Old Corruption, denouncing despotism, oligarchy and aristocracy, and their contempt for grandee corruption. They embraced the cause of the people, and propounded an Enlightenment faith in human betterment, to be achieved by the defeat of vested interest, the progress of science, and the diffusion of useful knowledge. . . . All believed the rights of man included the right to health, indeed, the right to its self-management" (Porter 1992, 217). Of the three, Buchan held the most radically democratic views on the dissemination of medical knowledge. He was a medical pragmatist, and believed that anyone could acquire sufficient basic skills to treat, or preferably to prevent, many of the more common physical complaints. He also worked closely with the poor, witnessing explicitly the squalor and disease they experienced.

However, even Buchan recognized the necessary dependence of the lay practitioner on the medical expert, and the authority of the physician over the patient: "[h]e had no desire to 'supersede' the physician . . . for 'to talk of making all men physicians, is the extreme of folly' " (Porter 1992, 220). His pledge was "to impart 'all the information in *my* power, both with regard to the prevention and cure of diseases' " (Porter 1992, 221, emphasis mine). Buchan and his peers were certainly motivated by a democratic ideal and a genuine concern for the wellbeing of the public. They nonetheless configured themselves as the possessors and sources of the specialized knowledge they disseminated, and the patient was still interpellated as the subject under the authority of the medical expert.

This interpellation of the patient as a subject lacking knowledge of and authority over his or her health was particularly pronounced in the case of advice books treating the medical management of children and infants. In lay medical texts intended to direct parents in the proper management of the health and growth of their children, there are two levels of interpellation in operation. First, the parent is interpellated as the subject requiring the expert advice of the medical authority in order to tend to the physical and psychological disorders of the child.[21] Second, the child, who of course was herself neither intended to read medical texts nor to apply the treatments and advice they contained, is interpellated as the subject lacking both the specialized knowledge needed to manage her own health and the faculty of reason needed to comprehend and utilize this knowledge.

One of the principal discursive techniques medical authors used to position themselves as scientific authorities over both their adult readers and child patients was the medical case study, which objectively narrated the progress and eventual cure of disease in a particular subject. Case studies were often couched in complicated medical language with which lay readers would not have been familiar, and often included footnotes citing medical authorities of whom their stated audience would often not have heard. This is true even of democratically minded medical writers, despite their assertions that they were removing any specialized terminology from their work for the benefit of their nonspecialist readers.

Ludmilla Jordanova rightly points out, in her article "The Popularization of Medicine: Tissot on Onanism," that modern readers of medical advice books cannot assume, in terms either of class or of education, a generic eighteenth-century readership for such works. They were often addressed to "specific social groups (women, mothers, families, people with a specific . . . occupation)" (68). Further, medical advice books were written with varying degrees of sophistication: "there were wide variations in the amount of technical and linguistic knowledge presupposed" (68). In the main, however, these texts shared certain characteristic narrative forms and stylistic traits such as the inclusion of "endless individual case histories," and the regular citing of authorities from both inside and outside of the field, "ranging from the expected use of Galen and Hippocrates to the more surprising invocation of literary sources like Horace and Plutarch, who are quoted in the Latin" (71, 70–71). It was common in the eighteenth century for medical writers to quote literary sources, or even to write medical treatises in verse (cf. Hugh Downman's *Infancy, or the Management of Children; a Didactic Poem,* 1803). Pope's *The Rape of the Lock,* for example, was even occasionally cited as a textbook example of female hysteria. One could argue that literature informed medicine as much as medicine informed literature, and that the exchange of information between the discourses ran both ways.[22]

In *Advice to Mothers on the Subject of their own Health, Strength, and Beauty of their Offspring,* William Buchan employs the increasingly common case history style to discuss the affliction of one Isabella Wilson, who suffered from fits and convulsions. He attributes her medical condition to the excessive parental tenderness exhibited by her mother, "more guided by love than reason, by the impulses of a tender heart instead of the dictates of an enlightened mind."[23] Isabella was "the object of her mother's idolatry" (222); she was indulged in her every caprice, fed on an extravagant diet, and dressed in the most fashionable clothes, all symptomatic of an unhealthy desire on her mother's part to make her an upper-class lady. Little did her mother suspect that "the taper form, the fine limbs, and laughing softness which she so admired, were the sure symptoms of debility and latent disease" (222). By comparing the extravagance and delicacy with which Isabella is raised to "idolatry," Buchan invokes the vice and irrationality middle-class political and pedagogical writers ascribed to the upper classes in the late eighteenth century.[24]

It is no coincidence that Buchan's pediatric writing should echo Locke and Rousseau in its condemnation of fashionable clothes and delicate diets for children, as he and many other medical experts on childhood regularly cited these two figures as authorities. Perhaps more interesting is the intersection of his critique of upper-class cultural practices with the empirical, "objective," and diagnostic language of physical illness and its causes. W. F. Bynum has indicated that in the late eighteenth century it was common for physicians to ascribe "nervous conditions" of the sort to which Isabella has fallen victim to the luxurious living enjoyed by the urban leisured classes. Eighteenth-century doctors, like their counterparts in the field of pedagogy, were informed by Rousseau in this matter: "[a] simple, energetic country life engendered health and vigour; anything which deviates from it is debilitating."[25] Deviations from the rustic ideal usually took the form of practices associated with the privileged classes who lacked the virtues of restraint and self-denial: "want of fresh air, highly refined foods, tea, excessive alcohol consumption, fashionable dress . . . novel reading, adultery, excessive passion" (93).[26] William Moss expresses the opinion of many of his peers when he asserts that "[t]he diseases to which the human body is liable by nature, are comparatively very few in number with those that are produced by art, or luxuries and excess" (2). As close a proximity as possible to a "state of nature," especially for children, was a middle-class ideal of physical and mental health shared by many across disciplines in the period.

Buchan proceeds to describe in considerable detail the various fits to which the overly indulged Isabella becomes prone: "In order to give a precise idea of this singular kind of fit, I shall call its first state active, and the second passive. During the former, the young woman made use of the most violent exertions. . . . At the same time, she uttered a sort of noise, consisting of three notes, which was more like the cry of some wild beast than anything human" (*Advice,* 224). This cataloging of the patient's symptoms, from the two stages of her fits to the three notes of her subhuman utterance, is typical of Enlightenment medical discourse. As Foucault remarks, the patient in this discourse becomes, in effect, the disease, and her behavior becomes the physical manifestation of her illness. The subject is thus contained here within a discourse of medical expertise through Buchan's precise examination of the features of her disease. Buchan goes on to list his observations on the quantity, consistency, and regularity of Isabella's bowel movements; the gaze of the enlightened medical practitioner takes in not only the minutiae of the subject's external symptoms, but the effluvia of her inner parts as well.

Once the first stage of his clinical case study, the meticulous cataloging of symptoms, is complete, Buchan describes the case history, placing particular emphasis on the effects inexpert medical practices have produced in the subject before his timely intervention. Following the advice of a family friend (presumably not a trained physician), Isabella is given a "cold bath" treatment to cure her fits. Her condition deteriorates so drastically as to provoke near hysteria in the local inhabitants: "the astonishing singularity of the girl's disorder . . . filled the minds of the country people all around with the wildest and most superstitious conjectures" (*Advice*, 227).

That the practice of cold bathing should produce such devastating effects in Isabella, and, subsequently, such paranoia in her neighbors, bears some further investigation, since it and the "cold regimen" of which it was a part, were the source of much controversy in medical circles in the eighteenth century. Bathing children in cold water, dressing them in loose-fitting, light clothing, and feeding them a simple diet were all strongly advocated by both Locke and Rousseau as a means of guaranteeing robust health. Medical experts of the late eighteenth century were strongly divided on the efficacy of the "cold regimen;" its prescription, or a practitioner's failure to do so, resulted in regular accusations of quackery in both camps. It was, however, normally only recommended as a preventative measure in already healthy patients, rather than as a curative.[27] Buchan discusses the cold bath at some length in *Domestic Medicine,* and provides an example of its proper use: "The cold bath . . . is peculiarly beneficial to the inhabitants of populous cities, who indulge in idleness, and lead sedentary lives. In persons of this description the action of the solids is always too weak, which induces a languid circulation, a crude indigested mass of humours, and obstruction in the capillary vessels and glandular system" (635–6). In such cases, the cold bath acts as a preventative measure against the circulatory disorders to which the inactive are prone. However, once an idle and luxurious lifestyle has already generated illness (as it apparently has in Isabella's case), the invigorating effects of cold bathing tend to compromise the already weakened state of the patient's health: "the cold bath will only aggravate symptoms, and hurry the unhappy patient to an untimely grave" (636). Presumably, the family's well meaning friend had heard of the potential health benefits of cold bathing, but, not possessing sufficient medical knowledge and authority, he misprescribes it—much to Isabella's detriment. The decision to apply such treatments must ultimately be left to the most skilled of physicians: "[i]t can only be accomplished by practitioners . . . who possessing minds superior to local prejudices, are capable of distinguishing diseases with accuracy, and of forming a sound judgment respecting the genuine effects of medicines" (634).

After Isabella's cold bathing mishap, the villagers, Buchan reports, begin to assume the girl is possessed by devils, and he describes a radical cure suggested by one of the local rustics: "[o]ne bold captain of horse, a man of more resolution than intellect, declared his readiness to expel the foul fiend by shooting the girl, if the parents would give him leave" (Buchan, *Advice,* 227). Buchan makes a fairly clear parallel: heeding ill-conceived and inexpert medical advice (here the unfortunate "cold bath") from an untrained and unenlightened source is tantamount to putting a bullet in the patient's head.

By including a description of the panic Isabella's degraded post-bath condition inspires in the local population, Buchan suggests the larger social role proper medical expertise was meant to play in the regulation of cultural practice. Not only does the unsupervised practice of medicine by nonexperts (Isabella's family and their misguided friend) jeopardize the girl's health, it has the potential to provoke public unrest. The superstitions of the "country people" become inflamed as a direct result of an abuse of proper medical authority by an unenlightened and unsanctioned practitioner. Buchan's intervention in Isabella's case, and his eventual success in curing her of her fits, performs both the stated medical function of administering to the individual patient in need, as well as the implicit middle-class ideological function of social reform by supplanting irrational popular superstition with reason and empirical medical practice.

When Buchan arrives on the scene, not a moment too soon, the third phase of the case study begins, that of effecting a cure through the controlled application of the approved medication: "the internal use of tonics, particularly chalybeated wine, and the compound of tincture of bark" (Buchan, *Advice,* 226). His footnote to this prescription is particularly revealing: "I have here omitted the detail of doses and effects, usually given in medical cases, as I am not writing instructions for the treatment of diseases, but cautions to mothers concerning the nursing of their children" (226). The intended audience is not Buchan's fellow medical authority, but mothers, who are here, quite explicitly, interpellated as subjects in need of expert advice, being themselves deficient in the knowledge required to manage the health of their children properly. Further, by withholding the full medical information needed to effect a cure, Buchan also positions the mother as the needful recipient of medical practice. He clearly implies that she should not attempt to mix and administer the tonics to Isabella herself; the physician alone is qualified for this level of practical expertise. Buchan shares some of the previously elite and guarded knowledge of his discipline with his lay audience while still retaining his authority as expert to whom the reader must defer.

Alexander Hamilton treats the administration of medicines similarly in his advice book, *A Treatise of Midwifery.* While it includes "prescriptions for women and children, and directions for preparing a variety of food and drinks," it generally excludes the particulars of mixing and dosages of medicines. These have to deal with the "technical and abstruse theories" with which lay practitioners "can not correctly concern themselves" (title page). Some texts, such as William Moss's *An Essay on the Management, Nursing, and Diseases of*

Children, from the Birth, addressed specialized, technical material in footnotes "To the Medical Reader," deliberately, if not altogether successfully, demarcating and distinguishing the textual terrain of the expert practitioner.

If the parent or guardian, for whom such texts as Buchan's were ostensibly designed, is construed as a subject in some degree deficient in the knowledge necessary to the proper rearing and management of children, the children themselves are doubly subjected. They are further removed from the authority and knowledge of the expert because they are the subjects of such texts, not the intended audience. Not only do children lack, as the parent or guardian does, specialized medical knowledge, they lack the very mental faculty on which it and all of the other rationalized discourses of the Enlightenment are founded: reason.

It is the very fact that children were deemed so far removed from what Althusser calls the "capital S" subject, or "subject par excellence" (in the discourse of the Enlightenment, Reason), that made them "others." Further, it created in the adult mind of the late eighteenth century the urgent necessity to contain and regulate this newly recognized otherness. In *A Familiar View of the Domestic Education of Children during the Early Period of their Lives,* German physician Christian Augustus Strüve strongly recommends that this otherness be visibly inscribed in children through their apparel: "*[t]he dress of children should be different from that of adults.*"[28] Children, being in all ways inferior to adults, especially in the capacity for reason, are only made "disgusting to behold" when given the outward appearance of adults; they "resemble a monkey rather than a human creature" when "disfigured by dress" (305). By carefully demarcating the difference between child and adult through dress, the subordinate station occupied by the child is reinforced: "their very garments should restrain them within the limits of childhood, and make them sensible to their infantile state" (306). To make children receptive to the efforts undertaken by their superiors for their management and improvement, they must be made palpably aware of their otherness; to make parents and guardians successful in these efforts, they must enforce this difference.

Strüve's work differs from that of Buchan in that the interpellation of the adult reader as subject in need of advice is less overt. He often refers to himself and his readers together as "we," while positioning children, the subjects of his examination, as "them." Following the lead of such pedagogical writers as Rousseau and Anna Barbauld, he discusses how such childhood passions, or "affections of the mind," as envy are better corrected by the use of example than by admonishment: "[a]dmonitions are likewise unavailing, or have but a faint and momentary effect on *those* who are unable to comprehend the tendency of *our* arguments. Hence *we* ought to pursue a [different] plan" (387, italics mine). This apparent collapsing of the space between expert author and nonexpert reader is, I believe, primarily a rhetorical strategy intended to make his advice appear as the "familiar view" suggested in his title. Strüve still occupies the position of authority (if he did not, why would readers consult his work?), employing such forms as the clinical case study and such scholarly apparatuses as citing other experts in footnotes to demarcate subtly the space between himself and his audience. Ginnie Smith observes that some authors of medical advice books employed a "more discreet professionalism" which "refrained from drawing attention in their advice books to the professional role": "they did not have to, it was there in their minute and conscientious attention to experimental detail" (274). The author's methodology itself, as well as his style of writing, served to designate him as expert and authority.

Although pediatric experts of the eighteenth century did not always agree on all aspects of medical theory or practice, they were generally united in their assessment of the physical and psychological deficiencies inherent to the state of childhood. David Hartley's observation that the "Erroneousness of the Judgment in Children and Idiots" should be held in direct contrast to "the Perfection of Reasoning natural to Adults" was joined with the immediately recognizable physical limitations of childhood to confirm the need for a rigorous discipline over this imperfect yet perfectible state.[29] Establishing the nature of the child's difference from adult perfection through observation and analysis was central to containing it within the discourses of both medicine and education. The growing body of medical knowledge about childhood in the eighteenth century was predicated on determining how the physical and psychological state of childhood deviated from a male-gendered adult norm of health, and how to correct these differences. Childhood was in itself implicitly conceived of as a state of, or potential state of, disease, lack, and deficiency, and the regulation and advice to parents proposed by medical experts were intended as steps toward effecting a cure.[30]

Perhaps the most obvious indication of the deficiency of childhood was the "Erroneousness of Judgment" identified by Hartley in his *Observations on Man*. Children's inability to think rationally, to ascribe correctly cause to effect, and their susceptibility to fits of passion were obstacles in the path to Enlightenment perfectibility and accounted for most of their miscarriages in behavior, as well as for many of their more serious psychological disorders. These mental or psychological aberrations were cataloged, alongside the physical disorders peculiar to children, in the medical treatises and advice books of the period.

The unformed state of the child's mind not only made the inculcation of vicious habits at an early age an alarming prospect, it opened the door for a variety of potential mental disorders to take root. Just as the frail bodies of children had to be conditioned toward hardiness through such regimens as exercise, simple diet, and light dress, their minds required fortification through stimulus. While Thomas Day may have taken Rousseau's injunctions to toughening the child's mind and constitution by exposing it to startling noises to an extreme—his notorious discharging of pistols by his son's ear—this sort of practice was recommended by some medical authorities. William Falconer warned against "the effeminizing effect" on both mind and body produced by parents who "foster the sensibility of their children, especially females, to an unnatural degree, by officious attention to remove every thing that can give the least interruption to pleasure, or even awake the mind to it [sic] natural and necessary exertions" (75). The absence of displeasure in the child's experience had a debilitating effect on the mind and, therefore, on the body as well. Once a child, through the misguided and excessive affections of a doting parent, has grown accustomed to always getting whatever she fancies, her passions become prone to dangerous overexcitement: "[a] vehement desire for any object whatever . . . excites the circulation and perspiratory discharge. . . . When very intense, it is said to have produced epilepsy, and . . . an aneurism of the aorta" (Falconer, 11–12).

Indulging the every desire and want of a child was never recommended by medical experts, but some, like James Forrester, opposed the child's exposure to startling noises and other disagreeable stimuli. In his *Dialogues on the Passions, Habits, and Affections Peculiar to Children* (1748), Forrester ascribes "the Origins of Fear" to the nurse who, trying to arrest the child's peevishness or crying, "dresses up an uncouth Figure, makes it come in, and roar and scream at the Child in ugly disagreeable Notes, which grate upon the tender Organs of the Ear."[31] The impact on the child is a weakened fearful mind: "by Degrees it becomes so fearful, that it can look at nothing, which is not familiar to it, whether the Figure be frightful or not" (32).

Forrester's account says as much about the dangers of exposing children to the irrational cultural practices of the plebeian classes (embodied here in the figure of the nurse) as it does about the precarious state of the child's mind.[32] That the child's mind needs strengthening to defend itself against the myriad psychological afflictions to which it is susceptible is not in question. Although Forrester may disagree to some extent with later Rousseauvian medical experts on the benefits of such methods as the use of surprise or loud noises in the fortification of the developing mind, he concurs that the psychological condition of the child is one prone to weakness, disease, and easily excitable states of passion. The real threat to the child's mental health lies in the plebeian influence of the nurse. Her child-rearing methods reproduce in the individual the irrational subjection and fear of things greater than oneself that perpetuate, in the minds of the middle classes, a stagnant class hierarchy and political order. If the middle classes of the eighteenth century were to succeed to their rightful place in English society, their children had to be raised with the mental vigor and strength needed to resist the fear of tyranny.

Michael Underwood's *A Treatise on the Disorders of Childhood, and the Management of Infants from the Birth; Adopted to Domestic Use* is an encyclopedic work in three volumes cataloging hundreds of physical and

psychological disorders, describing symptoms, providing case histories of individual subjects, causes of disease, and remedies. Underwood's credentials as
a medical expert are impressive; he was a member, specializing in midwifery,
of the elite Royal College of Physicians, a physician to Caroline, the Princess
of Wales, and senior physician to the British Lying-in Hospital. Although
his treatise is directed principally at mothers, its objective is not to enable
its nonexpert readers to become doctors, but rather to make them aware of
the signs and symptoms indicative of illness in the child. Like most of his
contemporaries, Underwood seeks to provide parents with enough empirical
information to dislodge the superstitions of unenlightened practitioners—the
"many prejudices very hurtful to the ease and health of children [that] still
prevail" (I:2).[33] At the same time, he reaffirms the need for trained physicians
in the medical management of the young: "is it Education, is it Observation
and long Experience, that can qualify a person for the superintendance of infants, or the treatment of their complaints?—Surely all these fall eminently to
the share of the regular practitioner, to the utter exclusion of illiterate nurses
and empirics" (I:8–9).[34] That quacks and the uneducated lower orders are
unfit for the task is here made explicit; implicitly confirmed is the notion that
even the book's rational, middle-class, and educated readership, themselves
not "regular practitioners," are also subjects lacking the requisite specialized
training needed to manage their children properly.

Underwood was certainly guided by a humanitarian concern for the welfare of the young, as well as a utilitarian concern for the improvement of the
rising generation and for the promotion of the social good: "the destruction
of infants is eventually the destruction of adults, of population, wealth, and
every thing that can prove useful to society, or add to the strength and grandeur
of a kingdom" (I:2).[35] Within his account of maintaining the health of children, however, and indeed in most other similar works of the period, the very
subjects of his treatise are elided by the discourse describing them.

In the case of preverbal infants, this elision is more manifest than with
older children who have developed language skills. One of the common objections to professionalizing pediatric medicine in the eighteenth century was that
infants were incapable of informing physicians of what ailed them. Acquiring
the necessary information to formulate a diagnosis relied on the verbal communication of the patient, and since infants could not perform this function,
perhaps leaving their medical care to the mothers and nurses most familiar
with them was the best course. Underwood's reply to this position reveals a
great deal about both the changing nature of medical knowledge and practice
in the period, and the creation of the modern medical subject: "their diseases
are all plainly and sufficiently marked by the countenance, the age, the manifest symptoms, and the faithful account given by the parent, or an intelligent
nurse" (I:7). The infant patient is reduced to a series of outward signs and

symptoms, relayed by a guardian and interpreted by the medical expert; the child becomes a text that the physician, equipped with the requisite specialized knowledge, can read.

The physician can interpret and understand his subject with the barest input from her parents, and without any input or agency on the subject's behalf. As George Armstrong remarks in his highly influential treatise *An Essay on the Diseases Most Fatal to Infants,* "though infants are not capable of expressing their complaints by words, the very symptoms will, for the most part, speak for them, in so plain a manner as to be easily understood."[36] The voice of the subject becomes unnecessary to the articulation of her discomfort because her disease speaks for itself, and in a language only the doctor can understand: "[e]very distemper may be said, in some sense to have a language of its own, and it is the business of a physician to be acquainted with it" (Underwood, I:7). In effect, far from being the least treatable of patients, the mute infant becomes the ideal medical subject, one in whom the signs and symptoms are given their freest expression, unhampered by potentially inaccurate or contradictory spoken communication.[37]

Older children are only marginally more difficult to read as medical subjects. Their ignorance of their own needs, their absolute dependence on the superior knowledge and expertise of their elders, and their proximity to a natural state, so admired by Rousseauvian pedagogues and physicians alike, permit the physician to read the manifest indicators of the medical condition of children without having to ask them to describe their complaints. Because they wear, without disguise, the signs of their conditions on their exteriors, the peevishness or contrariness common to child patients is circumvented in the process of diagnosis. In the second volume of his treatise, Underwood discusses "[e]very complaint of importance falling under the more immediate province of the surgeon" related to childhood (title page). As in Buchan's account, this takes the form of a series of case histories, focusing on and interpreting the symptoms exhibited by a variety of afflicted children. The children become the disease from which they suffer, reduced to a description of the symptoms they display. They are constituted within this discourse, through their difference from the masculine norm of adult health, as subjects requiring expert maintenance and management.

The boundaries between the categories of disease and childhood were often unstable because childhood itself was perceived, in medical discourse, as a state of deficiency, or as a surplus of negatives, in much the same way disease was. Children, for this reason, required greater medical supervision than adult patients; their inherent proximity to a state of illness accounts for their increased susceptibility to a wide range of life-threatening conditions. Underwood, for example, observes that "[i]nfants readily slide into diseases" (1:n.12), while William Forster remarks that "Children do easily fall into

Diseases."[38] The descent into a state of serious debility is an ever-present threat to children because they occupy by their very nature and constitution—by definition—a gray area that can never be fully described as healthy in the way a rational, male, adult ideally can.

It is perhaps for this reason that pediatric treatises of the late eighteenth century regularly included advice to parents concerning their management of "healthy" children. The third volume of Underwood's text deals with more general strictures on child rearing such as diet, exercise, clothing and sleep habits, and most of his contemporaries included similar remarks. Prevention of illness through dietary and exercise regimens was an important part of most works of domestic medicine treating health in adults as well, but in texts focusing on the health of children it was a paramount concern. Since the possibility of serious sickness was a constant of the state of childhood, all facets of the child's behavior and activity needed regular and close monitoring. Further, since parents—especially mothers—were generally not experts in the enlightened management of their offspring, specialists like Underwood considered it necessary to instruct them concerning such practices as the proper "posture of children when feeding" and "proper times of feeding" (III:66, 85).

B. C. Faust, a German physician whose *Cathechism of Health: for the Use of Schools, and for Domestic Instruction* was translated into English in 1794, demonstrates the double interpellation operating in works of medical advice as well as the need for careful regulation of the habits and appearance of the healthy child. His book is composed of a long series of questions revolving around the diet, exercise, and dress of children followed by the correct answers, which were to be committed to memory. Presumably both children and their guardians (teachers or parents) were intended to learn this catechism, as both were subjects lacking the specialized knowledge pertaining to the maintenance and promotion of children's health.

Of particular interest in this text is the section concerning appropriate dress for children. Following Locke and Rousseau, Faust advocates simple, light, loose-fitting clothing as most beneficial to the child's health. Like his contemporary and countryman Strüve, Faust requires that children's dress "be different in every respect from that of older or grown-up persons": "To induce children to live with less restraint and greater happiness in the society of each other, to impress upon their minds an idea of their weak, helpless condition, in order thereby to check the too early ebullitions of that pride which leads children to ape the customs and actions of grown-up persons; a practice unbecoming at their age, and dangerous, perhaps, to their health and morals."[39] Confirming and consolidating the difference between children and adults through the cultural practice of fashion serves to reinforce the weakness, dependence, and necessary otherness of the child; paradoxically,

Fig. 6   Frontispiece and title page: B. C. Faust, *Catechism of Health.* Courtesy of the Thomas Fisher Rare Book Library, University of Toronto

it promotes his physical health and moral development as well.[40] Moral, or psychological, disorders in children, in this case excessive pride, are linked to physical illness in the logic of the eighteenth-century model of psychological materialism fostered by the works of Hartley, Long, Falconer and others. In the child-subject who is *always already* in an ambiguous, if not precarious, state of health, transgressing age (and, in many senses, class) categories through dress was particularly dangerous to his psychological and physical wellbeing.

The emphasis in such medical advice books as those of Strüve and Faust on making childhood's difference from adulthood distinct through dress, diet, and routine served not only to demarcate the boundaries of childhood as other within the discourse and practice of medicine, but to impress this difference on the child's mind as well. In order for medical advice to prove effective, the subject's need for it had to be internalized. Parental and professional supervision of the subject-patient had to be diligent, but as Faust's catechistic method indicates, in order to guarantee the successful maintenance of health, the child had to supervise and regulate himself as well.

By demarcating the boundaries between adulthood and childhood, advice books and treatises on the medical management of children participated in the production of childhood as a new subject category. This newly imagined child-subject was maintained in medical discourse in large part through a variety of regimens designed to exercise a disciplinary power over the body and the mind (itself viewed as a machine like other organs). Medical regimen as a disciplinary strategy wedded itself well with the types of discipline promoted and developed in other discourses of childhood, including, as we shall see, pedagogical theory and books written for children themselves.

Chapter 4

Toward the Self-Regulating Subject: Teaching Discipline in Pedagogical Systems and Children's Books

Medical and psychological theories of childhood overlapped with pedagogical theory regularly in the period, and not simply in their shared reliance on the work of Locke and Rousseau.[1] Writers in one field regularly dabbled in the other. For example, Erasmus Darwin, a physician and scientist by profession (and Charles Darwin's grandfather), devised a plan for the administration of female boarding schools, *Female Education in Boarding Schools* (1797), and Joseph Priestley wrote on the subject of education as well. Most pedagogues and children's writers were themselves not experts in contemporary psychological or pediatric theory. Much of the information generated in these fields would, however, have reached them through such media as the lay medical advice book and pamphlets or journals summarizing recent developments in science for the nonexpert. Some pedagogical writers, such as Maria Edgeworth (whose brother-in-law was the physician Thomas Beddoes, discussed in the previous chapter), were obviously quite familiar with these specialized discourses. For educationalists and writers for children, knowledge of the workings of the human mind was essential, since their principal concerns were the formation of children's minds and the regulation of their behavior toward a greater social good. Since, in the period, it was widely accepted that body and mind were parts of the same machine, systems for managing the physical health of children would also have been of interest to the pedagogical writer.

In *Practical Education,* Maria Edgeworth and her father Richard celebrated the rationalization of practice and theory enjoyed by the natural sciences in the late eighteenth century, and envisioned the field of education reaping the same benefits. Where the education of children had once been "classed amongst the subjects of vague and metaphysical speculations," an enlightened new generation of pedagogues was placing it in "its proper station in experimental philosophy" (I:v). In this belief, they echo Joseph Priestley, who had made a similar claim about the scientific foundations of pedagogy some thirty-five years earlier in *An Essay on the First Principles of Government*: "Education is as much an art (founded, as all arts are, upon science) as husbandry, as architecture, or as ship-building. In all these cases we have a practical problem proposed to us, which must be performed by the help of *data* with which experience and observation furnish" (71–2). In the spirit of the age, education, like scientific inquiry and medical practice, was advancing through the application of reason towards the perfection of its methods and goals.

Hartley's associational psychology, which informed much of the later eighteenth century's medical literature on childhood disorders, echoes throughout the Edgeworths' educational theory as well. For them, as for such contemporaries in the medical field as William Falconer, the incorrect association of ideas was at the root of both physical and mental illness: "the false associations which have early influence upon the imagination . . . produce the furious passions and miserable vices" (Edgeworth and Edgeworth, II:727). They echo James Long as well in their psychological account of why ideas are more readily fixed in the child's mind than in that of the adult: "[y]oung children who have not a great number of ideas . . . associate those they acquire with tenacity" (I:158). Earlier educational writers such as Isaac Watts had made similar observations on the child's tendencies to form inaccurate ideas and to fall victim to exaggerated passions; children "love and hate too rashly and with too much vehemence; they grieve and rejoice too violently and on the Sudden, and that for mere Trifles."[2] By the end of the century, however, such observations took on the added authority and explanatory power of empirically derived, rationally substantiated, and accepted scientific discourse.

Catharine Macaulay, in her *Letters on Education* (1790), places perhaps the greatest emphasis on the importance of Lockean and Hartleyan associationalist/materialist psychology to the project of perfecting education and improving children: "without an adequate knowledge of the power of association, by which a single impression calls upon a host of ideas, which, arising in imperceptible succession, from a close and almost inseparable combination, it will be impracticable for a tutor to fashion the mind of his pupil according to any particular idea he may frame of excellence" (i–ii). Macaulay, a political radical and "rational utopianist" who subscribed to the doctrine of perfectibility, was keenly aware of the scientific advancements the Enlightenment had produced, and enthusiastically supported the possible benefits to society they promised. She was especially fluent in contemporary discourses of philosophy of mind, invoking throughout her treatise not only the authority of Locke (as most pedagogues did), but of Hartley and Tucker as well, and making the connection between mental health and a rational education abundantly clear: "The very maniac, who languishes out his miserable existence in the phrenzy of distraction, and that more unfortunate madman, who retains a sufficient semblance of reason to colour his misfortune with the deformity of turpitude, might have found a cure, or a softening remedy to their maladies, from the sources of philosophy, had its balsam been administered before the passions had taken root in the mind" (11). Macaulay alludes to the curative powers of reason (*i.e.* philosophy), as well as to its centrality in the prevention of diseases of the mind, echoing the language of contemporary medical advice, which stressed the role of preventative measures in the maintenance of health.[3]

For Macaulay, educating and raising the young was a practice necessarily informed by the medical discourse of her day. Like her contemporaries, she blended advice on reading and manners with advice on dress and diet, regularly citing or invoking the appropriate authorities. For example, when discussing diet for children and the inappropriateness of veal, she indicates that her recommendations are fully corroborated by the experts: "[i]t is I believe generally agreed by all the medical profession, that the flesh of well grown animals, is easier of digestion than the flesh of young ones." Her admonition against veal is also, it is worth noting, informed by the discourse of sensibility, it being cruel "to destroy life almost in the first moments of existence" (39). As well, she recognized, like her medical counterparts, that applying the wrong treatments for childhood disorders or miscarriages could prove fatal: "A child, who by the force of discipline had been made to belie her sentiments, and to return thanks for her mortifications, had a medicine administered to her; and after every bitter sip she made a curtesy, and called out as she had been taught, 'I thank you for my good stuff.' Unfortunately there was a mistake in the medicine; and the child, after having suffered great misery during the night, died the next day" (111). By associating the physical correction of children, against which Locke and his countless followers advised, with "bad medicine," Macaulay parallels the use of outdated disciplinary/child-rearing practices with the dangers of following inexpert medical advice.

The intersection between late eighteenth-century medical and educational discourses included the use of the case study to describe individual instances of disorder, illness, or misbehavior in children. In *Practical Education,* the Edgeworths use this discursive practice to demonstrate the causes and cures of childhood distempers: "H——, about nine months old when she first began to observe the hardness of bodies, let her hand fall upon a cat...she was surprised and terrified by the unexpected sensation of softness; she could not touch the cat, or any thing that felt like fur, without agitation, till she was nearly four years old...the antipathy was, however, cured at last, by her having a wooden cat covered with fur for a plaything" (I:156). In their account of the distemper afflicting H——, and in their account of the success of the rational cure effected in this case, the Edgeworths echo Buchan's account of Isabella's case of fits. Further, they echo the biographical case studies that were becoming increasingly common in medical texts describing mental illness in adults, most notably in cases of female hysteria.[4]

This direct reproduction of the increasingly accepted discursive techniques of medical reportage in pedagogical writing is revealing on a number of levels. It reinforces the medically held conception of childhood as a state of disease, or at least of constant potential disease. It also portrays childhood instances of misbehavior and faulty reasoning as manifestations of this diseased state. Further, it confirms the otherness of children by associating childhood behavioral miscarriages with pathological adult states, confirming Hartley's assertion about childhood's similarities to various forms of mental debility. Finally, the Edgeworths' use of the case study model confirms the parallel between education and health in the social program of the eighteenth-century middle classes. The development and regulation of the child's mind is as important as the maintenance and regulation of her body to ensuring a sound and productive next generation.

The widely-acknowledged and well-documented deficiencies of the state of childhood made children, in the view of eighteenth-century pedagogues (and medical experts), subjects singularly needful of discipline. As the reviewer of Wollstonecraft's *Original Stories* for *The Analytical Review* observes, "[c]hildren are, indeed, the proper objects of discipline. Their entire dependence on others, their ignorance, and above all, their exemption from confirmed habits, renders them teachable and submissive" (II:478). Disciplining children is, naturally, a practice as old as having children, but the methods and objectives of this practice were changing in the eighteenth century. The stated goal of the discipline to which such writers as the reviewer for the *Analytical Review* allude was not the punishment of a child's affront to the authority of her elder, but the correction and improvement of the child herself. Discipline, by the late eighteenth century, was increasingly viewed as an instructive, rather than retributive, tool; as the *Analytical Review* piece describes it, discipline entailed providing "the means of their thinking *right*, before they have learnt to act *wrong*" (II:478).

This shift in attitudes towards correcting rather than punishing the behavior of children has been attributed by historians of childhood to Locke's injunctions against the use of the rod in cases of childhood miscarriages. J. H. Plumb, for example, argues that "[t]he dominant attitude towards children in the seventeenth century had been autocratic, indeed ferocious" (287). Although Locke's *Some Thoughts* was not solely responsible for the shift toward a philosophy of gentler treatment of children, it marks a definite turning point: "Locke's book encapsulates what was clearly a new and growing attitude towards child-rearing and education which was to improve the lot of the child in the eighteenth century" (289). Christina Hardyment suggests that by the time Maria Edgeworth was writing, the influence of Locke and Rousseau had changed the rationale and methods of punishing children; the view "was not vengeance or expiation but a utilitarian view that the greatest possible happiness of society was the object achieved by the partial evil of punishment" (Hardyment, 25).

A concomitant shift in the logic of punition was occurring in the late eighteenth-century prison, toward, as Foucault demonstrates in *Discipline and Punish,* a rehabilitative model. Where the body of the criminal had once been the site upon which the state executed its vengeance, Enlightenment theories of materialist psychology, perfectibility, and utility promoted a prison technology geared toward the reform of the perceived mental deficiency that motivated unlawful behavior.[5] Destroying or injuring the body of the condemned came to be seen as counterproductive; rendering the prisoner's body submissive to authority (rather than lame or dead) was more conducive to utility and the social good: "the body becomes a useful force only if it is both a productive body and a subjected body" (Foucault 1977, 26). The irrationality of children, although not of the same caliber or severity as that of criminals, was similarly at the root of their undesirable behavior. The enlightened discourse of child management, like its counterpart of the prison, focused on mental discipline as the most effective mechanism for correcting the child's tendencies towards miscarriages in thought and deed.

In *Discipline and Punish,* Foucault famously discusses Jeremy Bentham's proposed new prison design, the Panopticon, as the articulation of the eighteenth century's changing discourse of punition and rehabilitation, and as an indicator of the changing nature and exercise of power in the period. Bentham envisioned a prison whose very architecture would foster a reform of inmate behavior. At the center of the structure stood a darkened guard tower from which all the inmates' back-lighted cells were open to surveillance; this arrangement "reverses the principle of the dungeon; or rather of its three functions—to enclose, to deprive of light and to hide—it preserves only the first and eliminates the other two" (Foucault 1977, 200). The Panopticon physically reproduces the central metaphor of the Enlightenment, illuminating through reason the darkened corners of society in which ignorance and "unreason" breed.

Whether or not an individual prisoner was being observed by the guards at any given time was not the point. The fact that the arrangement of the cells made such observation possible would, Bentham theorized, create in the prisoner the constant fear of detection and awareness of his visibility; it would "induce in the inmate a state of conscious and permanent visibility that assures the automatic functioning of power" (Foucault 1977, 201). The inmate thus internalizes the gaze of his keeper and modifies his own behavior in accordance with the desired standards of the prison authorities (and by extension, those of the dominant elements of society as well).

Foucault comments that this model of reproducing power, by making its subjects constantly aware of their possible observation and of the possible detection of their undesirable behavior, had applications beyond the regulation of prison inmates:

> If the inmates are convicts, there is no danger of a plot, an attempt at collective escape, the planning of new crimes for the future, bad reciprocal influences; if they are patients, there is no danger of contagion; if they are madmen there is no risk of their committing violence upon one another; if they are school-children, there is no copying, no noise, no chatter, no waste of time; if they are workers, there are no disorders, no theft, no coalitions, none of those distractions that slow down the rate of work, make it less perfect or cause accidents. (Foucault 1977, 200–201)

The order created by the panoptic exercise of power in the field of education was quite clearly understood by Andrew Bell, if we accept his account of the operation of the East India Company's orphan asylum he ran in Madras.[6] In *An Experiment in Education, Made at the Asylum of Madras,* he describes the success (and cost efficiency) enjoyed by the "monitorial" system of education he implemented for the instruction of half-caste boys. From the outset Bell suggests that this success could just as easily be reproduced in England among the children of the poor, "that class of children to whom it seems particularly adapted."[7]

Bell's task of establishing an efficient and productive school in India was, by his own account, no easy matter, as his students had already acquired many of the vices endemic to their class and, presumably, their race: "[t]he boys were, in general, stubborn, perverse, and obstinate; much given to lying, and addicted to trick and duplicity."[8] The *Dictionary of National Biography,* in its entry on Bell, was certainly not the only source to express sympathy for the problems he faced, but its sympathetic remarks are worth noting here: "[t]he work presented peculiar difficulties; for the teachers were ill-paid and inefficient, and the half-caste children little amenable to moral influences."[9] In short, the conditions Bell encountered were the very opposite of the order and regularity upon which any rational system—be it educational or productive—ought to be founded. Compounding Bell's difficulties was a shortage of finances needed to pay instructors and purchase school supplies. The system he devised to counter these obstacles is, perhaps, a testament to Scotch thrift and ingenuity, but more importantly speaks to the changing mechanisms of power, discipline, and normalization described by Foucault.

The first principle of Bell's monitorial system was the inculcation of self-reliance. As his institution was insufficiently staffed, he selected the best behaved and most reliable of the older students and put them in charge of their younger classmates, placing the bulk of the responsibility for the students' supervision and education on themselves and their peers. In this regard, Bell's implementation of peer monitoring to compensate for a lack of teachers parallels the colonial system of governance, with its use of a "native informant" class to oversee the rest of the population, which the British would eventually apply in India. Each student is held responsible for his own work and for keeping his materials in good order: "every scholar is made, at the first, to rule his own paper; and this he is at once taught to do as well as any master. No teacher, or other person, is ever allowed, at any time or under any pretext, to write a single letter in the scholar's copy, or cyphering, or other book, but himself" (14). The boys, who come from a class for whom nothing is done and who cannot expect to have servants, must be prepared from a young age to fend for themselves. This lesson in self-sufficiency, of course, was one the middle classes also perceived as valuable.

Once the scholar has learned a suitable writing hand, he signs a contract assuring that he will forever keep with it: "The boy then copies, in the next page, an example of that hand in these words: 'This hand I am to keep to in writing throughout this book; and should I deviate from this rule wilfully and through carelessness, I am to be brought to punishment according to the regulations of this school' " (16). This voluntary submission to punishment for any deviation from the established norm facilitates the internalization of the gaze of authority by forcing the student to blame himself for his own errors. As well, the contract compels a regularity in performance desirable in those who might have to perform repetitive tasks.

The secret to the hoped-for success of Bell's system lies in the combination of the constant supervision by monitors, peers and teachers to which the scholar is subjected, with the normalizing effects of routine and methodical repetition of tasks: "Every day he puts down in his book, with a pencil or otherwise, the day of the month, at the termination of his day's task. And, on a page at the end of his book, he daily registers the number of lessons said, pages written, sums wrought, tasks performed, & c. & c. & c. which the teacher compares to what he did the day before, and what the other boys do; and at the end of each month, these are all added by the scholar, and compared by his teacher with the former month, and what has been done by others in school" (16–17). As Bell observes, the constant surveillance and grinding repetition produce ideally self-regulating subjects: "they did not require looking after, as they of themselves habitually performed their daily tasks" (17).

Bell only hinted that his system of peer-run education could be applied in England; his primary objective was the inexpensive creation of a trained and docile labor pool in India to supply the needs of British colonial expansion. This objective can be usefully compared to Foucault's discussion of the production of "docile bodies" in *Discipline and Punish*. He describes how military discipline renders its subjects both able and submissive: "on the one hand, it turns [the body] into an 'aptitude,' a 'capacity,' which it seeks to increase; on the other hand, it reverses the course of energy, the power that might result from it, and turns it into a relation of strict subjection" (Foucault 1977, 182). In the same way, Bell's model of discipline in the Madras orphanage was meant to develop productive skills in the students, while ensuring their submission to colonial authority.

Joseph Lancaster adopted many of the practices of Bell's East Indian school and adapted them for use in his school for the poor in Southwark, established in 1798. As Alan Richardson points out, Bell's system for instructing colonized half-caste children lent itself well to Lancaster's efforts regarding their English, domestic counterparts: "[t]he 'mutual' approach, then, was concerned from the beginning with the disciplining of England's colonial subjects and the internal colonization of its unruly 'industrious classes,' and these twin problems inspired a single method of approach" (Richardson 1994, 96–97). Bell and Lancaster were the subjects of much controversy in the 1790s and early 1800s, largely because of perceived differences between Bell's adherence to Church of England religious training and Lancaster's nondenominational approach. These sectarian differences did not, as Richardson observes, override the middle-class ideological ends common to both: "The intensity of the Bell-Lancaster controversy should not obscure the fact, however, that writers on both sides of the debate were most often on ideological common ground, as evinced not only by the congruence of their principal arguments in favor of educating the poor, but also by their adoption of the same discursive conventions" (Richardson 1994, 103). In his *Improvements in Education, as it Respects the Industrious Classes of the Community* (1803), Lancaster would outline his version of the monitorial system for forming in the young of England's poor "habits conducive to the Welfare of Society" (44).[10]

Although similar to Bell's plan in design and execution, Lancaster's model includes certain innovations, such as a fairly elaborate system of rewards for good scholarship and behavior (absent in Bell's system perhaps because of a greater shortage of funds). Lancaster initiated a ranking system for his pupils, handing out tags bearing the designations 1st, 2nd, 3rd, and so on, and providing financial prizes of up to a shilling for exceptional performance.[11] He also had prizes of "bats, balls, and kites, & c. & c. in great variety;—thus they are kept on the tip-toe of expectation" (49). The logic of this reward system differs somewhat from that of the Marshall and Newbery stories discussed in chapter 1. Although in both instances rewards act to coax children into learning and to demonstrate how industry yield financial benefits, Lancaster's aim was also to foster in his students a proper reverence for their benefactor: "The influence a master has over his scholars is very great; the veneration wherewith they regard him is almost equal to idolatry . . . so much so that they are his willing servants, and doubly proud to be his embassadors on trivial occasions; his smiles are precious, and even bitter things are sweet, when bestowed by his hand" (50). Lancaster is preparing his scholars for a life of service suited to their class; subordination is their lot, and if they are made to see it as rewarding from a young age, they will grow up to be good and faithful servants.

Underpinning both Bell's and Lancaster's educational plans for the poor is the logic of industrial capitalism and of factory production.[12] The older boys function as the foremen, monitoring and ensuring the productivity of their younger peers, and the schoolmaster acts as the factory owner/manager. For Bell, part of the beauty of his system is that the schoolmaster is the only nonexpendable figure: "as matters now stand, the schoolmaster alone is essentially necessary at this school. He has the charge of the daily disbursements and monthly expenses" (24–5). As in the factory, labor is easily replaced; the money managers play the most pivotal role.

Both systems have an eye to cost-effectiveness as the bottom line: "[t]he class, by this means, will spell, write and read at the same instant of time. In addition to this, the same trouble which teaches twenty will suffice to teach sixty or a hundred" (Lancaster, 50). Lancaster, in fact, is so concerned with the production aspect of education that the students' spelling is measured in terms of output: "[i]f 20 boys spell 200 hundred words each, the same number spelt by 60 boys must produce a great increase of total" (59). He even goes so far as to calculate the total annual spelling output of his school of three hundred boys, arriving at the suitably impressive figure of two million words. The system's efficiency comes from its regularity (spelling, writing, and reading *at the same time*), and this regularity is maintained through the mechanism of constant surveillance, and the internalization and awareness of surveillance.

While the discipline promoted by Bell and Lancaster was intended for the regulation of the habits of the colonial subject or the domestic plebeian subject, it had its analogues in the education and rearing of the children of the English middle classes. Mrs. Teachum's girls school in Sarah Fielding's *The Governess, or Little Female Academy* operates on similar principles. Although Mrs. Teachum runs the school, she remains largely in the background as an observer, having delegated authority to the oldest and wisest of the girls, Jenny Peace. In *The Art of Teaching in Sport,* Eleanor Fenn also advocates delegating parental duty to the eldest child, in this case the eldest daughter, on the grounds that it provides useful training for her eventual maternal duties. Further, this eldest child can reproduce parental authority over younger siblings: "[t]his young lady is a good deputy parent; when occasion requires it, she will fulfill the more serious maternal duties; the man who marries her, will find in her, a Mother to their children!" (6). Investing the eldest child with authority over her younger siblings also serves to naturalize the gradations of the social hierarchy, instilling in young children different degrees of respect for their elders.

When conflict and disorder erupt in *The Female Academy* between the other girls (over who should receive the biggest apple) Jenny acts as mediator, pointing out to her peers their faults, and having them recognize the passions that have provoked their disorderly conduct: "[n]othing will shew your Sense so much, as to own that you have been in the Wrong.... All the Misses will be your Friends, and perhaps follow your Example."[13] After reflecting on Jenny's words, Sukey Jennett, one of the principals in the dispute over the apples, is overcome by a proper sense of shame at her own behavior and begins to internalize the lesson: "the more I reflect, the more I am afraid Miss *Jenny* is in the Right; and yet it breaks my Heart to think so" (9). Through the direct intervention of Jenny and the indirect gaze of Mrs. Teachum, the students learn to correct and regulate their own behavior and that of their peers.[14]

Richard Johnson's *Juvenile Trials, for Robbing Orchards, Telling Fibs, and Other Heinous Offences* describes a model of peer regulation of behavior in which children hold mock trials, judge each other, and hand down appropriate sentences for infractions. As he explains in the preface, the effect of this form of discipline is both greater and more enduring: "When they are corrected by the hands of their governor, it is no sooner over than forgotten, and their companions immediately crowd around them, to console them under a misfortune, which they know not how soon may be their own case; but when they are made judges of their own cause, with respect to harmony among themselves, it will become the interest of everyone to abide by the general determination, and the *shame* of being condemned by their own companions may have far greater effect than any other kind of correction possibly can."[15] This system of peer judgment utilizes the normalizing power of shame, which Locke touted as a desirable alternative to physical correction.[16] Foucault attributes the effectiveness of shame to its ability to point out the sinful pride of the subject: "[s]hameful punishments are effective because they are based on the vanity that was at the root of crime" (Foucault 1977, 107). It also represents the children's internalization of the rationalized adult judicial system, which defines and enforces socially acceptable behavior. The adult rules governing proper conduct in children are thus enforced and voluntarily followed by children, with an eye toward guaranteeing their continued acquiescence.

Like Mrs. Teachum in *The Governess,* the tutor in this story remains primarily in the shadows, allowing his rational influence to operate through the medium of one of the older children, Meanwell, who acts as judge in the proceedings. Although he does not preside physically over the proceedings, the tutor's rational influence and regulatory power are still felt: "[t]heir tutor had taken care to make every thing as solemn as possible, that it might make the greater impression on their tender minds" (29). Acting as the instrument of the tutor's authority, young Judge Meanwell clarifies for the other children the objective of the exercise: "to make you reflect on your own conduct, that you may now see your own errors, check folly in its growth, and thereby prevent your imbibing those notions, which, if not properly seen through in time, might one day unhappily bring you before a more awful tribunal. By being judges in your own cause, you will more readily sink into the recesses of your own hearts, and soon blush at the weaknesses you will there find" (31). Meanwell's speech combines the language of prevention central to pediatric writing and

Fig. 7   Frontispiece and title page: Richard Johnson, *Juvenile Trials*. London: T. Carnan, 1786.
Courtesy of The Osborne Collection of Early Children's Books, Toronto Public Library

medical advice with the discourse of discipline in the late eighteenth century. The subjects in this miniature judiciary internalize the gaze of authority, submit and defer voluntarily to the power of reason, and learn to regulate their own behavior in accordance with it.

Although similar at the level of promoting a self-regulatory form of discipline, Fielding's system differs from Johnson's in a decidedly gendered way. Jenny Peace acts as a mediator, reestablishing harmony in her circle; Judge Meanwell enforces the law, albeit with the consent of his peers and under the supervision of his tutor. While Jenny is being trained for the domestic sphere, the female duties of a mother and pacifier, Meanwell is being trained for public service, in the masculine discourse of judicial decision making.

Teaching children accountability for their actions was an essential part of the late eighteenth-century didactic goal of raising responsible, self-regulating subjects. The literature for children of the period was filled with examples of young people who, having internalized accepted models of behavior, no longer required the direct intervention of their parents and guardians to correct their own deficiencies. Such works often presented young readers with pseudobiographical or autobiographical accounts of the behavior and experiences of "real" children.

One of the more famous examples of this sort of pseudobiography is Mary Wollstonecraft's *Original Stories from Real Life,* which recounts the steps Caroline and Mary—aged twelve and fourteen—take toward rational improvement under the watchful eye of Mrs. Mason, their tutor. As Allan Richardson observes, "[t]he book is offered as a means to facilitate the girls' internalization of Mrs. Mason's pedagogy, by reconstructing their lives as a series of moral 'stories' calculated to illustrate her precepts" (Richardson 2002, 31). While Mrs. Mason's presence is ubiquitous throughout the girls' experiences, the objective of making Caroline and Mary self-regulating subjects is achieved by the end of the narrative: "[t]he girls no longer require the constant presence of a monitor only because they have learned to monitor themselves" (Richardson 2002, 31).

The pseudonymous Arabella Argus's (whose name, rather ominously, recalls the hundred-eyed giant of Greek mythology, Argus Panoptes) *The Juvenile Spectator* is an epistolary work taking the form of an advice column for children. In the preface, an elderly woman claims she has decided to write for the improvement of the young by inviting them to send letters asking her for advice on how they can improve themselves. What follows is a supposedly authentic series of letters from the children in her neighborhood. The first comes from a boy named William, who writes (unaware that Mrs. Argus is, in fact, his grandmother) because he realizes that "all children have faults" and has heard "that you would give us directions on how to be good and happy."[17] After confessing that he is "often very passionate" and naughty towards his sisters, William pleads for Mrs. Argus to help him cure himself: "What ought I to do?...Give me some directions, if you please, ma'am, and I shall be much obliged" (12).[18] William's appeal for guidance indicates not only an awareness of his own failings, but a voluntary submission to the improving inspection of adult authority necessary to effect a cure of his passions.

Mary Cockle's *The Juvenile Journal; or, Tales of the Truth* posits a similar, albeit more invasive, model of discipline employing pseudoautobiographical confession. In order to promote the improvement of Caroline Montgomery, an ill-behaved and spoilt young girl, Mrs. Villars (an enlightened governess) proposes she keep a journal of her daily activities. Caroline is a fairly typical product of upper-class overindulgence, which naturally manifests itself in the state of her health: "your pale cheeks and heavy eyes discover to-day, as they too frequently do, how much your health has suffered from indulgences."[19] Her diary is not meant for private reflection, but as an account to be regularly inspected: "[it] will be read every day by your papa and mamma, and by any of their friends who will do us the favour to look at. They will therefore all, in future, be fully acquainted with your merit, as well as your failings" (19). Caroline's life is to become a text opened to the scrutiny of her elders so that the shame of detection of her misdoings will help her modify her behavior. The effectiveness of this method depends again on the subject's seemingly voluntary participation in her own objectification; her own written articulation of her errors is necessary to their correction.

like Sherwood

Ideally, such methods of discipline will produce children capable of governing their own passions and punishing themselves for their infractions. The protagonists in *The History of Young Edwin and Little Jessy* are portraits of this sort of voluntary submission to disciplinary power. Although the siblings are generally model children, honest, industrious, and dutiful to their parents, Edwin does misbehave on one occasion. When a poor, lame soldier comes to him complaining of hunger, "Edwin told him that he should give him nothing, and that he might go away."[20] After his father explains to him the naughtiness of his lack of charity, Edwin seeks out the appropriate punishment for his own miscarriage. After locating the poor soldier, Edwin brings the man to his father, announcing his intention of self-correction: "'Now,' said Edwin to his father, 'I beg you will let me punish myself. Pray allow me to give this poor man my dinner, and I will fast until supper time'" (43). Edwin is a middle-class parent's fantasy of obedience, proper submission, and discipline. Not only are his transgressions extremely rare, he supplicates his father to allow him to punish himself for the few that he does commit. In addition, he derives the appropriate lesson from the whole exercise: "[w]hen he felt hungry, and very hungry he was, he reflected how often probably the poor creature, whom he had so ill treated in the morning, had suffered more severely from want of food" (45). He has worked out for himself the rationalized logic of the punishment, identifying how it proceeds naturally from his crime, and how it is designed to improve his future behavior.

Physical punishment, especially the use of the rod, in the correction of children was, as I have already remarked, decidedly out of favor with the late eighteenth century's generation of pedagogues and pediatric writers, as well as with many middle-class children's writers. The impact on actual child-rearing practices of Locke's recommendation to replace this mode of discipline with the mechanisms of shame and reward is debatable, and despite the ubiquity of writers following his advice, representations of physical correction in children's literature of the period persisted. While, as Foucault observes, the *fin-de-siècle,* saw "the disappearance of punishment as spectacle" and the decline of the "ceremonial of punishment" (Foucault 1977, 8), their equivalents in the disciplining of misbehaving children were still in use in the works of such writers as Dorothy Kilner.

The Village School; or, a Collection of Entertaining Histories, for the Instruction and Amusement of all Good Children (1795), for example, depicts a method of discipline seemingly out of step with the pedagogical authorities of the age. Miss Betsy and Miss Polly, despite repeated admonishments from their teacher, Mrs. Bell, persist in playing with their toys in school. In order to correct their misconduct, Mrs. Bell "[took] a piece of string, [and] tied the doll round Miss Polly's neck, and the tea-chest round Betsy's and then placed them in two corners of the room" (I:12). The toys are later confiscated. This punishment seems to function on the principle of correction through shame:

"they were so ashamed of the manner in which they lost [their toys], and indeed knew they deserved to have them taken away, that they made no complaints" (12). However, the fact that Betsy's and Polly's shaming should become a public spectacle seems at odds with the self-reflection and internalization of shame most contemporary pedagogues deemed necessary to the subject's improvement.

Ben Heady, another student from Mrs. Bell's school, receives similar, albeit more severe, punishment for his repeatedly disruptive behavior. After destroying a classmate's nosegay and refusing to apologize, his teacher confines him in "a little closet, where he was very uncomfortable" for the duration of the school day: "it was not high enough to stand upright, nor wide enough to let him sit upon the ground with his legs straight out before him, so that he could only stand stooping, or else sit all on a heap, with his knees up to his chin" (II:81–82). He is eventually released, but only after he makes a solemn "promise to be good" (82). As in the case of Betsy and Polly, there is, on one level, a clear logic to the punishment; he has deprived someone of the

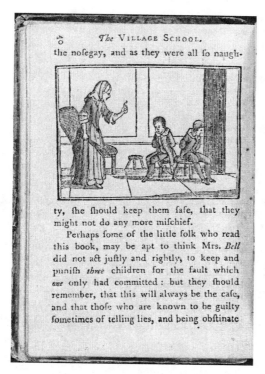

Fig. 8   Dorothy Kilner, *The Village School*. London: J. Marshall, c.1795. Courtesy of The Osborne Collection of Early Children's Books, Toronto Public Library

object of her enjoyment and should therefore be punished by a suspension of the freedom of mobility he enjoys and misuses. On another level, because of the emphasis placed on his discomfort, Ben's confinement seems more like retribution than reform. The ideal of promoting self-regulation by making the subject comprehend the irrationality at the root of his bad behavior is lost. Ben's promise comes as the result of the fear of enduring physical discomfort again, rather than of a voluntary subjection to an authority he perceives as natural and rational.

Betsy, Polly, and Ben are described as "repeat offenders"; they are subjected to their humiliation because they do not heed their teacher's continued warnings. Children who are permitted to continue in their disobedience and who will not learn to regulate themselves seem to be the proper objects of more extreme forms of disciplinary action. In *Little Stories for Little Folk*, Kilner tells the story of Sally Sting, "a child no one was fond of, for she was a cross girl, and took pleasure in hurting anything that was less than herself."[21] Sally's misbehavior is not the product of the usual deficiencies to which children are prone: "[she] had sense to know what was right, and she knew it was wrong to hurt anything" (18). Her case clearly requires, even in Lockean terms, special measures, as she evinces the "manifest Perverseness of the Will" that Locke conceded merited the use of corporal punishment (*Some Thoughts*, 141).

After Sally beats her poor cat one time too many, her mother is compelled to resort to extreme methods: "she made her stand in the corner, with her hands tied behind her, for as she made so bad use of them, it was not fit she should be let to have them" (Kilner, *Little Stories*, 18). This punishment does not modify her behavior in the long run, for as soon as she is freed she beats her cat again, believing it to be the cause of her confinement. In Sally's case, the irrational pattern of behavior is so entrenched that it directs her for the rest of her life: "when she grew to be a woman, she did just the same; and used to beat and whip her children for nothing" (23). Physical punishment is a last resort; it does not promote improvement or self-regulation, but only restricts the subject temporarily from acting upon an inherent psychological perversity.

Sally is something of an anachronism in children's literature of the late eighteenth century. She exhibits the sort of innate wickedness earlier Puritans like John Bunyan or James Janeway ascribed to childhood, and defies attempts at improving her character, seemingly contradicting the notion of perfectibility through proper education. Although a rarity in children's literature of the period, such characters as Sally point to some of the contradictions of enlightened pedagogical and psychological theories of childhood. It is difficult to reconcile the notion of the *tabula rasa* with that of a "manifest Perverseness"—suggestive more of innate ideas, a psychological theory widely discredited by this time. Aberrations like Sally, defying the best efforts at improvement, remain, however, in such narratives as Kilner's, and require at least some disciplinary mechanism for their containment.

Such textual representations of the use of physical correction on children in the late eighteenth century may or may not be evidence that such disciplinary methods continued to be applied through the period, despite the advice of the majority of pedagogical and pediatric authorities. What is clear from the late eighteenth-century literature for and about children is the belief that they, by their deficient or unformed nature, required discipline if ordered subjects were to be formed out of the disordered state of childhood. Instilling discipline, and ideally the mechanisms for self-discipline, was as essential to the discourse of middle-class pedagogy as it was to the discourse of medical management. Discipline was necessary to promote the regularity of thought and habit in the young that would allow the morality, economic practices, and, in short, the ideology, of the middle classes to take root successfully in the rising generation. In essence, it was, in the minds of writers for and about children, an essential ingredient to the successful dissemination and reproduction of this ideology.

Chapter 5
Molding the Middle-Class Subject of the Future: Applied Lessons and the Construction of Gender Roles

The cornerstone of late eighteenth-century middle-class pedagogy was the formation of healthy, ordered subjects capable of resisting destructive passions and of disciplining themselves. Once this groundwork was in place, the child would be capable of acquiring the specific skills needed to perform his or her eventual adult role productively within the changing social and class structures of the period. This chapter will explore how the practical skills and lessons parents and pedagogues deemed essential were represented and taught in the literature for and about children. It will also investigate how the evolving middle-class distinction between male public sphere and female domestic sphere manifested itself in the educational practices of the late eighteenth century. Simple distinctions between what constituted male and female types of learning in the late eighteenth century cannot be made. Boys and girls of the middle classes were expected to acquire many of the same skills; at the same time, the proper objectives and extent of female education was the subject of much debate in the period.

Roy Porter has remarked that in response to the increasing complexities of an emerging industrial and capitalist economy in eighteenth-century England, such efforts "to make life more regular and predictable" as standardized times of day and weights and measures evolved: "[t]he hurly-burly of life was taken under control in new attempts to stabilize the environment, predict the future and protect investments" (*English*, 281, 282). For middle-class children to meet the challenges of a fast-changing social and economic environment, they had to learn the techniques of efficient management of its two most prized commodities: time and money.

Children's writers, especially the Puritan authors of the late seventeenth century, had long advised their young readers to employ every moment of the day in some useful activity, in large part to help them avert the many vices accompanied by idleness. The representation of time as a commodity with a limited supply, however, suggests the changing modes of production of an evolving system of industrial capitalism. By 1810 Arabella Argus, for example, in *The Juvenile Spectator,* describes time in terms of a material resource, and warns young readers against wasting "our most valuable, yet most fleeting possession, *time*" (54). *Mental Amusements,* a collection of stories and essays for children, contains an essay "On the Management of Time" which provides a mathematical, rather than the traditional moral, argument for early rising: "[i]n the course of forty years, supposing we go to bed at our accustomed hour, the difference between rising every morning at six or eight o'clock, amounts to three years, one hundred and seventeen days and twelve hours; which would supply twelve hours a day for almost seven years."[1] Although early rising and avoidance of idleness were long considered important virtues, this precise calculation of lost hours over the long term points to the types of future planning characteristic of the middle class's investment mentality. It points as well to the forecasting and management of human resources necessary for a company's or industry's sustained economic growth in an uncertain capitalist economy.

La Comtesse de Genlis, author of such influential children's books as *Tales of the Castle* (1785), performs a similar tabulation of time lost due to inefficient execution of daily activities. In an essay entitled "Of the Employment of Time," she suggests a variety of time-saving methods for children to adopt: "It ought further to be recommended to youth to give themselves a habit of acting in everything with attention and celerity; slowness of movement is the occasion of a vast loss of time. They ought also to consider the different manner of performing all those little things which daily occur, such as folding letters, putting them in their covers, sealing them, &c. and to prefer that which is most prompt in its execution."[2] Genlis' recommendations for improved efficiency resonate with the economy of motion needed in factory production. Her audience, however, was the children of the middle and upper middle classes for whom the elimination of wastefulness and the maximization of productivity were of equally great concern as future heads of households or of businesses.[3]

As early as the 1760s, John Newbery published *The Important Pocket Book, or the Valentine's Ledger,* with its telling title page inscription: "He that keeps his Accounts may keep his Family, but he that keeps no Account may be kept by the Parish."[4] While this was a common refrain in children's literature of the period as well as in the Cheap Repository Tracts and other similar texts designed for the moral and fiscal reformation of the poor, *The Important Pocket Book* actually contains a daily calendar and ledger designed to help children keep their own accounts.

The ledger portion of the book contains both a "Money Account" and a "Moral Account," the first with columns for registering moneys "Received" and "Paid," the second with columns for registering "Good" and "Bad" deeds performed. Newbery includes a number of sample entries to demonstrate to the young reader how to use the ledger. Not surprisingly, the sample money paid columns include a number of expenditures for other Newbery books purchased (*History of Giles Gingerbread, History of Little Goody Two-Shoes,* etc.). In the sample "Moral Account" columns appear such entries as "Relieved a poor Woman," and "Gave a very poor Boy—1p." By promoting this dual system of accountancy, *The Important Pocket Book* introduces the young reader to both the bookkeeping practices necessary for financial success and to the moral responsibility incumbent on a middle class seeking to assume the role of benefactor of society.[5]

By 1790, William Darton was publishing a day planner for children entitled *The Minor's Pocket Book.* According to Christina Duff Stewart, these books enjoyed a lengthy run with the Darton and Harvey publishing house, coming out annually until well into the 1840s.[6] The 1791 edition, held in the Opie Collection at the Bodleian, opens with "A Short Account of the Life of John Howard, Esq. F. R. S."—a celebrated philanthropist who visited and relieved imprisoned debtors—for the moral edification of the young owner of the book. The book also contains a few riddles and anecdotes on such virtues as "Patience" and "Forbearance," thereby combining the practical tools for planning one's day with instruction and delight. Later editions would also contain riddles and puzzles, the solutions for which were published in the next year's *Pocket Book.* The Darton and Harvey firm held an annual poetry

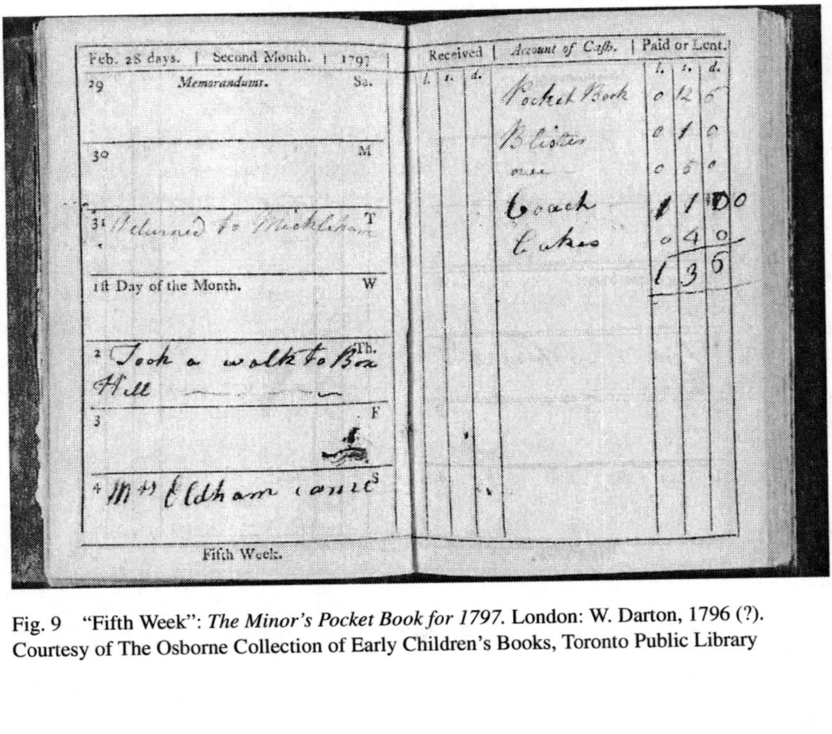

Fig. 9   "Fifth Week": *The Minor's Pocket Book for 1797.* London: W. Darton, 1796 (?). Courtesy of The Osborne Collection of Early Children's Books, Toronto Public Library

competition, the winners of which were published in the *Pocket Book* as well. In her autobiography, the famous writer of children's poetry, Anne Taylor credits the *Pocket Book* not only with publishing her and her sister Jane's juvenile work, thus starting their illustrious careers, but with giving them a greater sense of purpose: "It was the purchase, accidental, shall I say? of the pocket book for 1798 that gave direction, and I hope usefulness to our lives."[7]

In its design, the pocket books resemble more upscale organizers and day timers of the present; they were usually bound in leather, and the binding included pouches for notes, bills of sale, and so on. The books were relatively expensive items, costing between 1s and 1s 6d, depending on the quality of the binding. They contained a full day-to-day calendar on the left side of the text in which the child could write her appointments, along with columns for daily expenditures and receipts on the right side.[8] Also included were tables of weights and measures, money calculations (indicating, for example, how £1 breaks down into shillings and pence), a list of hackney coach fares and the best places in London to catch coaches. Although they lacked the ledger for moral accounts of Newbery's earlier publication, they provided the middle-class child with the tools to document how every minute and penny was spent, and with the practical information needed to navigate through the complex urban environment of late eighteenth-century London.

Both boys and girls of the eighteenth-century middle classes would commonly have received an allowance of pocket money to spend on treats, books, toys, or in small acts of charity, and would have been included in shopping and sightseeing trips to the city. Their mobility would have been limited, especially that of young girls who would almost always have been chaperoned by a governess, maid, or adult relative.[9] Keeping personal financial records, knowledge of coach fares and stops, and how to make correct change in a shop or with a street vendor would, however, have been directly applicable for all middle-class children, as well as useful training for their adult years. Indeed, the full title of the 1824 edition directly addresses a mixed audience: *The Minor's Pocket Book, for the Use of Both Sexes.*

Children of both sexes received training in the fundamental business skills of time and money management, and were both, to a point, made familiar with the business and industrial practices of the period. *The Book of Trades, or Library of the Useful Arts* (1806) was one of many similarly conceived books designed to familiarize boys and girls with the various occupations of the English people. It provides full-page illustrations of each of the 65 trades described, along with such matter-of-fact information on each profession as standard wages. *The Book of Trades* acted as a guide to the more respectable and useful forms of labor, and to the professional trades into which boys of the middle classes could eventually expect to enter. *The Cries of London; or Child's Moral Instructor,* however, dealt exclusively with the lower ranks of society and how they earned their living, cataloging the metropolis's

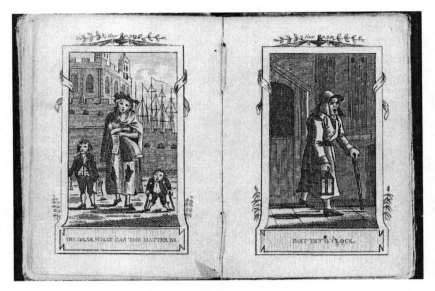

Fig. 10 *The Cries of London.* London: c. 1796. Courtesy of The Osborne Collection of Early Children's Books, Toronto Public Library

itinerant sellers and laborers, and their wares and services. This widely circulating and regularly reprinted text was designed to help middle-class children identify the cries used by the various street hawkers and to recognize which ones to avoid (such as "The Old Cloathes and Bottle-Woman," who is only marginally better than a common thief), and which ones could be safely pitied and patronized (such as "The Shoe-Black," who is represented as an unfortunate orphan). Unlike *The Book of Trades,* which celebrates English business and industry, *The Cries of London* acts as a field guide to the different species of urban plebeian fauna, describing which are benign and which are dangerous.

Although science, industry, and business were primarily part of the masculine social domain, both boys and girls were trained in the scientific discourse on which these pursuits were founded. Specialized texts in applied mathematics, for example, such as Robert Arnold's *The Arithmetical Preceptor; or, Practical Assistant* were addressed specifically to adolescent boys, because they provided training for the world of finances. As the title page remarks, Arnold's book contains "Such Rules in Arithmetic as are deemed necessary to be taught Youth designed for business OR Rules for measuring, as are sufficient to form the Man of Business."[10] Zoological texts such as Stephen Jones's *The Natural History of Beasts,* which condensed the works of Carl Linnaeus and Georges Buffon for children, were designed for both sexes.[11]

Jones's bestiary is, according to its preface, designed for "the generality of readers" and does not specify the age or gender of its intended readership (v). The fact that it was published by Elizabeth Newbery and cataloged in the Opie Collection indicates that it was intended for the use of children. It contains a surprisingly sophisticated account of the debates surrounding systems of animal classification in the eighteenth century, and describes the strengths and weaknesses of treatises by a variety of specialists in the field. Jones comments, for example, on the failings of Klein's taxonomy: "by a servile regard to a method taken from the number of toes, he has jumbled together most opposite animals; the camel and the sloth, the mole and the bat, the glutton and the ape" (viii). What separates this text from other works on natural history is, according to the author, its focus on practical utility: "the uses of the various products of nature in medicine, mechanics, manufactures, dying, painting, &c." (v–vi). While some of the particulars of the debates in the field may be of little use to young readers, it provides them with a glimpse into how knowledge is generated and scientific authority constructed. By describing the utility of such natural resources as animals, Jones demonstrates to middle-class children the connections between the mastery of science and nature and the increasingly industrial economy in which they live.

Representing children engaged in rational diversions—the application of useful knowledge to play—in juvenile literature was a widely used device for acquainting them with the advances of the scientific and industrial revolutions, and of providing them with an early mastery of the world they inhabited. Lady Eleanor Fenn's *Rational Sports in Dialogues Passing Among the Children of a Family* was one of the many texts advancing this brand of instruction and delight. In the first dialogue, "Trades," the children play out a number of different occupations learning and teaching each other the functions of a milliner, a cooper, a druggist, and so on. One child calls out a trade and assigns another child to describe it:

> George: Draper!–when you are asked what your linen is made of, answer, hemp or flax.—They are both plants.—You know what the woolen cloths are made of?
> Susan: O yes.
> Jane: Brasier! What is your brass made of?
> George: Copper ore melted with caliminaris.[12]

The professions the children play act are almost exclusively ones men would occupy, but gaining detailed knowledge (such as the chemical composition of brass) and the ability to categorize this information provides children of both sexes with the understanding of their environment they will need to function effectively in it.

In the third dialogue, the children contrive a game in which the names of countries are written on ivory counters, deposited in a jar and drawn at random:

"the girl was to tell what that country produced—which she chanced to draw ... and if it was a great girl, the situation, soil, climate, and other particulars" (44). Knowledge of geography, and specifically of the raw materials, resources, and agricultural conditions of a given country, was of increasing importance at a time of colonial expansion and broadening international commerce. That the participants in this geography game are girls suggests that such information was considered useful not only to the young man who may seek his fortune in trade or in managing a plantation. As such writers on female education as Mary Wollstonecraft, Priscilla Wakefield, and Catharine Macaulay, discussed later in this chapter, argued, it was useful information for his future wife and partner as well.

The middle-class pedagogical practice of combining useful learning with play and domestic leisure time has been quite thoroughly discussed by both historians of childhood and literary scholars, and I wish only to add a few remarks on the subject.[13] Anna Barbauld and John Aikin's *New Christmas Tales* chronicle the nightly activities of a model middle-class family who have made the domestic sphere a place of important learning and humble amusement. Each evening's rational diversion takes the form of a story highlighting a suitable moral such as charity, kindness to animals, or fortitude in the face of adversity. This is followed by a lecture on a scientific topic. The twenty-third evening, for example, begins with the story "Generous Revenge," in which "the son of a base mechanic" in Genoa rises by his virtue and industry to prominence. The accompanying scientific discourse is an investigation into the structure and properties of "Cruciform-Flowered Plants" (424).

The Harcourt family in Priscilla Wakefield's *Mental Improvements: or the Beauties and Wonders of Nature and Art* follows a similar plan of domestic education, discussing on different evenings religious subjects ("Of the sacred writings"), natural history ("The spider described"), and manufacture ("Of making glass"). In her preface, Wakefield remarks on the utility of this type of rational diversion, as well as the necessary shortcomings of her text: "As improvements in various manufactures are daily taking place, of course, in a work like this, variations will be observed in the production of art and labour, as, even during the printing of this book, important alterations have occured [sic], in the process of making more than one article."[14] Her concern that her information on science, technology, and industry may no longer be up-to-date mirrors the concerns of middle-class parents in the period over the education their children received. Wakefield, like many of the parents who bought her book, was keenly aware that hers was an age of rapid change, and the well-informed child needed constantly to keep pace.

To promote and maintain children's interest in the useful fields of maths and sciences, and more generally to exercise the child's rational faculties, such popular literary (originally oral) forms as books of riddles were adapted to middle-class pedagogical ends. Chapbooks often contained riddles and other similar amusements; so as to disassociate themselves from these plebeian origins, books of rational or scientific riddles often underscored the utility of riddles in honing intellectual faculties. The preface to *Food for the Mind: or, a New Riddle-Book*, for example, speaks of the riddle's ancient and noble lineage: "[n]or has it been confined to common people, as a certain author supposes; for Kings, and even some of the wisest of them, are said to have been adepts in the science."[15] By invoking the term "science" to describe the telling and deciphering of riddles, the author appeals to the middle-class parent seeking rational and useful diversions for her child. The utility of riddles is made even clearer later in the preface: "its utility is unbounded and may be extended with propriety and benefit to every part of life, and every branch of learning" (vi). While this celebration of the humble riddle is made, to some extent, tongue-in-cheek (cf. the assertion that riddling constitutes "the art of dissembling and undissembling" and, therefore, would be useful to the future politician), the desire to make this form more palatable to a middle-class audience is sincere.[16]

Making math and sciences enjoyable to children by presenting them in the form of riddles and puzzles was the objective of M. L. Despiau's *Select Amusements in Philosophy and Mathematics; Proper for Agreeably Exercising the Minds of Youth*. The first part of the text is a collection of mathematical rules and equations, which, if the child learned them, could be applied to the riddles in the second part. Using science to explode irrational superstitions and practices was one of the objectives of the Enlightenment intellectual enterprise, and Despiau set his sights on the popular misconceptions surrounding gambling and luck: "[t]hough nothing, on the first view, seems more foreign to the province of mathematics, than games of chance, the powers of analysis have, as we may say, enchained this Proteus, and subjected it to calculation" (75). To the practical utility of statistical analysis in science and industry is here added an empirical proof against the lottery mentality of the plebeian classes, who view luck as the key to success, as well as the oft-derided upper-class penchant for gambling. Despiau's metaphor for statistical probability as a chaining and restraining power over protean uncertainty echoes the efforts of the middle classes, described by Roy Porter above, to control their environment through the discourse of the rationalized sciences.

Books of games and pastimes sought not only to make the learning of science and other rational discourses fun but to demonstrate how traditional games themselves could be viewed from a scientific perspective as well. *The Universal Conjuror; or, the Whole Art of Legerdemain*, for example, provides the young reader with both the mechanics for performing small feats of magic or harmless sleights of hand and the scientific basis for these tricks.[17] Richard Johnson (writing as Michael Angelo) playfully applies the technical terminology of the scientific treatises of the age to traditional children's games in his *Juvenile Sports and Pastimes*. The result is quite comic, with such chapters as

"Important considerations on tops," in which he discusses "new improvements in the instrument of so much pleasure as a good top affords us," "Strictures on the game of trap-ball," and "A dissertation on marbles," which comes complete with diagrams and tables distinguishing the "three different species or kinds" of marbles (69, 100). This rather unique combination of instruction and delight has more than just humor value; it familiarizes the child with the kind of language specific to scientific discourse. As well, it introduces children to the methods of ordering and controlling information, by distinguishing differences and forming categories and epistemes. Such discursive techniques were central to the production and dissemination of scientific knowledge in the late eighteenth century.

Children's games and toys reflecting the trend in instructional play proliferated in the marketplace of late eighteenth-century England.[18] For the most part, the board games of the period operate along much the same principles as many of their present-day incarnations; dice rolls or the spinning of a "totum" (a needle in a dial) determine the player's progress around the board, and she must avoid various pitfalls to reach a final goal. The movement of the pieces on the board was generally accompanied by some lesson in history, geography, or by moral instruction on virtues to be practiced or vices to be avoided.

Many board games from the earlier part of the century were not necessarily designed for the amusement of children; they involved gambling (an activity later expunged from most rational games), and were often devoid of any clear pedagogical purpose.[19] An early version of "snakes-and-ladders," *The Royal Passtime of Cupid, or the New and Most Pleasant Game of the Snake,* for example, posits the game's final objective as entry into "the delightful Garden of Cupid." The garden features a picture of a dancing couple holding a pitcher of wine, with Cupid playing a lyre for their amusement, seemingly celebrating drinking and license as the winner's reward.[20]

As with children's books of the period, rational and instructive games espousing the middle-class virtues of useful education and investment in one's future existed alongside games with a decidedly plebeian lottery sensibility. John and Edward Wallis, among the most prolific and successful producers of board games in the late eighteenth and early nineteenth centuries, published many examples of the useful, instructive brand of amusements, such as *Wallis's Tour Through England and Wales, a New Geographical Pastime.* The board takes the form of a map of England and Wales dotted with 117 numbers representing various towns across the country. Players start in London and race around the map until they return again to England's economic and cultural center. Along the way, they must stop for a prescribed number of turns to take in the various points of interest at whichever town their totum-spin determines: "50. Worcester—A city, and capital of the county; also the see of a bishop. It has nine parish-churches, besides a cathedral. Here the traveller must stay two turns to see the several manufactures of china, gloves, &c." The clear focus of the game is the familiarization of children with the local geography and its principal industries.[21]

By contrast, *The Game of Chance, or Harlequin Takes All,* published in the same year, is, as the title suggests, a game of pure and random chance, involving such vices as gambling and the suggestion of drinking that would have vexed many middle-class parents and pedagogues. Each player must "stake in" an undetermined amount of money to commence play, and add more to the pot, or withdraw from it, depending on where they land on the board. The player who lands on No. 10 (the image for which depicts two men with full tankards sitting on a barrel) must "Take up 5, and Drink to your friend;" the player who lands on No. 23 (which depicts a dog) must "Pay 5, forfeit all claim to the Game, and Bark till it is over." The game is won when a player lands on the Harlequin, No. 13, and collects the whole pot. With its emphasis on gambling, depictions of ribald activity, and its implication that chance alone determines one's fortunes, *The Game of Chance* depicts the same lottery mentality as the chapbooks middle-class pedagogues and children's writers sought to banish from the middle-class nursery. Many of these early games were, of course, not designed originally as diversions exclusively for children, but found their way, like chapbooks and other elements of plebeian culture, into the nurseries of the more affluent classes. That such games were still being produced in 1794, and for a market catering to and largely dominated by the middle classes, suggests the survival of plebeian culture in an environment increasingly hostile to its influence on the impressionable minds of children.

The Newbery publishing house, the leader in the instruction-and-delight market, manufactured a number of board games in the late eighteen hundreds, often publishing them in association with John Wallis's firm. *The Royal Genealogical Pastime of the Sovereigns of England* describes itself in its rule booklet as "a scientific Game, in which the Amusement and Instruction are equally considered." Starting from the square representing King Egbert (ruled 827–837), the child spins the totum, advances the corresponding number of chronologically arranged squares, then reads from the rule booklet the description of the monarch represented on that square. If the child lands on a good monarch like Queen Elizabeth at No. 43, she advances an extra two squares. The penalty for landing on Henry VIII at No. 40, however, is a return to the beginning of the game, "Henry VIII having been so cruel as to have his wives unjustly put to death." Similarly, the player landing on No. 11, the bad Prince Edwy, "must put down two of his Counters for getting into such bad Company." Children are meant to learn not only the names and dates of their country's rulers, but to abhor cruelty and keep themselves from vicious company.

Perhaps the most value-laden of the Newbery-Wallis board games was *The New Game of Human Life,* which had the players spinning a totum and progressing through the seven stages of life, "Infancy to Youth, Man-Hood,

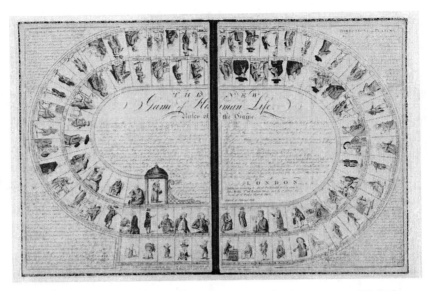

Fig. 11 *The New Game of Human Life.* London: E. Newbery, 1790. Courtesy of The Osborne Collection of Early Children's Books, Toronto Public Library

Prime of Life, Sedate middle-age, Old age, Decrepitude, & Dotage," and arriving finally at No. 84, "The Immortal Man." The progress of human life, as depicted in the game, reflects the middle-class ideology of progress through education and industry. If a player lands on No. 15, "The Assiduous Youth," he is promoted immediately to No. 55, "The Patriot." Landing on No. 7, "The Studious Boy," results in automatic advancement to No. 42, "The Orator." Parallel to this ideology of progress is one of failure and regression through succumbing to vice; the player who lands, for example, on No. 63, "The Drunkard," must "go back to the Child at 2." The lack of reason evinced by the alcoholic makes him, following the Hartleyan psychology of the age, analogous to the infant.[22]

While Newbery-Wallis board games espoused the middle-class ideological concerns of rational education and advancement through industrious application, they contain, like many of the hybrid Newbery books discussed in chapter 1, residual elements of plebeian culture. Advancement, though in theory the result of keeping good company, such as that of Queen Elizabeth, or of being a "Studious Boy," comes in practice through the random chance of a die roll or the spin of a wheel. Further, given the collapsing of time represented in *The New Game of Human Life,* the child's experience of reward is immediate; the player is taken from his lowly station of child to the exalted position of, for example, "The Orator" in one quick and simple step.

Representations of rational play were common in children's stories of the late eighteenth century, and, if we are to believe such historians as J. H. Plumb and Isaac Kramnick, reflected in large part the lived experiences of middle-class children as well. Activities and instruction for boys and for girls shared much common ground but differed considerably along gender lines, although perhaps not quite as considerably as one might assume. When buying suitable toys for her young charges of both sexes, Mme. de Rosier, "The Good French Governess" of Maria Edgeworth's *Moral Tales for Young People,* takes them to a shop "under the direction of an ingenious gentleman, who had employed proper workmen to execute rational toys for the rising generation."[23] The boys and girls take equal delight in the cabinets "for young mineralogists," the "botanical apparatus," the microscopes, and the miniature garden implements for sale at the rational toy shop.[24]

Davidoff and Hall have remarked that although certain activities, such as tending miniature gardens, were engaged in by both sexes, gender differences were still inscribed in these shared forms of rational play: "[g]irls' gardens concentrated on flowers, while boys might plant trees and ferns" (344). In the works of such writers as Edgeworth, Barbauld, and Fenn these distinctions are not so apparent; their texts often represent both sexes receiving the practical, useful training often considered exclusively the domain of boys. Davidoff and Hall's observation that while boys engaged in more rigorous physical activities, "girls played with dolls, doll houses, needlework and miniature work baskets," is, however, born out by representations of male and female activity in much of the children's literature of the period (344). Girls were often represented as participating in many of the same rational pursuits as boys, but that they were also being trained for more domestic duties is clear.

Mary Ann Kilner, whose *Adventures of a Pincushion* was written for a female audience, later wrote a companion piece for boys entitled *Memoirs of a Peg-Top.* She discusses her rationale for writing different stories for the different sexes in the preface to the second text: "for although the laws of justice, probity, and truth are of general obligation, yet, it was imagined, that by consulting different amusements and pursuits, and recommending the accomplishments separately, in which each sex were more particularly concerned, the subjects would . . . have . . . a better chance of approbation" (vi). The accomplishments specific to the female sex to which Mary Ann Kilner alludes are those of the devoted mother, celebrated by her sister-in-law, Dorothy Kilner, in her dedication to *The Doll's Spelling Book:* "[t]o every Doll's Mamma in the Kingdom of Great Britain. . . . As every Parent is desirous of seeing their Children Good, Wise, and Happy, I doubt not but you also are anxious for the welfare of your dear little families, whether they are composed of Wax, Wood, Leather or Rag."[25] That the dedication conflates adult mothers with girls playing at being mothers only reinforces the centrality of domestic duty to the construction of female identity in the children's literature of the late eighteenth century.

In its design, *The Doll's Spelling Book* mirrors such books of instruction for very young children as Barbauld's *Early Lessons* and Fenn's *Cobwebs to Catch Flies,* except that here it is a young girl teaching her doll rather than a mother performing this duty for her child: "[c]ome, my dear doll, though you can not talk, I will make-be-lieve that you can. So come, my child, sit in my lap, and tell me if you know what you are made of? DOLL: I am made of paper. MAM-MA: O, you sil-ly thing! do you not know bet-ter than that? You are made of wood" (39–40). Using the question and answer method of Barbauld's and Fenn's works, the girl teaches her doll to read, describes how the wax from which it is partially composed is manufactured, and provides it moral lessons like "[t]o be good is bet-ter than to be pret-ty" (50).[26] The child is, of course, still in the process of learning such lessons herself, but at the same time she is in training for her future maternal role of instructor to her own children.

The Female Ægis; or, the Duties of Women from Childhood to Old Age outlines for its young female readership the three areas in which "the influence of the female character is most important":

> 1) In contributing daily and hourly to the comfort of husbands, of parents, of brothers and sisters . . . in the intercourse of domestic life, under every vicissitude of sickness and health, of joy and affliction.
> 2) In forming and improving the general manners, disposition, and conduct of the other sex, by society and example.
> 3) In modeling the human mind during the early stages of its growth, and fixing, while it is still ductile, its growing principle of action.[27]

The text advocates a kind of educational reform for young women, "drawing forth the reasoning power of girls into action" through their instruction in "[g]eography, natural history, portions of general history, and popular facts in astronomy, and in other sciences" (19–20). Although the author makes this plea for female education in the more masculine discourses, he or she does not go so far as to suggest female participation in the male public sphere: "[i]n the science of legislation, of political economy, the arts of attack and defense, of commerce and government, man was alone destined to preside" (8). This construction of female duty and education restricts women's roles to the rearing of children and providing comfort in the domestic circle. It is decidedly conservative in comparison with the work of Mary Wollstonecraft or Catharine Macaulay, yet provides a useful index to the types of arguments for broadening, and indeed for completely overhauling, the field of female education that were gaining wider acceptance by the end of the century.

Earlier models of female education focused on cultivating the delicacy of manner and genteel *politesse* many in the middle classes of the late eighteenth century had come to associate with the decadence of the aristocracy. Books of conduct, such as *The Polite Academy,* provided young women with instruction not in the useful arts and sciences, nor in domestic duties, but in how to present themselves gracefully and agreeably in polite society: "A young Woman of Virtue and good Sense, will never think it beneath her Care and Study to cultivate the Graces of her outward Mien and Figure, which contribute so considerably to making her Behaviour acceptable . . . where we see a young Lady standing in a genteel Position, or adjusting herself properly, in Walking, Dancing, or Sitting, in a graceful Manner, we never fail to admire that exterior Excellence of Form."[28] The specific lessons contained in *The Polite Academy* reflect the highly formalized and codified behavior characteristic of court and aristocratic culture. They provide the young reader with precise directions on how to bow, enter or retire from a room before company, and how "To offer or receive any Thing":

1. Whenever you give or receive, take it in your Right-Hand.
2. Bow your Head and Body gently forward.
3. Let your Body rest upon the Left-Leg, which must bend a little; then keeping the other straight, let the Head of that Foot touch the Ground.
4. The Right-Arm should be held forward, and gently bent at the Wrist and Elbow. (44)

The attention here is on graceful physical displays and the superficial beauty so many children's books of the late eighteenth century instruct their readers to mistrust, rather than on intellectual or spiritual concerns.

The Abbé D'Ancourt, in *The Lady's Preceptor. Or, a Letter to a Young Lady of Distinction upon Politeness,* placed an even more pronounced emphasis on surface appearances in female education. His treatise on "the Philosophy of Manners" gestures to, for example, the importance of female piety, but puts its focus on how a lady should conduct herself and *appear* in church ("Of Behaviour at Church"): "[d]uring the Time of the Sermon always *behave* with Gravity and Attention, which is a thing too much neglected by young Ladies of this Age, who come to Church merely to see and be seen."[29] D'Ancourt is promoting the performance of piety, perhaps because a complex engagement with religious matters is, in his estimation, beyond a lady's capacities: "[a]nother Particular . . . which I would at the same time caution you against, is the attempting to dogmatize, or form Difficulties with regard to Religion. . . . Neither is it the Business of one of your Sex, Madam, to concern themselves about the Rites and Ceremonies of the Church she adheres to" (7). As Davidoff and Hall observe, serious commitment to, and the rationalization of, religion was one of the hallmarks of middle-class culture in the late eighteenth century for both sexes, especially in Dissenting circles.

Just as serious religion had little place in D'Ancourt's plan for a lady's proper education, strenuous intellectual accomplishment was also out of her purview: "[i]t is not necessary for a young Lady to be a Scholar" (58). She needs, for example, only enough arithmetic to prevent her being deceived by merchants; her time would be better spent working on her handwriting, as letter writing is the most "improving" and "agreeable Entertainment" for a lady (59). The field of knowledge that D'Ancourt believes should remain most closed to women is philosophy, especially its natural (scientific) branch: "Philosophy, I think, Madam, is a Study without a Lady's Sphere; and if you are either told or read enough of it to know, that the Earth moves round the Sun, and not the Sun round the Earth ... that Thunder and Lightning are mere natural Causes, and that when it hails there is no Fracture in the Skies, as the poor *Pagans* believe ... when your reading in this Branch of Literature, I say, has gone as far as all this, Madam, 'tis full time for you to put a Stop to its farther Progress" (61). The infantilizing tone in which D'Ancourt addresses his female reader and the implicit comparison between female and pagan ignorance clearly reflect the received wisdom of limiting female education.

By the end of the eighteenth century, middle-class notions of female virtue and sense had less to do with elaborate, superficial, and exterior graces. Texts such as *The Polite Academy* and *The Lady's Preceptor,* however, never went out of fashion, as their continued publication history demonstrates. Indeed, Nancy Armstrong convincingly traces current women's magazines back to this form of conduct literature.[30] While middle-class culture was in many ways based on its opposition to upper-class excess, emulation of the cultural practices and modes of consumption of the most privileged classes was still a very strong competing impulse. An increasing number of late eighteenth-century texts promoting a more practical middle-class model of female education coexisted, however, with more conventional conduct literature and provided an alternative ideal of womanhood and of its role. Practicality, morality, and domesticity were increasingly favored over aristocratic notions of refinement in the period, and the woman's role as conveyor of these virtues to her husband and children would become a central concern in the education of girls.[31]

Calls to reform female education were not new to the end of the eighteenth century. At the end of the previous century, Mary Astell in England and François Fénelon, a Catholic priest in France, wrote in favor of replacing the traditional cultivation of ornamental graces with a rigorous intellectual and physical training for girls. Fénelon's observations on female education in his 1688 treatise *De l'Education des Filles* were considerably ahead of their time in a number of respects. He described, for example, the acquisition of knowledge in children using, and predating, the Lockean terminology of impressions on soft, unformed matter: "the substance of their minds is soft, and it hardens more each day ... this softness of the mind allows for easy impressions."[32] He also advocated regular exercise and early rising for children of both sexes, before either Locke or Rousseau did so: "moderate sleep, along with regular exercise, make a person cheerful, vigorous and robust" (94). Fénelon also bemoaned the contemporary practice of keeping young girls inactive and of filling their time with reading vain romances. He describes the importance of a well-educated woman to both the domestic and social good: "A judicious woman, devoted and full of religion, is the soul of a great house; she keeps both worldly goods and health in order. Even men, who have all the public authority, can bring about no good effect in their deliberations if women do not help them in the execution" (92). The argument that the wellbeing of the public sphere rested on the moral and physical health of the family unit—for which the mother must be largely responsible—would be restated and elaborated by later writers on female education.[33]

Mitzi Myers has remarked that the reform of fashionable models of genteel female socialization through more rational, practical education and training in domestic duty was an objective shared by late eighteenth-century women of the middle classes regardless of political or religious affiliation: "Such alternate (but not mutually exclusive) domestic ideologies as More's model of Evangelical femininity and Wollstonecraft's rational womanhood are parallel, even symbiotic, female responses to political upheaval, attempts to take advantage of national unease to repattern domestic life through new schematic images of social order. Both were part of the larger and eventually successful bourgeois campaign to rehabilitate a degenerate culture through propaganda for enlightened domesticity and societal reform" (Myers 1982, 211–12). Alan Richardson's objection to Myers's recuperative placing of widely divergent authors under the rubric of early feminism is worth noting here: "[h]er grouping of 'sister authors for the young,' for example, collapses together such ideologically disparate positions as the outspoken radicalism of Wollstonecraft, the liberal compromises of Edgeworth and Barbauld, and the deep-seated conservatism of Trimmer and More" (Richardson 1994, 168). As Richardson observes, many of the women writing about female education and social reform in the late eighteenth century saw little common ground between themselves, and even rejected attempts to unify their literary efforts. Nonetheless, an unacknowledged allegiance based on shared class interests and class culture unifies many texts, originating in different political camps, that advocate the reform of female education.

Richardson points to Barbauld's refusal to participate in "a 'periodical paper' featuring the work of 'all literary ladies of the present day' on the grounds of political difference" as an indication of the ideological differences between pedagogical reformers (168). Ideology, however, gains its power, as Althusser observes, by unifying diversity and contradiction beneath a "ruling ideology" (Althusser 1971, 139). While there is clearly a difference between the positions held by Wollstonecraft or Macaulay, and those held by Trimmer or More on the matter of female education and duty, their works do overlap at the level of promoting the centrality of the domestic sphere in the construction of the middle-class subject.

Perhaps one of the most significant points of difference between radical and Evangelical or conservative positions on the need for more rigorous and rational female education concerned the "natural" differences perceived between the sexes. More conservative views, such as that of the anonymous author of *The Female Ægis* and of Thomas Gisborne in *An Enquiry into the Duties of the Female Sex,* considered that inherent weaknesses in the female sex made females prone to inattention and the love of superficiality: "The gay vivacity and the quickness of imagination . . . have a tendency to lead to unsteadiness of mind; to fondness of novelty; to habits of frivolousness, and trifling employment; to dislike of sober application; to repugnance to graver studies, and a too low estimation of their worth; to an unreasonable regard for wit, and shining accomplishments; to a thirst for admiration and applause; to vanity and affection."[34] More radical writers such as Wollstonecraft and Macaulay rejected the inherency of such predilections, extrapolating from Locke's rejection of innate ideas that there were no natural intellectual differences between the sexes. Centuries of cultural prejudice had, in Macaulay's estimation, produced the false notion of female mental inferiority: "It is from such causes that the notion of a sexual difference in the human character has, with a very few exceptions, universally prevailed from the earliest times, and the pride of one sex, and the ignorance and vanity of the other, have helped to support an opinion which a close observation of Nature, and a more accurate way of reasoning, would disprove" (203–204). Wollstonecraft places the blame for female weakness and vice, to which Gisborne alludes, squarely on "libertine notions of beauty" and "the desire of establishing themselves—the only way women can rise in the world—by Marriage."[35]

Wollstonecraft had little regard for such conservative efforts to reform female manners and education as *The Female Ægis* or Gisborne's *Enquiry,* as they reinscribed notions of inherent female weakness: "[t]he education of women has of late been more attended to than formerly; yet they are still reckoned a frivolous sex, and ridiculed or pitied by the writers who endeavour by satire or instruction to improve them" (*Vindication,* 83). An upbringing devoid of any intellectual rigor made "mere animals" out of women, and rendered them "weak beings . . . only fit for a seraglio" (83).[36]

Traditional forms of social conditioning were responsible for creating the perceived vices, weakness, and servility of the female sex in the eyes of more moderate writers as well. Contrary to Thomas Gisborne, the relatively conservative Priscilla Wakefield argued that the refined education to which women had been subjected did not exaggerate their predisposition to frivolity and idleness. Such flaws in the female character were the product of a system that suppressed a woman's innate potential as a rational being: "[t]he intellectual faculties of the female mind have too long been confined by narrow and ill-directed modes of education, and thus have been concealed, not only from others, but from themselves, the energies of which they are capable" (*Reflections,* 5). Wakefield was certainly less radical than Wollstonecraft or Macaulay, but she did propose such forward-thinking changes as equality of wages between the sexes: "[a]nother heavy discouragement to the industry of women, is the inequality of the reward of their labour, compared with that of men; an injustice pervades every species of employment performed by both sexes" (*Reflections,* 151). Validating the rational utility and moral authority of the domestic sphere was, for many late eighteenth-century feminist writers, the key to redressing this injustice and to redirecting female energies to the benefit of women, the family, and society.

The types of training girls received for their future domestic roles went well beyond the general instruction in time and money management discussed earlier in this chapter. They extended past the maternal nurturing skills depicted in *The Doll's Spelling Book* and such miniaturized forms of domestic industry as playing with work baskets, pincushions, thimbles, needles and thread as well.[37] Mary Wollstonecraft's exhortation to "give their activity of mind a wider range," so as to promote intellectual curiosity and the "nobler passions" in young women, was reflected in books of natural history written by women and sometimes depicting girls engaged in scientific inquiry (*Vindication,* 181).

Priscilla Wakefield was one of the foremost writers of children's science books in the late eighteenth century. Although she wrote primarily on scientific subjects such as botany and zoology, which did not have the same male cultural capital as "harder" sciences like chemistry, her books for children display a sophisticated knowledge of the material and a facility with the scientific discourse of her age. *An Introduction to Botany, in a Series of Familiar Letters* aims, according to its preface, to reform fashionable models of female education: "[m]ay it become a substitute for some of the trifling, not to say pernicious, objects, that too frequently occupy the leisure of young ladies of fashionable manners, and, by employing their faculties rationally, act as an antidote to levity and idleness."[38] By framing her study of plants as a series of letters between two young sisters, Wakefield reinforces the reform agenda of her work. The fashionable epistolary novel, often regarded by educational writers as one of the "trifling" and "pernicious" diversions on which young women wasted their time, is here adapted and converted to rational pedagogical ends.[39]

Wakefield promises in her preface to divest the text of complex scientific jargon and Latin terminology in order to render her work more accessible to young readers. The fact, however, that Felicia's letters to her sister still contain Latin genus names and that the text comes equipped with footnotes citing the relevant scientific authorities indicates that the young reader is meant to come away from this text with more than just a cursory, superficial knowledge of the

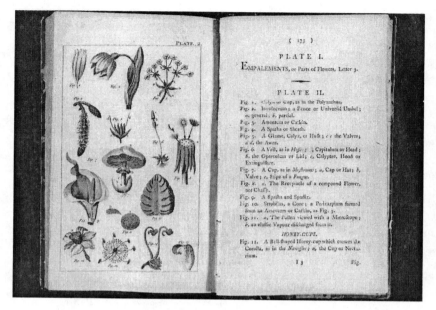

Fig. 12   Priscilla Wakefield, *Introduction to Botany.* London: E. Newbery, 1796. Courtesy of
The Osborne Collection of Early Children's Books, Toronto Public Library

field. In one letter, Felicia provides her sister with a clever mnemonic device
for retaining the botanical classification system:

> Vegetables resemble Man,
> Classes, Nations of Men,
> Orders, Tribes, or Divisions of Nations,
> Genera, the Families that complete the Tribes,
> Species, Individuals of which Families consist,
> Varieties, Individuals under different Appearances. (Wakefield,
> *Introduction,* 29)

Not only is the young botanist learning about the different structures of a plant
and the Latin names for them, she is acquiring the methods of classification as
well. She is not simply learning scientific trivia, but scientific methodology,
the tools to organize information into distinct sets, and the ways of knowing
instrumental to late Enlightenment scientific discourse.[40]

Wakefield's *Introduction to Botany* follows the pedagogical model of
monitored peer instruction and autodidacticism discussed in chapter 3. The
sisters inform each other of their discoveries through their correspondence:
"[y]ou may compare my descriptions with the flowers themselves, and, by
thus mutually pursuing the same object, we can reciprocally improve each

other" (2). Directing Felicia's botanical excursions in the background is the figure of the rational governess: "Do not think, dear sister, that I am capable of methodizing so accurately, without the kind assistance of one, who superintends my letters, and points out what I should write; it is not necessary to say, that Mrs. Snelgrove is that affectionate friend, who will not allow me to do anything without some degree of regularity" (29). That the governess should fulfill the panoptic function of monitoring the activities of the child and foster self-regulation in the child was common, as we have seen, in the children's literature of the period. That the governess or mother should be configured as an authority on scientific discourse, training girls and boys in this form of knowledge, suggests an unprecedented degree of female input in the dissemination of specialized scientific knowledge.

Evangelical writers such as Sarah Trimmer were also interested in having children acquire the knowledge of the natural world that had been validated by Enlightenment science. The last portion of the title of Trimmer's *An Easy Introduction to the Knowledge of Nature, and Reading the Holy Scriptures* (1780) suggests the devotional nature of the scientific inquiries she proposes: to have children garner a better understanding of the works of the Supreme Being. She does, however, hope that by her work children "might be brought in their early years to attend scientific accounts of causes and effects, [and] to enter far into each particular branch."[41] Once again, the discourses of useful knowledge and religious duty overlap in the figure of the female instructor, be she of an Evangelical or rational disposition.

In *Domestic Recreation; or, Dialogues Illustrative of Natural and Scientific Subjects,* Wakefield combines the acquisition of scientific knowledge with domestic activity again, presenting the reader with a series of "miscellaneous conversations, between a well informed mother [Mrs. Dimsdale] and her daughters [Emily and Lucy]."[42] While this text is not particularly detailed or sophisticated in its reproduction of scientific knowledge and discourse, other of Wakefield's works were. Mrs. Dimsdale does not wish to "burthen" her daughters' "memories with the Latin names of the orders," but it is clear that she is herself familiar with both the Latin terminology and the recognized authorities (12). She is simplifying the specialized vocabulary of the discipline out of consideration for the age of her children.

Mrs. Dimsdale's science lessons are broad and generalized, and her objective is to introduce her daughters to such important scientific innovations as the microscope, and such pivotal advances as Newton's discoveries on light and the color spectrum.[43] The book closes with a lengthy discussion on the "Progress of Civilization," in which Mrs. Dimsdale traces the rise of the liberal arts and sciences in the classical period, their descent in the "dark ages," and their reascendance and trajectory toward perfection in the present age of the late Enlightenment. She singles out the advent of print and the spread of literacy as the harbingers of the age of perfectibility: "[s]ince that time, science in general has advanced with hasty steps; the manners of all ranks are improved; the principles of religion are better understood; and morality more generally practised: for knowledge and virtue mostly attend each other,—vice and ignorance are inseparable companions" (Wakefield, *Domestic,* 214–15). Wakefield, through the mouth of Mrs. Dinsdale, sums up one of the governing principles of Enlightenment philosophy: that the advancement of knowledge amounts to the advancement of virtue. By portraying this endorsement through a mother's instruction of her daughters, Wakefield creates a space for female participation in the enlightened improvement of society and signals the expansion of domestic training and duty beyond the moral support of husbands and the nurturing of children.[44]

Ann Shteir, in *Cultivating Women, Cultivating Science,* remarks that women's inclusion in the study of science began early in the Enlightenment, and went beyond pursuits in the field of botany: "[p]romoters of science for women recommended astronomy, physics, mathematics, chemistry, and natural history as activities for moral and spiritual improvement" (2). The study of the sciences by nonspecialists was not conducted strictly for utilitarian ends such as promoting industry and manufacture, but "was part of general and polite culture," and was conceived as "an antidote to frivolity and an alternative to the card table" (2). Girls were already gaining, alongside their male counterparts, general scientific information by the middle of the century through such texts as Newbery's *A Museum for Young Gentlemen and Ladies; or, a Private Tutor for Little Masters and Misses* (1760, 3rd ed.). With its encyclopedic scope and survey approach to useful knowledge, this work and others like it, served to provide boys and girls with enough information to enable the type of rational conversation required for participation in the polite society of the enlightened age.

It was not until the 1790s that women's consumption of scientific discourse truly translated into the production and dissemination of scientific knowledge. Women's writing of books of science arose out of a "new maternal ideology in the eighteenth century," which "lent authority to women in scientific education and popular science writing" (Shteir, 4). Although books on botany designed for the young were the principle avenues of this scientific authority, women wrote on other fields of natural history as well.[45]

Studying and writing science not only contributed to the domestic authority of women, it provided a sanctioned form of professional employment: "[b]otany as a popular subject for informal education also attracted women who wanted to earn money by writing for the juvenile market, women, and general readers" (Shteir, 5). Female education, in particular the acquisition of scientific knowledge, connected women to the Enlightenment goal of improving society by spreading scientific knowledge: "[t]heir pioneering contributions to the textbook tradition merged gender and genre and helped make science into popular and improving hobbies for the middle ranks of society" (Shteir, 81). It also connected them to the middle classes' ideological project of establishing themselves as the productive center of English society. By disseminating to the rising generation the information and systems of knowledge central to the promotion of technology, industry, and manufacture, women demonstrated their utility to the Industrial Revolution, and the middle classes demonstrated their status as society's most progressive force. In addition, women engaged directly in the marketplace and the capitalist enterprise through their participation in the publishing industry and by choosing educational writing as a profession.

Joseph Priestley had argued, like a number of his contemporaries, that the education of daughters would contribute to their personal virtue and happiness, and would help them to become better wives and mothers: "[i]f their education has been virtuous and proper, and at all liberal, they will be valuable wives to men of liberal minds and better fortunes, and will be particularly well qualified to conduct the education of others" (*Miscellaneous,* 137–38). He also recognized the value of some degree of professional training for girls of more moderate fortunes to ensure their future economic independence: "[i]f . . . parents . . . take care to have their daughters taught such things as women can maintain themselves by doing, they will never be under a necessity of living in a servile dependence upon any person" (137). Priestley is here referring to possible means of survival and upward class mobility for daughters of lower middle-class families and of the improvement-minded lower classes. Girls of the more comfortable middle and upper middle classes could expect to apply their learning more exclusively within the domestic context. His advice concerning female education was valid for them as well, however, considering the volatile nature of the early capitalist market in which middle-class families lost their fortunes as quickly as they made them. Priscilla Wakefield, for example, came to a career in writing in her forties as a result of "[w]orries over her husband's lack of business acumen and a son's legal expenses" (Shteir, 87).

Increasingly in the late eighteenth century, the writing of educational books for children was one of the things middle-class women could do to earn a living. A rigorous and comprehensive education in the liberal arts and sciences was, for Priestley, as much an investment against possible future misfortunes for girls as it was for boys, since it provided them both with a variety of marketable skills. Such flexibility would help middle-class subjects of both sexes to defend against the arbitrary forces of chance that might otherwise reduce them to a state of financial debt and to the "servile" reliance on others so antithetical to the middle-class ideal of the industrious, self-reliant and self-made individual.

Conclusion

The Trajectory of Children's Literature into the Early Nineteenth Century: Moving Toward a Middle-Class Form of Fantasy

This book starts from the premise that the training and management of children was a focal point for a number of middle-class ideological concerns in late eighteenth-century England. Children's reading and education was more closely scrutinized and took on a greater urgency in this period than ever before, as parents, writers, and pedagogues saw the conditioning of the rising generation as essential to creating and sustaining a new social and class order with the middle classes at its moral and productive centre. The widely diverging opinions of individuals and groups within the middle ranks of English society on such matters as religion, the monarchy, civil society, and the duties of women were, to a large extent, superseded by issues of class, social, and pedagogical reform. Rationalists and Evangelicals, republicans and monarchists, proponents and opponents of expanded women's rights found some agreement on what children needed to know and how they should behave. They all sought to expunge vicious plebeian influences from the nursery environment and to impart such virtues as industry, obedience, disdain for finery, and charity to animals and the deserving poor. Concern over the state of their young fostered in the middle classes an ideological cohesion that would, by the nineteenth century, allow for the creation of a new middle-class form of fantasy literature for children.

At the same time, as I argue in chapter 1, the plebeian culture of chapbooks continued to survive, at least residually, in the nurseries of the middle classes, despite concerted efforts by middle-class pedagogues to keep children from its influence. The appropriation and transformation of chapbook characters and narratives in children's books of the second half of the eighteenth century did not represent the triumph of middle-class ideology over plebeian culture. Rational, moral, and more or less strictly didactic children's books coexisted with works combining plebeian constructions and middle-class objectives, and with traditional chapbooks and fairy tales in the children's book market.

The fact that Sarah Trimmer still found it necessary in the opening years of the nineteenth century to warn middle-class parents against *Blue-Beard, Valentine and Orson,* and *Cinderella* in her reviews for *The Guardian of Education* indicates that such texts were still in wide enough circulation to constitute a legitimate threat to her notions of proper children's reading.

The ideological battle the middle classes were waging in the public and political arenas manifested itself in the rational and moral children's books of the late eighteenth century. Children's literature played a vital role in middle-class efforts to reform the vices of the classes below and above by pointing out to young readers such evils as plebeian prodigality and upper-class license. The emphasis on charity in children's books of the period coincides with attempts by the middle classes to disrupt traditional patronage, aristocratic dispensing of monies, and state sponsored charities with individually motivated acts of giving. For the children of the middle classes to assume their future roles as society's benefactors and primary producers, they had to learn to distinguish themselves from the other classes and to recognize their duty to the deserving poor.

As I remark in chapter 2, middle-class children's literature did not uniformly vilify the lower classes in order to point out to the young reader the nature of their difference. Middle-class children were presented with countless portrayals of a contented, industrious, rural plebeian class, living out the Rousseauvian ideal of simple, honest labor, and having no aspirations for class advancement. More often than not, the villainous plebeian figures in children's books of the period came from the servant classes. Their proximity to luxury and a mode of consumption out of their economic reach bred in them a dishonesty and vanity that threatened the developing morality of the child as well as her understanding of the class structure and her place within it.

The lessons middle-class parents sought to impart on their offspring regarding their class position and personal and social duties, were constantly under threat by undesirable influences (from servants, nurses, and so on). Accompanying the desire to improve the morality and intellect of children was a newly conceived understanding of the fragility and malleability of their mental and physical states. John Locke, David Hartley, and the medical writers who followed the sensationalist theory of the brain's workings had demonstrated that the minds of children started as unformed masses, which gradually took the shape determined by the stimuli and impressions to which they were subjected. Middle-class parents and pedagogues had to pay special attention to the types of influences young children received to ensure that their lessons took root, and that their ideological goals were achieved.

Given the natural instability of both the mental and physical state of childhood, order and discipline, the subjects of chapter 4, came to be viewed as the foundations upon which any practical instruction must lie. Regulating one's habits from an early age was the key to the future happiness and success of children, as it served to counteract both the child's inclination towards disorder and unreason, and the uncertainties of a society moving toward a capitalist economic structure. As John Aikin and Anna Barbauld remark in an essay entitled "The Power of Habit," self-regulation serves very practical and utilitarian ends: "[o]f what importance then must it be towards a happy life, to regulate our habits so, that in the possible changes of this world we may be more likely to be gainers than losers" (*New Christmas,* 493). Control over a changing social environment could be achieved by a rigorous education in the useful fields of knowledge, but for these efforts to succeed, children needed to learn mastery over themselves.

With their passions held in check by the authority of their guardians and by their own burgeoning self-discipline, middle-class children could acquire the types of skills and information that would guarantee their success and utility in the adult world. Chapter 5 considers the forms of training parents and children's writers deemed necessary for boys who would go on to careers in commerce, science, or industry, and for girls whose principal future roles revolved around managing the domestic sphere. While certain forms of specialized training were reserved for boys once they reached adolescence (more advanced accountancy, for example), younger children of both sexes acquired the rudiments of the Enlightenment scientific discourses of the day.

For girls, this constituted a shift away from, or at least a supplement to, the ornamental, refined forms of accomplishment which had become associated with aristocratic decadence, and which were increasingly distasteful to both radicals and moderates in the middle classes. Many proponents of more rigorous female education viewed their endeavors as a means of circumventing potential vice in young women, and of improving their utility as companions to their husbands and educators of their children. However, scientific instruction for girls in the late eighteenth century also helped create unprecedented career opportunities for women. Women like Priscilla Wakefield made successful careers from writing educational science books, thereby gaining authority in the marketplace as producers of text, and in the realm of the sciences (most notably in botany) as producers and disseminators of scientific knowledge. Women had also, of course, long participated in the children's book market, writing stories and educational books. However, science writing allowed them to bridge the accepted female genre of instruction for children and the conventionally more masculine genre of science writing.

The practical education of children and their training from a young age in the useful sciences, so germane to middle-class pedagogical and ideological objectives, had many opponents in the late eighteenth and early nineteenth centuries. Samuel Johnson, for example, asserted that the minds of young children were much better suited to the fantasy constructions of chapbooks than to the new type of rational and moral pedagogy now being promoted. James Boswell recalled a conversation at Langton in 1780: "The next day I dined at Langton's with Johnson, I remember Lady Rothes spoke of the advantage children now derived from the little books published purposely for their instruction. Johnson controverted it, asserting that at an early age it was better to gratify curiosity with wonders than to attempt planting truth, before the mind was prepared to receive it, and that therefore, *Jack the Giant-Killer, Parismus and Parismenus,* and *The Seven Champions of Christendom* were fitter for them than Mrs. Barbauld and Mrs. Trimmer."[1] The rigorous education of young children was, in Johnson's estimation, a "useless labour": "[s]uppose they have more knowledge at five or six years old than other children, what use can be made of it? It will be lost before it is wanted, and the waste of so much time and labour of the teacher can never be repaid" (Boswell, II:408). Johnson challenges the middle-class logic of early knowledge acquisition on its own terms; if educating the very young is intended as an investment in the child's future, it is one that does not pay dividends.[2]

Johnson's support of chapbook reading stems, in part, from an antiquarian interest in the tales of bygone cultures: "for it is to be apprehended, that at the time when very wild improbable tales were well received, the people were in a barbarous state, and so on the footing of children" (Boswell, IV:17). Far from endorsing children's consumption of a living plebeian culture, Johnson is suggesting, rather, the Rousseauvian construction of the child as primitive. Further, he implies that the culture that produced chapbooks and fairy tales is safely contained in the realm of the archaic, much as childhood itself is contained in the past by the adult discourse of nostalgia.

A number of Romantic writers, Charles Lamb and William Wordsworth for example, held similar views to those of Johnson. They believed that the pedagogy and children's literature of the late eighteenth and early nineteenth centuries were usually oppressive of childhood's natural energies, imagination, and sense of wonder. Lamb—himself a successful writer for children—rails against the rational and moral (and female) didactic writers of his age in a letter to Coleridge, dated November 4, 1802. After wondering what would have become of his idol, "if instead of being fed with tales and old wives' fables in childhood, [he] had been crammed with geography and natural history," he can barely contain his anger against the perceived enemies of the imagination: "Hang them!—I mean the cursed Barbauld crew, those blights and blasts of all that is human in man and child."[3]

In *The Prelude,* Wordsworth combines his critique of rational and moral pedagogy with the highly idealized construction of childhood characteristic of Romantic discourse. In Book V, Wordsworth laments at length the model of the rational child, "Full early trained to worship seemliness" (*Wordsworth,* 1.298):

[. . .] he can read
The inside of the earth, and spell the stars;
He knows the policies of foreign lands;
The whole world over [. . .]

> [. . .] he sifts, he weighs;
> All things are put to question; he must live
> Knowing that he grows wiser every day
> Or else not live at all.   (ll.317–25)

For the unfortunate product of this unnatural, regimented learning Wordsworth blames the pedagogues of the age: "Some intermeddler still is on the watch/ To drive him back, and pound him like a stray,/ Within the pinfold of his own conceit" (ll.334–36). The "modern system" of education would have divinely imaginative children behave "Like engines" (1.295, 1.368).

At the heart of this romantic condemnation of the new pedagogy of the late eighteenth century is a nostalgic conservatism, a longing to return to simpler and more innocent times. In "Ode: Intimations on Immortality," Wordsworth expresses his dismay that "The things which I have seen I now can see no more," and his sadness over the loss of his own idealized childhood innocence motivates his reaction against the changes imposed on contemporary children by the pressures of modernity (1.9). For Wordsworth, the state of childhood is connected to what can be seen as a conservative fantasy of an idyllic past; he uses the evocation of lost childhood innocence to celebrate an ideal, organic past, removed from the noisy and dirty realities of his industrialized present.

William Blake, too, mistrusted the modern system of education, which he believed stifled the child's natural imaginative faculty. However, rather than situate childhood in some nostalgic recollection of an almost mythical, pastoral past, he addresses issues of contemporary economic inequality and social injustice through the media of childhood innocence and experience. In "The Chimney Sweeper" of *Innocence,* Blake suggests the possibilities offered by the imagination to help child laborers escape, temporarily, the miseries of their daily existence. Following a long day of cleaning the chimneys of London, Tom Dacre dreams of angels liberating him and his fellows from their "coffins of black" to "rise upon clouds, and sport in the wind."[4] His dream, or fantasy, provides him the strength to face another day of potentially deadly or crippling labor ("Though the morning was cold, Tom was happy and warm" [*Blake's,* 1.23]), in much the same way that chapbook fantasies often projected plebeian desires for a better life.

For Blake, the connection between children and plebeians was one loaded with the potential for revolutionary change in the present, rather than a hearkening back to a better past. In "The Chimney Sweeper" of *Experience,* the child blames his plight on the chief authorities of his day, "God and his Priest and King" (*Blake's,* 11). The pedagogues and educators of his day were also to blame for the oppression Blake perceived children to be suffering, "binding with briars, [their] joys and desires" ("Garden of Love" in *Blake's,* 1.12). The perceived affinity between plebeians and children, seen by many middle-class children's writers of the late eighteenth century as an impediment to children's improvement, becomes for Blake a means for expressing his outrage at the injustices suffered by both. As a result, his critique of the modern systems of education and philosophy possesses a subversive quality lacking in that of Wordsworth. The child, for Blake, is a subject, living in the present, upon whom the various forces of authority exercise power, and his celebration of the child's imagination is constructed as a direct and radical challenge to the authorities of his day.

Perhaps Blake's most biting satire on the modern philosophy that had engendered the pedagogical practices of the late eighteenth century is his early prose work *An Island in the Moon,* which contains many of his *Songs* in an early form. Through the mouth of his child character, Aradobo, he lampoons Chatterton and the rationalized sciences of the Enlightenment: "In the first place I think...I think in the first place that Chatterton was clever at Fissic, Follogy, Pistinology, Aridology, Aragraphy, Transmography, Phizography, Hogamy, Hatomy, and hall that, but, in the first place, he eat wery little, wickly—that is, he slept very little, which he brought into a consumption; and what was that he took? Fissic or somethink—and so died!" (*Blake's,* 381) Blake turns the tables on Enlightenment discourse; it is the branches of science in this mangled catalog that are the subject of ridicule, not the child for whom the terms are all nonsense.[5]

Unlike most other Romantics, who came from privileged families, Blake was from lower middle-class artisan stock. He was largely an autodidact and was apprenticed at a young age to an engraver, the trade that supported him throughout his writing career. The childhood depicted by Wordsworth is one characterized by leisure, holiday walks in the country, and much free time for enjoyable reading—a childhood only the monied classes were at liberty to enjoy. Such sorrows as child labor, abandonment, and life in an orphanage, endured by countless English children, do not encroach on most romantic childhood utopias, as they do on Blake's vision of childhood.

Romantic rhapsodizing over childhood innocence and criticism of spirit-crushing pedagogies did not extend to the children of the lower orders, as Alan Richardson's account of the Lake poets' enthusiasm for Andrew Bell's and Joseph Lancaster's systems of education indicates: "Southey, Coleridge, and Wordsworth in *The Excursion* were quite active in framing and disseminating the ideology of the monitorial system. It represented for them a radical cure for England's social ills and political unrest, a means for facilitating and justifying colonial expansion, and (in Bell's version) a prop for that great edifice of stability, the Established Church" (Richardson 1994, 95).[6] Blake showed up the hypocrisy of such models of plebeian training provided by orphanages and Sunday Schools in his two "Holy Thursday" poems. In the "Holy Thursday" of *Innocence,* he describes an annual display of charity in which the orphans of London were paraded through the streets in their new clothes, arriving finally at St. Paul's cathedral: "The children walking two & two in red & blue & green" (2). The parade, intended as evidence of the gentle care the city takes of its destitute children, becomes in Blake's account a paean to the majesty and divinity of the singing children rather than to the "Grey headed beadles" and "the aged men wise guardians of the poor" (3, 11).

Of the few contemporary readers of "Holy Thursday," it seems some missed the irony in Blake's treatment of this noble expression of humanitarianism. Benjamin Heath Malkin, in *A Father's Memoirs of His Child* (1806), saw the poem as expressing "with majesty and pathos, the feelings of a benevolent mind, on being present at a sublime display of national munificence and charity."[7] Blake engraved the frontispiece for this work, a tribute to Malkin's departed son who was the middle-class ideal of the self-disciplining child: "a tutor to himself; requiring neither excitement nor coercion to regulate his habits of employment" (35). The frontispiece subverts this ideal of the rational child by depicting a radiant boy carried up to heaven by an angel, leaving behind his governess, pens, books, and most notably, a compass, in Blake's iconography the Urizenic instrument of confinement.

Blake's outrage at the conditions in which orphaned children lived explodes from the opening lines of "Holy Thursday" of *Experience:* "Is this a

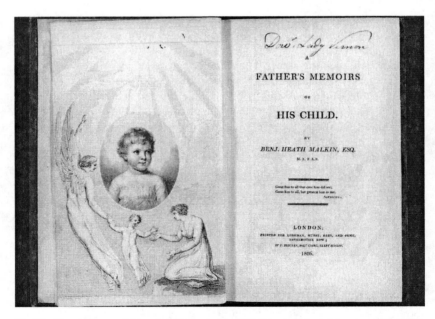

Fig. 13   Frontispiece and title page: Benjamin Heath Malkin, *A Father's Memoirs of His Child.* London: Longman, Rees, Hurst, and Orme, 1806. Courtesy of The Osborne Collection of Early Children's Books, Toronto Public Library

holy thing to see,/ In rich and fruitful land,/ Babes reduced to misery,/ Fed with cold usurous hand?" (1–4). In his representation of the suffering and victimization of London's orphans, Blake takes the opportunity to portray a revolutionary re-visioning of the just society: "For where-e'er the sun does shine,/ And where-e'er the rain does fall:/ Babe can never hunger there,/ Nor poverty the mind appall" (13–16). This is a far cry from Wordsworth's sentimental recollections of the idyllic world of his childhood.

For Alan Richardson, the difference between Blake's critique of contemporary pedagogy and its ideological underpinnings and that of Wordsworth is that the latter saw childhood as inherently apolitical: "Unlike William Blake, whose *Songs of Innocence* . . . expose and deconstruct the disciplinary strategies informing contemporary children's literature, schooling, and religious instruction alike, Wordsworth responds to the politicization of childhood in the 1790s by idealizing the child and attributing to it an 'ideology-proof, organic sensibility' naturally resistant to radical and conservative indoctrination alike" (Richardson 1991, 48–9). Blake's unflinching engagement with the plight of London's disenfranchised children serves as an urgent critique of social injustice and of the emerging middle-class ideology. Wordsworth's lament over the modern child's subjection to a rational education defuses the revolutionary potential of its subject by employing nostalgia, thus distancing childhood from the material concerns of the present.

Blake's *Songs of Innocence* and *Songs of Experience* were not written as children's literature and were not considered as such until much later. His construction of childhood was at odds with the prevailing opinions of the age; he believed that childhood was not a state of mental weakness or deficiency, but one of imaginative and creative power: "Neither Youth nor Childhood is Folly or Incapacity. Some Children are Fools and so are some Old Men. But there is a vast Majority on the Side of Imagination or Spiritual Sensation."[8] That he should praise fantasy and the imagination as beneficial to the child, while condemning the middle-class pedagogy of his age is not surprising considering his radical departure from much Enlightenment thinking. By the opening decade of the nineteenth century, however, middle-class writers who did not share in Blake's radicalism were seemingly beginning to disregard the warnings of Trimmer's and Barbauld's generation concerning the dangers of fantasy and nonsense. A new brand of imaginative, fantasy writing for children, largely divested of potentially subversive and plebeian sources, was emerging as a precursor to the so-called Golden Age fantasy of the Victorian period.[9]

By 1801, Lucy Aikin, in her preface to *Poetry for Children*, had mollified Anna Barbauld's position on the unsuitability of poetry for children, claiming that the regular and ordered structure of poems produced a beneficial "taste for harmony" in the young reader.[10] She suggests that the suspicion of fancy that had informed so much of the rational and moral middle-class children's writing of the previous two decades was, by the beginning of the nineteenth century, no longer as pressing a concern:

> Since dragons and fairies, giants and witches, have vanished from our nurs-
> eries before the wand of reason, it has been a prevailing maxim, that the
> young mind should be fed on mere prose and simple fact. A fear, rational
> in its origin, of adding, by superstition and idle terrors, to the weakness
> of childhood, or contaminating, by any thing false or impure, its truth and
> innocence—has, by some writers, and some parents, been carried to so great
> an excess, that probably no work would be considered by them as unexcep-
> tionable for the use of children, in which any scope was allowed to fancy or
> fiction. (iii)

Aikin suggests that the ideological work of the previous generation's didactic brand of children's literature has been largely completed: it has accomplished its goal of banishing the bugbears of plebeian culture from middle-class nurseries. Since reason has triumphed over superstition, and the mechanisms for regulating childhood weakness and producing rational, moral children are firmly in place, the door can safely be opened to the creative and cultivating influences of poetry.[11]

Writing for children in verse already had a long history in England, dating back considerably further than the puritanical verses of John Bunyan's *A Book for Boys and Girls* (1686) and the devotional poems of Isaac Watts's *Divine Songs* (1715), even to Chaucer and Lydgate. Despite Barbauld's concerns that the noble form not be debased to suit the capacities of children, several of her contemporaries penned original poems for the child reader, including Dorothy Kilner (*Poems on Various Subjects, for the Amusement of Youth*), and later, Ann and Jane Taylor (*Original Poems, for Infant Minds; Rhymes for the Nursery*).[12] Kilner defended her use of rhyme on the basis of its mnemonic utility: "the jingle of the rhyme, it was imagined, would be an agreeable exercise to the memory, at a time of life when that faculty is peculiarily strong, and must have some subject for its employment" (v–vi). Much of the poetry for children, for Kilner, the Taylors, and their contemporaries, contained the same sorts of instruction regarding industry, honesty, and charitable duty, and performed largely the same middle-class ideological work, as its prose counterparts. "The Child's Monitor" from the Taylors' *Original Poems,* for example, describes the ideal, self-regulating middle-class child discussed in chapter 4:

> When I would do what is forbid,
> By something in my heart I'm chid;
> When good, I think, then quick and pat,
> That something says,—"My child do that."
> When I too near the stream would go,
> So pleas'd to see the waters flow,

> That something says, without a sound,
> "Take care, dear child, you may be drown'd"
> And for the poor whene'er I grieve,
> That something says,—"A penny give." (1.47)

The Taylors' "Poor Children" from *Rhymes for the Nursery,* cited above in chapter 2, is an example of a lesson, in poetic form, in the avoidance of plebeian vices.

In 1807, William Roscoe's *The Butterfly's Ball and the Grasshopper's Feast* was published, a "magical" work which Patricia Demers and Gordon Moyles have described as an example of "[s]heer delight," divested of any overt moralizing or didacticism. Within a year, Roscoe's very amusing poem about a variety of insects gathering for an evening of innocent revelry and entertainment spawned numerous imitators: *The Peacock "At Home:" A Sequel to the Butterfly's Ball* (1807); *The Elephant's Ball, and Grand Fete Champetre* (1808); *The Fishes Grand Gala* (1808); *The Fishes' Feast, with a Mermaid's Song* (1808); *The Lion's Parliament, or The Beasts in Debate* (1808); *The Lobster's Voyage to the Brazils* (1808); and *The Tyger's Theatre* (1808), among others. These playful accounts of the adventures and gatherings of anthropomorphized animals differ substantially from such predecessors as Trimmer's *History of the Robins* and Kilner's *The Rational Brutes.* They steer clear of the charity-to-animals-and-the-lower-orders message, and venture into territory Lewis Carroll would later map in "The Lobster's Quadrille" of *Alice's Adventures in Wonderland.*

I would like, in closing, to take a closer look at one poem of this genre, *The Horse's Levee, or the Court of Pegasus,* and to suggest how and why this brand of fantasy literature entered a middle-class children's book market that had so recently favored its seeming opposite. The authors of such works were not of the lower classes, just as such later writers as Lewis Carroll and Edward Lear were not, and the fantasy literature they produced was of a decidedly middle-class timbre, bearing little resemblance to chapbook fantasy narratives. William Roscoe was very much a middle-class figure, a "[h]istorian, attorney, banker, and rare book collector" (Demers and Moyles, 249). Many of the poems emulating Roscoe's enormously successful work were authored anonymously, but Catherine Dorset (née Turner), author of *The Peacock "At Home,"* came from the middle ranks of English society as well. All of the texts I list above were printed by such reputable publishers as J. Harris of London. They contain elaborate and skilfully executed copper-engraved illustrations, which further mark their difference from the cheap printing, rough woodcuts, and cultural environment of chapbook production.

The anonymously published *The Horse's Levee* describes Pegasus's reception of the various characters of the zodiac to his court. The mythical steed's soirée is a fanciful one; representatives of each constellation visit him and describe the various attributes and astrological features of their homes. The reminders to obey one's parents, avoid idleness, and give a penny to the unfortunate beggar, typical of late eighteenth-century children's books, are nowhere to be found. The text is, however, spotted with footnotes explaining points of Greek mythology, providing current scientific perspectives on the movements of the heavenly bodies and their locations in the night skies, along with geographical information about the New World, and even explaining such operatic terms as "Solo," "Duetto," "Glee," and "Quartetto."[13] Although this information is not dryly presented as facts to be retained, the instructional value of the text is still present, albeit in a less explicit form. Along with a sense of delight, *The Horse's Levee* provides children with useful instruction about the world and universe in which they live, as did such earlier works as Eleanor Fenn's *Rational Sports,* but in a more fanciful form.

Considering the often bludgeoning nature of the instructive literature for children of the preceding two decades, such poems as *The Horse's Levee* and *The Butterfly's Ball* are quite remarkable in their levity. The fantasy constructions they present, however, have little to do with the plebeian fantasies of the chapbooks and fairy tales about which earlier pedagogues and children's writers worried. These works are whimsical, but safely so; they contain none of the ribald, subversive humor of chapbooks, and rarely invoke fairies, giants, or other supernatural agents. The lottery mentality, by which plebeian chapbook

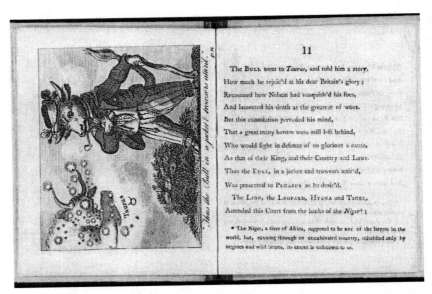

Fig. 14   *The Horse's Levee; or, The Court of Pegasus.* London: J. Harris, 1808. Courtesy of The Osborne Collection of Early Children's Books, Toronto Public Library

figures dramatically advance their class station—through luck, guile, beauty, or the medium of magical assistance—plays no role in these middle-class fantasies for children.

The advent of this form of middle-class fantasy writing in no way signals the absolute triumph of middle-class ideology over plebeian culture in the nursery, touted by Lucy Aikin in her preface to *Poetry for Children.* Chapbooks, and the plebeian culture they articulated, continued to thrive throughout the nineteenth century, even within the middle-class nursery, giving the lie to such a notion. Texts like *The Butterfly's Ball* and *The Horse's Levee,* however, do suggest a degree of comfort with the accomplishments of the moral and rational middle-class pedagogies of the late eighteenth century that ultimately enabled them. Twenty years earlier the middle classes viewed themselves as the outsiders of English society; the reforms of the class structure and social morality they sought to effect were still unrealized, and the ideological work of pedagogy was by necessity more polemical. By the early nineteenth century, a safe place for fantasy was emerging within a middle-class ideology and pedagogy.

The "re-emergence" of fantasy in the early nineteenth century does not represent the radical break from an earlier oppressive, dreary, and pedantic style of children's writing that such historians of children's literature as Percy Muir have suggested. Nor does the fantasy writing that followed the more overtly moral and rational models of the late eighteenth century signal the apotheosis of childhood or the triumph of fun and nonsense over didacticism; it was, rather, the logical extension of the middle-class ideological work performed by the children's books of a generation before. Early nineteenth-century fantasy for children was still designed to serve productive and pedagogical ends, but these ends were more concealed in delightful packaging. The late eighteenth-century recognition of childhood as a precarious state requiring rigorous rational and moral training, and constant supervision and discipline, speaks to the anxieties and pressures of an emerging middle class struggling to forge its identity in a time of social and political change and uncertainty. This earlier ideological groundwork allowed later writers to satirize an already entrenched and effective pedagogy, and made possible the "golden age," Victorian construction of childhood as a period of wonder, playful nonsense, and uninhibited imagination.

Notes

Introduction

1. Asa Briggs, *A Social History of England* (1983; reprint, Harmondsworth: Penguin Books, 1987), 159; hereafter cited in text.
2. Mitzi Myers, "Reform or Ruin: 'A Revolution in Female Manners,' " *Studies in Eighteenth-Century Culture* 11 (1982): 203; hereafter cited in text.
3. Ludmilla Jordanova, "Conceptualizing Childhood in the Eighteenth Century: The Problem of Child Labour," *British Journal of Eighteenth-Century Studies* 10 (1987a): 191; hereafter cited in text.
4. Douglas Hay and Nicholas Rogers, *Eighteenth-Century English Society* (Oxford: Oxford University Press, 1997), 191.
5. Joseph Priestley, *An Appeal to the Public, on the Subject of the Riots in Birmingham* (Birmingham: n.p. 1791), 132.
6. J. C. D. Clarke, *English Society, 1688–1832: Ideology, Social Structure, and Political Practices During the Ancien Regime* (Cambridge: Cambridge University Press, 1985), 71.
7. J. M. Golby and A. W. Perdue, *The Civilization of the Crowd. Popular Culture in England 1750–1900* (London: Batsford, 1984), 30–31; hereafter cited in text.
8. Conservative descriptions of a traditional, codified, and universally accepted system of deference and paternalism have been disputed by many historians, most notably E. P. Thompson in his *Cultures in Common* (New York: The New Press, 1993).
9. Isaac Kramnick, *Republican & Bourgeois Radicalism: Political Ideology in Late Eighteenth-Century England and America* (Ithaca: Cornell University Press, 1990), 16; hereafter cited in text.
10. Gary Kelly, "Class, Gender, Nation, and Empire: Money and Merit in the Writing of the Edgeworths," *The Wordsworth Circle* 25.2 (1994): 89.
11. A few remarks on my use of the often elusive term "ideology" may be necessary here. Kramnick, a Marxist historian, posits ideology as a false consciousness, designed to conceal or disguise the true nature of material relations. Such

a definition is limiting in at least two ways: it does not take into account ideology's ability, in Terry Eagleton's words, not only to "shape the wants and desires of those subjected to [it]" but also to "engage significantly with the wants and desires that people already have" (Terry Eagleton, *Ideology: An Introduction* (London: Verso, 1991), 14–15). Further, the emphasis on ideology as illusory belief neglects its "reality" as material practice (see, for example, Louis Althusser's comments on the "material existence" of ideology in "Ideology and Ideological State Apparatuses (Notes towards an Investigation)" in Louis Althusser, *Lenin and Philosophy and Other Essays,* trans. Ben Brewster [London: New Left Books, 1971]; hereafter cited in text). Finally, the "obviousness" or "naturalness" of ideological belief and practice makes the notion of a totally deliberate and cynically self-interested agenda of deceit difficult to accept.

12. Leonore Davidoff and Catherine Hall, *Family Fortunes: Men and Women of the English Middle Class, 1780–1850* (London: Hutchinson, 1987),176; hereafter cited in text.

13. Raymond Williams, *Problems in Materialism and Culture* (London: Verso Editions, 1980), 39; hereafter cited in text.

14. John Locke, *Two Treatises of Government,* ed. Peter Laslett (1960; reprint, Cambridge: Cambridge University Press, 1990), 271; hereafter cited in text as *Two Treatises.*

15. John Locke, *Some Thoughts Concerning Education,*. ed. John W. and Jean S. Yolton (1693; reprint, Oxford: Clarendon Press, 1989); hereafter cited in text as *Some Thoughts,* was in itself not designed as a guide for raising economically successful middle-class children, although his theories were often adopted to this end by late eighteenth-century pedagogues. Locke was far more concerned with "the Welfare and Prosperity of the Nation" than with individual success (*Some Thoughts,* 80). In his dedication, Locke makes clear that his work is designed to produce useful citizens of every rank, but especially of the highest ranks, the children of Gentlemen, whose example the rest of society would follow: "[f]or if those of that Rank are by their Education set right, they will quickly bring all the rest into Order" (*Some Thoughts,* 80).

16. The table of contents in the first volume demonstrates the remarkable scope of this journal; it is divided into the following subjects: Theology, Sacred Criticism, Ecclesiastical History, Philosophy, History of Philosophy, Arts, History of Academies, History, Biography, Law, Natural Knowledge, Botany, Chemistry, Medicine, Anatomy, Surgery, Mathematical Sciences, Music, Poetry, Mathematics, Astronomy, Commerce, Voyages and Travel, the Drama, Fine Arts, and Miscellanies. Each volume also contained extensive reviews of children's books and systems of education.

17. *The Analytical Review; or, History of Literature, Domestic and Foreign, on an Enlarged Plan,* 28 vols. (London: J. Johnson, 1788–1798), ii; hereafter cited in text as *The AR.*

18. The *AR's* republican political sympathies were often quite explicitly stated, as its review of Burke's *Reflections on the French Revolution* demonstrates: "[w]e cannot, *as cool and dispassionate persons,* subscribe to Mr. Burke's extravagant idolatry of ancestry and rank" (8:303).

19. Isaac Kramnick, "Children's Literature and Bourgeois Ideology: Observations on Culture and Industrial Capitalism in the Later Eighteenth-Century," *Studies in Eighteenth-Century Culture* 12 (1983): 15; hereafter cited in text.

20. J. H. Plumb, "The New World of Children in Eighteenth-Century England," in *The Birth of a Consumer Society: The Commercialization of Eighteenth-Century England,* ed. J. Brewer, N. McKendrick and J. H. Plumb, (London: Europa Pub., 1982), 290–91; hereafter cited in text.

21. Ludmilla Jordanova, "New Worlds for Children in the Eighteenth Century: Problems of Historical Interpretation," *History of the Human Sciences* 3.1 (1990): 72; hereafter cited in text.

22. Plumb does not deal much with the education of girls in the period; expectations of boys and of girls in terms of education and social roles were distinctly different. Boys and girls often shared similar curricula to a point (for example reading and writing skills). Training in the "harder" sciences and in such fields as accounting—fields tailored to the developing marketplace of the early industrial revolution—was reserved mainly for boys (for a more detailed discussion of children's gender training see chapter 4).

23. Christopher Hill's observation that "[m]uch of the social content of puritan doctrine was ultimately accepted outside the ranks of the noncorformists and even by the apparently triumphant Church of England" seems useful for understanding how ideas originally connected to dissent went beyond sectarian confines (cited in Golby and Purdue, 45).

24. Joseph Priestley, *Miscellaneous Observations Relating to Education* (London: R. Crutwell, 1778), 116; his emphasis; hereafter cited in text as *Miscellaneous*.

25. Mary Wiseman, *A Letter from a Lady to her Daughter, on the manner of Passing Sunday Rationally and Agreeably* (London: J. Marshall, 1788), 20.

26. Asa Briggs, *The Collected Essays of Asa Briggs, Vol. 1: Words, Numbers, Places, People* (Brighton: Harvester Press, 1985), 9.

27. See Hans Blumenberg, *Work on Myth,* trans. Robert M. Wallace (Cambridge, Mass.: MIT Press, 1985). I am indebted to Gary Kelly for the terms "investment mentality" and "lottery mentality" to describe differences in ideology and worldview between the middle classes and plebeian classes respectively. See Gary Kelly, "Revolution, Reaction, and the Expropriation of Popular Culture: Hannah More's Cheap Repository," *Man and Nature/ L' Homme et la Nature* 6 (1987): 147–59; hereafter cited in text.

28. Sarah Trimmer, *The Œconomy of Charity; or, an Address to Ladies Concerning Sunday-Schools; the Establishment of Schools of Industry Under Female Inspection* (London: J. Johnson, 1787), 14; her emphasis; hereafter cited in text as *Œconomy*.

29. John Belcham, *Industrialization and the Working Class: The English Experience, 1750–1900* (Brookfield, V.: Gower Pub., 1990), 55; hereafter cited in text.

30. Philippe Ariès argues that the modern family as we understand it today—an enclosed social unit, ideally separated from the world of communal activity—arose out of a growing middle-class disdain for contact with the lower orders (see Philippe Ariès, *Centuries of Childhood: A Social History of Family Life,* trans. Robert Baltick [New York: Vintage Books, 1962], 406–7.)

31. Joseph Priestley, *An Essay on the First Principles of Government; and the Nature of Political, Civil, and Religious Liberty* (London: J. Johnson, 1768), vi–vii; hereafter cited in text as *Essay*.

32. While they would probably have distanced themselves from Sarah Trimmer's conservative political views, writers in *The Analytical Review* generally agreed with her on the subjects of education and plebeian reform: "We perfectly coincide with her thinking, that by means of the Sunday Schools, the poor and rich being brought together, the most salutary effects may be produced . . . indeed nothing can be better calculated to bind two separate, yet dependent classes, than this kind of intercourse" (Review of *The Sunday-School Catechist*, 1788, 1: 475–76). Wollstonecraft herself regularly wrote for the journal.

33. Mary Wollstonecraft, *Original Stories from Real Life*, in *The Works of Mary Wollstonecraft Vol. 4*, ed. Janet Todd and Marilyn Butler (1791; reprint, London: William Pickering, 1989); hereafter cited in text as *Original*; and Sarah Trimmer, *Fabulous Histories; Designed for the Instruction of Children, Respecting their Treatment of Animals* (1786; reprint, New York: Garland Publishing, 1977); hereafter cited in text as *Fabulous*.

34. Alan Richardson, "Mary Wollstonecraft on Education," *The Cambridge Companion to Mary Wollstonecraft*, ed. Claudia Johnson (Cambridge: Cambridge University Press, 2002), 24; hereafter cited in text.

35. In *The Disappearance of Childhood* (New York: Delacorte Press, 1982), Neil Postman argues that the distinction between adult and child arose, in early modern Europe, through a differentiation between the categories of literate and illiterate: "[t]he printing press created a new definition of adulthood *based on reading competence,* and, correspondingly, a new conception of childhood *based on reading incompetence*" (18; italics his). By the time of the Enlightenment, the distinction would be based more broadly on the presence/absence of reason, and in medical discourse, by a careful articulation of physical/psychological difference.

36. To use the term "pediatrics" to describe late eighteenth-century medical writing on children is anachronistic, since it only came into common usage in the second half of the nineteenth century. I use it here and throughout the text because the terminology of the period is so cumbersome. Medical texts describing the state of children's health generally used such terms as "management of childhood illnesses" or "complaints" or "passions." The term "management" to describe what medical writers were trying to accomplish is particularly appropriate in describing the forms of control over children's bodies and minds they were undertaking.

37. Michel Foucault, "The Politics of Health in the Eighteenth Century," in *Power/Knowledge: Selected Interviews and Other Writings*, trans. and ed. Colin Gordon (New York: Pantheon Books, 1980), 172; hereafter cited in text.

38. The emphasis on individual cases in medicine is connected to the closer inspection of disease (and its manifestation in the individual patient) necessitated by the changing discourse of illness (see Foucault's account of Johann Georg Zimmermann's *Traité de l'expérience* (1800), in *The Birth of the Clinic: An Archaeology of Medical Perception*, trans. A. M. Sheridan Smith [1973; reprint, New York: Vintage Books, 1994], 15.)

39. William Buchan, *Advice to Mothers on the Subject of their own Health, Strength, and Beauty of their Offspring* (Philadelphia: John Bioren, 1804); Maria Edgeworth and Richard Lovell Edgeworth, *Practical Education,* 2 vols. (1798; reprint, New York: Garland Publishing, 1974); both hereafter cited in text.

40. Michel Foucault, *Discipline and Punish: the Birth of the Prison,* trans. Alan Sheridan (New York: Pantheon Books, 1977), 192; hereafter cited in text.

41. Foucault defines episteme as "the total set of relations that unite, at a given period, the discursive practices that give rise to epistemological figures, sciences, and possibly formalized systems," Michel Foucault, *The Archaeology of Knowledge,* trans. A. M. Sheridan Smith (1969; reprint, London and New York: Tavistock Publications, 1972), 191. See chapter 5, "Classifying," in Michel Foucault, *The Order of Things: An Archaeology of the Human Sciences,* trans., ed. R. D. Laing (1966; reprint, New York: Vintage Books, 1970), 125–65, for the sort of shift in scientific discourse I am discussing here.

42. Allegorical narratives designed to instruct children certainly did not disappear altogether in the period, as the number of new editions of Aesop's *Fables* indicates. "Real life" stories of credible individuals did become the principal instructional narrative.

43. Samuel Pickering argues that children's narratives remained allegorical in the late eighteenth century, citing the repetition of situations and continued use of allegorical "character" names (Miss Steady, Master Bold, etc.). What changed was the nature of the allegories: "[b]y the end of the eighteenth century, most allegory written for children had been thoroughly secularized," Samuel F. Pickering Jr., *Moral Instruction and Fiction for Children, 1749–1820* (Athens: University of Georgia Press, 1993), 18.

44. The novel, itself a fairly recent narrative innovation in the eighteenth century, with its concern for individual authorship and the internal psychological workings of individual characters, represents a similar shift in focus. Cf. Ian Watt, *The Rise of the Novel: Studies in Defoe, Richardson, and Fielding,* chapter 1, "Individualism and the Novel" (Berkeley: University of California Press, 1957).

45. In *Some Thoughts,* Locke does not make it clear at what age shame becomes an effective tool for the regulation of children's behavior. He does suggest that children reach the "age of reason" at a certain undefined point (depending on their individual development and the assiduity of their parents in their upbringing), at which time (in his treatise) the physical regimen of conditioning the child's body gives way to the rational conditioning of the child's mind. I would hazard to guess that the age of seven, which Postman describes as the preprinting press age at which infancy ended, may apply here (see Postman, 18).

46. Locke's use of an animal metaphor ("Reins") to describe the method of controlling the subject lacking reason exemplifies the frequent association between irrational children and the lower orders of creation. This association between brute creation and lack of reason would become quite common in discourses of childhood in the eighteenth century, as well as in discourses concerning the plebeian orders with whom children were regularly compared. Earlier in *Some Thoughts,* when discussing the mischief overindulgent parents

cause children by allowing bad habits to form, Locke makes the comparison quite clear: "[t]ry it in a Dog or an Horse, or any other Creature, and see whether the ill and resty Tricks, they have learn'd when young, are easily mended when they are knit" (104).

47. In his defense, Locke demonstrates surprising lenience when discussing what sort of behavior required correction. For example, children's play was, in his estimation, natural and no cause for alarm: "All their innocent Folly, Playing, and *Childish Actions, are to be* left perfectly free and unrestrained" (*Some Thoughts,* 119; italics his). Children should be left to play, but this play must still be subject to parental scrutiny.

48. It is worth adding here Raymond Williams's remark that economic structures are not static "realities," but systems always in flux: "when we talk of 'the base,' we are talking of a process and not a state" (1980, 34). The fluctuating and varied forms of superstructure are homologous with an ever-changing economic base.

49. Raymond Williams, *Marxism and Literature* (Oxford and New York: Oxford University Press, 1977), 94; hereafter cited in text.

Chapter 1

1. A version of this chapter appeared under the title "The Coach and Six: Chapbook Residue in Late Eighteenth-Century Children's Literature" in *The Lion and The Unicorn* 24 (2000): 18–44, and is reproduced here with the permission of *The Lion and the Unicorn.*

2. *A Little Pretty Pocket Book* (London: J. Newbery, 1744), hereafter cited in text as *Pretty*; *The History of Little Goody Two-Shoes, Otherwise Called Mrs. Margery Two-Shoes* (London: J. Newbery, 1766), hereafter cited in text as *Goody*; *The Friends; or, the History of Billy Freeman and Tommy Truelove* (London: J. Marshall, c. 1790, n.d.), hereafter cited in text as *Friends*; and *Nurse Dandlem's Little Repository of Great Instruction for all who Would be Good and Noble* (London: J. Marshall, c. 1784, n.d.), hereafter cited in text as *Nurse.*

3. Sarah Trimmer, ed., *The Guardian of Education,* 5 vols. (London: J. Johnson, 1801–1805), 4: 74–75; hereafter cited in text as *Guardian.*

4. J. Hamilton Moore, ed., *The Young Gentlemen and Ladies Monitor* (London: J. H. Moore, c. 1772, n.d.), 1.

5. Catherine Macaulay, *Letters on Education; With Observations on Religious and Metaphysical Subjects* (1790; reprint, London and New York: Garland Publishing, 1974), 53; hereafter cited in text.

6. Victor Neuburg, *The Penny Histories: A Study of Chapbooks for Young Readers Over Two Centuries* (Oxford and New York: Oxford University Press, 1968), 3; hereafter cited in text.

7. Harry B. Weiss, *A Book about Chapbooks: the People's Literature of Bygone Times* (1942; reprint, Hatboro, Penn.: Folklore Associates, 1969), 1; hereafter cited in text.

8. Mary V. Jackson, *Engines of Instruction, Mischief, and Magic: Children's*

Literature in England from its Beginnings to 1839 (Lincoln, Nebr.: University of Nebraska Press, 1989), 16; emphasis mine; hereafter cited in text.

9. "The Monstrous Regiment," in which he singles out female writers of children's literature such as Wollstonecraft, Edgeworth, and Trimmer as cold-hearted suppressers of the imagination, and "The Triumph of Nonsense" are the titles of chapters 3 and 5 respectively in Percy Muir's *English Children's Books 1600–1900* (London: B. T. Batsford, 1954); hereafter cited in text; "The Right to Laugh, the Right to Dream" is the title of Jackson's chapter 10.

10. Mary Cooper's *The Child's New Play-Thing: being a spellingbook intended to make the learning to read a diversion instead of a task* (1742; 2nd ed., London: Printed for the author, 1743) also has a claim to this title. Although essentially a primer and spelling book (a very old genre indeed), its playful, secular, rhyming alphabet was a previously unseen feature in children's books ("D was a Drunkard, who had a red Face.... Z was a Zany, and talked like a fool"). Also, its use of games, such as drawing letters from a hat and having children identify them and an object that begins with the letter drawn, was quite a revolutionary form of pedagogy.

11. *The History of Jack and the Giants, The First Part* (n.p.: J. Eddoes, n.d.), 4; hereafter cited in text as *Giants*.

12. Geoffrey Summerfield, *Fantasy and Reason: Children's Literature in the Eighteenth Century* (London: Methuen, 1984), 93; hereafter cited in text.

13. Patricia Demers and Gordon Moyles, *From Instruction to Delight: an Anthology of Children's Literature to 1850* (Toronto: Oxford University Press, 1982), 105; hereafter cited in text.

14. Dorothy Kilner, *The Rational Brutes; or, Talking Animals* (London: J. Harris, 1803); hereafter cited in text as *Rational*.

15. Later in the second part, after Goody's remarkable dog saves children from a collapsing school house, there is another bizarre fantasy incursion into the story when the Man in the Moon makes a recommendation for standardized building codes: "Had Mankind half the Sagacity of Jumper, they would guard against Accidents of this Sort, by having a public Survey ... of all the Houses of every Parish ... so friends, take Care of yourselves, and tell the Legislature, they ought to take care of you" (*Goody,* 100).

16. *The Life and Death of Robin Hood, the Renowned Outlaw. And the Famous Exploits Performed by Him and Little John* (Glasgow: n.p., n.d.), 19.

17. John Rowe Townsend, *John Newbery and his Books: Trade and Plumb-Cakes For Ever, Huzza!* (Metuchen, N.J.: Scarecrow Press, 1994), xi; hereafter cited in text.

18. Newbery died in 1767. His stepson, Thomas Carnan, and his son, Francis, carried on the business for some twelve years. John's nephew, also Francis, struck out on his own and proved to be a successful publisher of children's books himself. Francis died in 1780, and his wife Elizabeth ran the business until her retirement in 1802. Her manager, John Harris, took over from there. (See Townsend, 155–56, and the "Introduction" to S. Roscoe, *John Newbery and His Successors: A Bibliography,* Wormley: Five Owls Press, 1973).

19. While most of *Primrose Pretty Face* was, in Trimmer's mind, "fit for the perusal of children," the protagonist's rise to Lady of the manor she views as a very dangerous precedent to set. As she observes in her review of the book for *The Guardian of Education,* "it certainly is very wrong to teach girls of the lower order to aspire to marriages with persons in stations so far superior to their own, or to put into the heads of young gentlemen, at an early age, an idea, that when they grow up they may, without impropriety, marry servant-maids" (1:436). Perhaps surprisingly, Trimmer was very fond of *Goody Two-Shoes,* which she called a "great favourite." Her primary objection to it was over its antiaristocratic sentiment: "in these times, when such pains are taken to prejudice the poor against the higher orders, we could wish to have a veil thrown over the faults of oppressive squires and hard-hearted overseers" (1:430–31).

20. Alan Richardson, "Wordsworth, Fairy Tales, and the Politics of Children's Reading," in *Romanticism and Children's Literature in Nineteenth-Century England,* ed. James Holt McGovern (Athens: University of Georgia Press, 1991), 37; hereafter cited in text.

21. *The Natural History of Beasts, Compiled from the Best Authorities,* 1793; *Rudiments of Reason, or the Young Experimental Philosopher,* 1793; and *An Introduction to Botany, in a Series of Familiar Lessons,* 1796 are a few examples of the books of rational diversion published by the Newbery house.

22. *The History of Young Edwin and Little Jessy,* (London: E. Newbery, 1799), for example, shows the title characters engaged in domestic gardening (a favorite rational pastime of the period), learning their arithmetic lessons, and so on, with no reference whatsoever to giant killers or beanstalks. *The Silver Thimble* (London: E. Newbery, c. 1800, n.d.), ascribed by the Opies to Sarah Trimmer, preaches industry, utility over beauty, and charity for the deserving poor, arguably the three most popular lessons in the canon of middle-class late eighteenth-century children's books.

23. Harry B. Weiss refers to three publishers bearing this name, all operating in London in the second half of the eighteenth century. The publisher of the works I am citing and to which I am referring is almost certainly "John Marshall of 4 Aldermary Church Yard" who, according to Weiss, "published nothing but children's books of good quality" (25). Samuel Pickering, in his book *John Locke and Children's Books in Eighteenth-Century England* (Knoxville: University of Tennessee Press, 1981), provides an extensive critical study of Marshall's books. He comments that although Marshall's early books (his example is *Nurse Dandlem,* which I discuss below) had only "a modicum of digestible instruction," and "seemed to be fashioned out of rubbish and lumber" (178, 179), he enjoyed a conversion of sorts by 1785, and was led "to change his ways and make his publications more original and instructive" (180). This may very well have been the case, but his earlier, more chapbook-influenced books remained in print in the last decade of the century and beyond.

24. Pickering, again, would probably disagree with this assertion, and point rather to Marshall's affiliation with Trimmer, the Kilners, More, and the Cheap Repository. However, part of our difference in opinion arises from the fact

that where Pickering reads a text like *The Wisdom of Crop the Conjuror* as a principally moral and didactic work, I read it as an example of how chapbook themes and elements coexist with middle-class pedagogy (see my discussion of this text below).

25. Many of Marshall's children's books (and, indeed, many other children's books of the period) do not provide a date of publication. In these instances I follow the approximate dates suggested by the Opies in the catalog of their collection at the Bodleian Library.

26. Mary Wollstonecraft, *Thoughts on the Education of Daughters,* in *The Works of Mary Wollstonecraft Vol. 4,* ed. Janet Todd and Marilyn Butler (1787; reprint, London: William Pickering, 1989), 7; hereafter cited in text as *Thoughts.*

27. In the 1850 edition of *The Prelude,* Wordsworth laments the replacement of chapbook tales of fantasy and adventure with the rational diversions of the late eighteenth century. His remarks provide a useful (albeit biased) indication of children's supposed reading preferences in the period: "Oh! give us once again the wishing-cap/ Of Fortunatus, and the invisible coat/ Of Jack the Giant-Killer, Robin Hood,/ and Sabra in the forest with St. George!" William Wordsworth, *Wordsworth: Poetical Works,* ed. Thomas Hutchinson (Oxford and New York: Oxford University Press, 1969), 343–44; hereafter cited in text as *Wordsworth.*

28. See chapter 2 for a fuller discussion of how this equation is worked out in a middle-class moral economy.

29. For many educational writers of the late eighteenth century, making reading attractive by concentrating on the outward appearance of the book reinforced a mistaken notion of virtue. This is the sort of connection, of "virtue with personal charms," Macaulay objects to in *Letters on Education:* "This teaches the young mind always to look for virtue where it is, perhaps, for very obvious reasons the seldomest to be met with. This confounds the superior with the inferior excellence; and, as sensible objects strike the most forcibly on the imagination, must occasion youth and inexperience to lose every idea of the one, in the attraction of the other" (54).

30. See Laszlo Tarr, *The History of the Carriage,* trans. Elisabeth Hoch (London: Vision Press, 1969).

31. *The Twelfth Day-Gift: or, the Grand Exhibition,* 2nd ed. (London: Carnan and Newbery, 1770), 24.

32. *The History of Master Billy Friendly, and his Sister, Miss Polly Friendly* (London: J. Marshall, c. 1787, n.d.), 12–13; hereafter cited in text as *Billy.*

33. John Feather, *The Provincial Book Trade in Eighteenth-Century England* (Cambridge: Cambridge University Press, 1985), 41.

34. *The History of Tommy Sugar Plumb, and his Golden Book* (Gloucester: John Pytt, c. 1773, n.d.), 10.

35. *Mother Shipton's Legacy* (York: Wilson, Spence and Mawman, 1797); hereafter cited in text as *Shipton.* Sarah Trimmer, in *The Guardian of Education,* writes of this particular work that it is "filled with nonsense and mischief," and that it "ought to be thrown entirely aside, so as never to meet the eyes and ears of children" (1:430).

36. Mole interpretation was a fairly standard feature of chapbook fortune-telling texts. Cf., for example, *The Old Egyptian Fortune-Teller's Last Legacy,* London, c.1775.

37. *The Juvenile Cabinet of Amusement; Consisting of Pleasing Fairy Tales* (Gainsborough: Mozley and Co., 1795), is a true collection of fairy tales, unaffected by middle-class reforms of children's books. The continued existence of such works of fantasy and folklore speaks to the survival of plebeian culture in an age when its consumption by children was viewed with increasing suspicion.

38. *Father Gander's Tales, or, Youth's Moral Companion,* 2 vols. (London: H. Roberts, c. 1800, n.d.), 3,2. Also of interest here is the representation of plebeian "nonsense and absurdity" as a female idiom (Mother Goose), and of reason and morality as a male idiom (Father Gander).

39. Mitzi Myers, "'Servants as They are Now Educated': Women Writers and Georgian Pedagogy" *Essays in Literature* 16.1 (1989), 60; hereafter cited in text.

40. Susan Pederson, "Hannah More Meets Simple Simon: Tracts, Chapbooks, and Popular Culture in Late Eighteenth-Century England," *Journal of British Studies* 25.1 (1986), 88.

41. See Pederson for a more complete account of publication and distribution.

42. This method of distributing morally-improving literature for the poor was not unique to the CRTs. Sarah Trimmer's *Plan for Promoting the Religious Observance of the Sabbath-Day: and a Friendly Remonsterance, Designed for the Adult Poor* (1790), for example, was "sold by itself for 3d. or 20s. per hundred, and is a valuable present to the poor, and to young people in general" (*The AR* 7: 224).

43. For example, such children's book collections as the Osborne and Opie Collections generally catalog them as eighteenth-century children's books.

44. *The Cottager's Saturday Night* (London: J. Evans, c. 1794, n.d.).

45. Benjamin Franklin, *Franklin's Way to Wealth; or, Poor Richard Improved* (London: W. Darton, 1814), 10; hereafter cited in text as *Franklin's.*

46. The Newbery publishing house was enormously prolific and successful; Roscoe estimates the number of Newbery titles, including new editions and reprints, to be in the neighborhood of 2,400. It should be noted, however, that "so far as money-making was concerned, medicines were at all times John Newbery's concern" (Roscoe, 4).

47. Gillian Avery, *Childhood's Pattern: A Study of the Heroes and Heroines of Children's Fiction: 1770–1950* (London: Hodder and Stoughton, 1975), 15; hereafter cited in text.

Chapter 2

1. Peter Earle, *The Making of the English Middle Class: Business, Society and Family Life in London, 1660–1730* (Berkeley and Los Angeles: University of California Press 1989), 218. From his survey of households in Augustan London, Earle calculates an average of 1.9 domestic servants per household: "one or two servants, usually female, was . . . the normal domestic staff" (218).

Four out of every five of these servants were female; retaining a male domestic servant (as opposed to an apprentice in the master's business or trade, who usually would have lived with the family) indicated a middle-class family of higher status and greater wealth.

2. Bridget Hill, *Servants: English Domestics in the Eighteenth Century* (Oxford: Clarendon Press, 1996), 1; hereafter cited in text.

3. *Some Thoughts Concerning Education* contains numerous warnings about the detrimental influence of servants. Locke recommends, for example, the minimum possible contact between servants and children; parents must "carefully preserve him [the child] from the influence of ill Precedents, especially the most dangerous of all, the Examples of the Servants; from whose Company he is to be kept" (147).

4. Mitzi Myers sees Locke's attitudes towards servant-child contact as defining those of late eighteenth-century pedagogy: "Repeatedly, he contrasts the rational and moral cultivation of good parenting with the psychological warping induced by servants who spoil, neglect, or terrify their charges with scary fairy stories, thus initiating the opposition of backward servants and modernist parents which dominates Enlightenment educational discourse" (1989, 52).

5. Lady Eleanor Fenn, *The Art of Teaching in Sport* (London: J. Marshall, 1785), 16.

6. William Godwin, *The Enquirer; Reflections on Education, Manners, and Literature* (London: G. G. and J. Robinson, 1797), 204; hereafter cited in text.

7. Bridget Hill observes that the servant class was seen as representative of the various orders of the laboring poor: "Service. . . . served to distance the upper classes from contact with the poor and provided the only close contact most of the middle and upper classes had with the labouring class. Perhaps this goes some way to explaining why in literature domestic servants were for long the only members of the labouring class represented. They came to stand for the whole of that class" (5–6). Perhaps inspired by Rousseau, children's literature did often feature the agrarian laborer; however, the urban plebe was almost always a servant.

8. Cf. Mrs. Mason in Wollstonecraft's *Original Stories from Real Life,* who congratulates her young charges for finally acting "like rational creatures" and raising themselves above brute creation by endeavoring to correct their tendency to be cruel to animals (370).

9. See also chapter 5 in Hill's *Servants,* "Opportunity, Identity, and Servility."

10. *Scenes for Children* (London: J. Marshall, c. 1790, n.d.), 2; hereafter cited in text as *Scenes.*

11. Maria Edgeworth, *The Parent's Assistant,* 2 vols. (New York: Garland Publishing, 1974), II:18–19; hereafter cited in text as *Parent's.* Wollstonecraft had earlier observed in *Thoughts on the Education of Daughters* that deceit is inherent to the domestic servant: "[a]rt is almost always practiced by servants" (14). As a result, children left in the care of a maid would inevitably learn "cunning, the wisdom of that class of people" (13).

12. William Godwin, despite his view of the inherent wickedness of servants, also blamed the deceit and covetousness of servants on the decadent displays of

their wealthy masters: "The individuals of the first class have each a purse well furnished. There is scarcely a luxury in which they are not at liberty to indulge. There is scarcely a caprice which crosses their fancy, that they cannot gratify.... This monstrous association and union of wealth and poverty together, is one of the most astonishing exhibitions that the human imagination can figure to itself" (205–7). The vices of domestics stem, in large part, from the gross discrepency between their own economic position and that of the people they serve.

13. Priscilla Wakefield, in her *Reflections on the Present Condition of the Female; with Suggestions for its Improvement* (London: J. Johnson, 1798), goes so far as to suggest that love of finery can lead middle and lower middle-class girls to a fallen life: "[f]alse notions of enjoyment, and a dangerous taste for elegance ... have been the unhappy means of casting many women so situated into the abyss of prostitution" (60).

14. Rosamond learns this lesson in "The Purple Jar," when she recognizes that a new pair of shoes might have been a more useful purchase than a glass jar filled with colored water. Miss Steady from *The Silver Thimble* (c. 1790) has fully internalized the middle-class equation of virtue with utility. When she buys a thimble from an itinerant vendor, she scorns the more lavishly adorned models "of highly polished silver, with blue enamel edges, inlaid with curious mottos" in favor of a simpler steel-topped model: "I think they look quite as well as the others; and I like them best because they are more durable," *The Silver Thimble* (London: E. Newbery, c. 1800, n.d., 10, 11).

15. Cf. Gary Kelly's remarks on the Cheap Repository Tracts cited in chapter 1.

16. *The History of a Pin* (London: E. Newbery, 1798) contains a similar episode of plebeian honesty. A poor girl finds a gold coin (here part of a miser's treasure) and begins to contemplate all the useful things she could buy for her mother. She quickly comes to her senses: "[o]h dear heart ... what was I going to do? I thought so much about my dear mother, I had almost *forgot myself,* and that I had no right to the money—it is not mine" (51; italics mine). Fortunately, she does remember herself, and her class position, before committing the transgression of spending money she has not earned.

17. John Aikin and Anna Laetitia Barbauld, *New Christmas Tales (Being the Second Part of Evenings at Home)* (London: n.p., c. 1790, n.d.), 451–52; hereafter cited in text.

18. The futility of teaching by precept was almost universally acknowledged by pedagogues and children's writers of all stripes. In her essay "On Education," Anna Barbauld argued that children learn best from watching the behavior of those around them, and that they are generally resistant to sermonizing: "[i]f you would know precisely the effect these set discourses have upon your child, be pleased to reflect upon that which a discourse from the pulpit, which you have reason to think merely professional, has upon you" (312). Henry Fielding's *Joseph Andrews* opens with the remark. "It is a trite but true observation, that examples work more forcibly on the mind than precept" (59).

19. Sarah Trimmer's "The Murmurer Corrected" provides yet another example of the contented laborer: "[t]he rich ... seldom have such a hearty appetite to their

food as labour gives us; and I must question whether their sleep is as sound" (*A Selection,* 50). It also suggests a logic to preferring poverty over wealth: "the rich [are] subject to as many real evils as the poor, and more imaginary ones" (54).

20. Dorothy Kilner, *The Village School; or a Collection of Entertaining Histories, for the Instruction and Amusement of all Good Children,* 2 vols. (London: J. Marshall, c.1795, n.d.), further suggests that the poor will be content in their poverty if they absorb a reduced form of middle-class morality and recognize their utility to the rest of society: "[p]oor people, if they be good, are as useful in the world as the rich, and those who behave as they ought to do, though they be ever so poor, will be much more happy than naughty people, though they may have as many guineas as they are able to count" (I:44).

21. *The Entertaining and Instructive History of John Trueman* (Gainsborough: Henry Mozley, c. 1800, n.d.), 10; hereafter cited in text as *Entertaining*. Trueman is clearly an allegorical name of the type popular in moral and didactic writing since *Pilgrim's Progress*. Although the use of such allegorical names to label one-dimensional characters was still very common in late eighteenth-century children's books, these figures and their stories are by now mostly grounded in everyday, "real-life" adventures rather than in fable and allegory.

22. As spokesperson for the reform-minded middle classes, Mrs. Trueman's efforts echo Priscilla Wakefield's agenda for the "civilization of the poor" in *Reflections on the Present Condition of the Female*: "teaching them how to cut out their own clothes; to give the best relish to their homely fare...to regulate the disposal of their small pittance to the best advantage; to procure an increase in comfort, by a greater degree of cleanliness, order and good management" (111). In both cases, the absurdly patronizing notion that the poor are incapable of managing their meagre resources is clear.

23. As self-professed regulator of her class's propriety, Betty warns her daughter, a servant in a nobleman's house, to avoid the temptations of finery such as wearing "dirty bits of gauze and ruffles, and handkerchiefs, and bunches of nasty ribbons about your hat": "[s]uch things do not become young women at service; nor farmers' daughters; nor any people in low stations" (*Entertaining,* 26).

24. Sarah Trimmer, *The Charity School Spelling Book, Part I,* 11th ed. (London: F. C. and J. Rivington, 1808); hereafter cited in text as *Charity*.

25. In *The Œconomy of Charity,* Trimmer describes a similar case of the fortunate salvation of a destitute woman through such modest domestic industry. As Patricia Demers remarks, however, this type of industry for the poor promoted in charity schools serves the interests of their social betters as much as it does the poor themselves: "[t]he woman's situation is desperate, and Trimmer's pragmatic solution of learning a trade seems a real lifeline. But it is also a demonstration of middle-class interventionism inuring the poor to serve, accept, and obey" (46–47).

26. The subgenre in children's literature of commonplace inanimate objects narrating their adventures was among the most popular of the period. Cf., for example, Richard Johnson's *The Adventure's of a Silver Penny* (1787); Mary

Ann Kilner's *The Adventures of a Pin-Cushion, Designed Chiefly for the Use of Young Ladies,* 2 vols. (c. 1780), *The Adventures of a Whipping-Top* (c. 1790) and *Memoirs of a Peg-Top* (c. 1790); John Atkin's *The Adventures of a Marble* (c. 1790); Sarah Trimmer's (?) *The Silver Thimble* (c. 1795) and Miss Smythies's *The History of A Pin* (1798).

27. Despite its title and this injunction, the book is not a traditional fable. The adventures of the robin family coincide with "real life" portrayals of Harriet and Frederick, who discover the robins in their father's garden.

28. The Truemans in *The Entertaining and Instructive History of John Trueman,* who also observe the dietary and sumptuary restrictions appropriate to their class, provide a human counterpart to the respectably poor robin family.

29. The beehive has often been used as a model of productive society and labor efficiency (cf., for example, Mandeville's *Fable of the Bees*). However, the eighteenth-century washerwoman and poet Mary Collier, in *The Woman's Labour,* describes the beekeeper's hive as a site of labor exploitation: "So the industrious Bees do hourly strive/ To bring their Loads of Honey to the Hive;/ Their sordid Owners always reap the Gains,/ And poorly recompense their Toil and Pains" (24).

30. John Brand, *Observations on the Popular antiquities of Great Britain: Chiefly Illustrating the Origin of our Vulgar and Provincial Customs, Ceremonies, and Superstitions,* 3 vols., ed. Sir Henry Ellis (1848–49; reprint, New York: AMS Press, 1970), II:59, 57; hereafter cited in text.

31. Brand's assertion that this practice is "now almost entirely forgotten" in England is contradicted by his own evidence; he provides numerous examples of its continued survival across the country from sources dating as late as 1791 (cf. 77–81). Further, he indicates that throwing at cock was a vice practiced, like cockfighting, by not only the plebeian class, but the aristocracy as well: "[i]n King Henry the Seventh's time it should seem this diversion was practiced even within the precincts of the court" (79).

32. Edward Jenkins's cruelty to animals and enjoyment of plebeian pastimes is undoubtedly connected to the fact that he was left "to the care of a governess, who perhaps was never instructed herself to be tender to animals" (*Fabulous,* 78).

33. Richard Johnson's *The Toy-Shop; or, Sentimental Preceptor; Containing some Choice Trifles, for the Amusement of Every Little Miss and Master* (London: E. Newbery, c. 1787, n.d.) provides an excellent analog to Mrs. Addis in the decadent and misguided figure of Lady Fanciful. Her unnatural pampering of her pets is even more extreme: "[she would] have the nicest fowls sometimes dressed for [her] dogs, suffer them to feed off the cleanest napkins, and drink out of silver basons [sic], while a servant is ordered to attend them, as they do their masters and mistresses" (40).

34. The narrative device of having animals gather together, exchange stories, and shed light on human vices and follies has a long history. The implications of this particular gathering are not as satirical as Chaucer's *Parliament of Fowles* or Orwell's *Animal Farm.*

35. Priscilla Wakefield takes up Wollstonecraft's claim that children are incapable of human charity, suggesting everyone should try to assist the needy: "We are apt to suppose, that children have no power to assist the distressed,

but...benevolence and a desire to do good enable everyone to be useful to their fellow creatures, according to their respective situations," *Juvenile Anecdotes, Founded on Facts* (London: Darton and Harvey, 1798), 162–63.

36. Cf. Macaulay's citation of Rousseau on this subject: "[a] child would sooner give a beggar a hundred guineas, than a cake; but require the little prodigal to give away his playthings, his sweetmeats, and other trifles he is fond of, and we shall see whether or not we have made him truly liberal" (116). Paradoxically, the very mechanism of individual charity, which the middle classes sought to inculcate in opposition to state charity, is here seen as engendering upper-class arrogance.

37. Lady Eleanor Fenn, *Cobwebs to Catch Flies; or, Dialogues in Short Sentences, Adapted to Children from the Age of Three to Eight Years,* 2 vols. (1783; reprint, London: J. Marshall, 1800); hereafter cited in text. Another similarly conceived work, with a heavy emphasis on early development of the charitable impulse, is Dorothy Kilner's *The Good Child's Delight; or, the Road to Knowledge in Short Entertaining Lessons of One or Two Syllables* (1785?).

38. In case the reader has missed the point, the first variation appears on the title page as well.

39. In *Heaven Upon Earth,* Patricia Demers comments on the "ethic whereby privileged children give and the disadvantaged receive" characteristic of narratives like *The Orphan Boy*: "[t]he exchange is piddling and paltry, designed not to transform but to solidify inequities" (47). The middle classes were motivated, perhaps, by a genuine humanitarian concern to assist the poor, but not to facilitate any possibility of substantial class advancement.

40. The anonymously published *Juvenile Dialogues; or, Entertaining Conversations for the Improvement of Youth* (c. 1799) contains a similar instance of the charity giver scrutinizing the recipient before providing the requested aid. After young Miss Goodwill locates the apparent subject in need of assistance, she informs her mother, who determines the veracity of the poor woman's claim to charity: "you have found a warm advocate in my daughter; she thought by your looks you were distressed, and has entreated me to look up a few old things. If I may judge by appearances her charity will not be ill disposed" (12).

41. Thomas Percival, in *A Father's Instructions to his Children,* makes it quite clear who is truly at the center of English society: "[y]ou live in a mercantile country, my son, and I wish you to think respectfully of the character of a merchant," *A Father's Instructions to His Children* (London: n.p., 1775), 154. He goes on to cite Voltaire extensively in his attack on the attitudes of the nobility: "In France, says Voltaire, the title of Marquis is given gratis to any one who will accept it... with money in his purse, and a name terminating in *ac* or *ille,* [he] may strut about and cry, Such a man am I! and may look down upon a trader with sovereign contempt.... However, I need not say which is most useful to a nation; a lord powdered in the tip of the mode ... or a merchant who enriches his country... and contributes to the felicity of the world!" (155–56)

42. Joseph Priestley attacks the upper classes for their irreligion in *Miscellaneous Observations Relating to Education* (1778), stating that a "just sense of religion" is "very rarely found in the higher ranks of life, except in the form of a mean and abject superstition, similar to that in which the violence and

licentiousness of the feudal lords, in this and other countries, often terminated" (110–11). To my knowledge, children's books of the period never went so far as to suggest the upper ranks lacked the fundamentals of the Christian faith.

43. A virtually identical version of this story (minus the woodcuts) entitled "The Basket-Maker" appears in *The Twelfth Day-Gift: or, the Grand Exhibition*, 2nd ed. (London: Carnan and Newbery, 1770).

44. Cf. my remarks on *The History of Little Goody Two-Shoes* above in chapter. 1.

45. Children's books of the period took occasional jabs at such aristocratic figures as the courtier. The shopkeeper in Richard Johnson's *The Toy-Shop*, remarks of a tiny box in his shop that it is "the least box that ever was seen in England, and yet, would you think it, madam? In this same box, a courtier may deposit all his truth and probity" (19).

46. The review of Day's book in *The Analytical Review* celebrates its antipathy to the practices of the nobility and its favoring of middle-class values: "[a]mong the useful books which have been lately published, Mr. Day's Sanford and Merton, stands conspicuously formost. He aims at educating a man, and not . . . a nobleman" (*The AR,* 5: 217).

47. Mr. Barlow, the minister for the parish in which Sanford and Merton live, provides a fairly radical definition of the privileged gentleman: "one, that, when he has abundance of everything, keeps it all to himself; beats poor people if they don't serve him for nothing; and when they have done him the greatest favour, in spite of his insolence, never feels any gratitude, or does them any good in return" (I:36).

48. In Dick's case, it is not, in fact, a middle-class family with whom he finds his ultimate comfort, but an upper-class family "of distinction" who have adopted a middle-class model of domesticity: "[h]appy in domestic society and the company of a few friends, they seemed to enjoy life in the most rational manner" (173).

49. It should be noted here that Dick is not solely subjected to ill treatment. At one point he falls under the ownership of a generally well-intentioned, but drunken and lazy farmer who doesn't put him to the work natural to a creature of his station. As a result, Dick grows idle himself, and begins to evince some of the vices endemic to those classes that do not need to labor for their bread: "I grew wild and untractable for want of exercise, and acquired such a load of flesh that I was quite a burden to myself. . . . I became languid by indulgence, and the very idea of exertion was painful, except when it was to show my capricious freaks, and to bid defiance to the groom when he meditated an approach" (102–3). Dick demonstrates here the natural consequences of an indigent lifestyle, and exemplifies the middle-class platitude that only industry and utility can render one happy.

Chapter 3

1. For a detailed discussion of Locke's influence on pedagogy and children's literature, see Samuel Pickering's *John Locke and Children's Literature in Eighteenth-Century England.*

2. Joseph Priestley, *Hartley's Theory of the Human Mind, On the Principle of the Association of Ideas* (London: J. Johnson, 1775), iii; his emphasis; hereafter cited in text as *Hartley's.*

3. Priestley actually traces vibration theory to Newton's *Principia Mathematica* and his *Optics,* and argues that Hartley built his system on these earlier observations (*Hartley's,* ix–x).

4. John W. Yolton, *Thinking Matter: Materialism in Eighteenth-Century Britain.* (Minneapolis: University of Minnesota Press, 1983), 183.

5. [James Long?], *An Enquiry into the Origins of the Human Appetites and Affections, Shewing how each Arises from Association, with an Account of the Entrance of Moral Evil into the World, Four Early Works on Motivation,* ed. Paul McReynolds (1757; reprint, Gainsville, Fla.: Scholars Facsimile and Reprints, 1969, 27; hereafter cited in text). The authorship of this text is disputed. John Yolton has proposed that its author is actually Hartley, but I have followed Paul McReynolds, who edited the facsimile edition I cite here for the series *Four Early Works on Motivation* (1969).

6. Pierre Brouzet, *An Essay on the Medicinal Education of Children, and the Treatment of their Diseases* (London: Thomas Field, 1755), viii.

7. John Kruger (Johann Krueger), a professor of medicine at the University of Helmstadt, frames the connection thus in *An Essay on the Education of Children* (1765): "soul and body are so closely united as that it is scarce possible for us to correct the failings of the one without recollecting at the same time some defect in the other," 43.

8. William Falconer, *A Dissertation on the Influence of the Passions Upon Disorders of The Body* (London: C. Dilly, 1788), 2.

9. Alexander Hamilton, *A Treatise of Midwifery, Comprehending the Management of Female Complaints and the Treatment of Children in Early Infancy* (London: J. Murray, 1781), xvii.

10. William Moss, *An Essay on the Management, Nursing, and Disease of Children, From the Birth: and on the Treatment and Diseases of Pregnant and Lying in Women: with Remarks on the Domestic Practice of Medicine,* 3rd ed. (Egham: C. Boult, 1800), 13; hereafter cited in text.

11. William Cadogan. *An Essay upon Nursing, and the Management of Children, from their Birth to Three Years of Age,* 6th ed. (1748; reprint, London: J. Roberts, 1753), 3–4; hereafter cited in text.

12. John Leake, *A Lecture Introductory to the Theory and Practice of Midwifery,* 3rd ed. (1773; reprint, London: R. Baldwin, 1776), 3; hereafter cited in text as *Lecture.*

13. William Dease, *Observations in Midwifery, Particularly on the Different Methods of Assisting Women in Tedious and Difficult Labour; to which are Added Observations on the Principle Disorders incident to Women and Children* (Dublin: J. Williams, 1783), i–ii.

14. Medical experts on midwifery sometimes trod some contradictory ground when it came to representations of class (in much the same way children's writers did—cf. chapter 2). While condemning the plebeian figure of the midwife, they still followed Rousseau in his celebration of the virtues and health benefits

of the simplicity of the agrarian laborer. William Cadogan avers that "[i]n the Country, Disease and Mortality are not so frequent, either among the Adult [sic], or their Children," and that "[t]he Mother who has only a few Rags to cover her Child loosely, and little more than her own Breast to feed it sees it healthy and strong" (7). Paradoxically, the rural poor are healthy enough that their young do not need the help of medical experts, yet their influence on the children of the more affluent classes is a noxious one.

15. In his article "Honour and Property: the Structure of Professional Disputes in Eighteenth-Century English Medicine," in *The Medical Enlightenment of the Eighteenth Century,* ed. Andrew Cunningham and Roger French (Cambridge: Cambridge University Press, 1990), 138–164, David Harley remarks that the development of a medical orthodoxy was also hampered by the fact that its principle governing body, the College of Physicians, only had power to enforce restrictions on medical practice within a seven mile radius of London. Most practitioners lived and operated outside the city limits.

16. Roy Porter, *Health for Sale: Quackery in England 1660–1850* (Manchester: Mancheter University Press, 1989), 43.

17. Ginnie Smith, "Prescribing the Rules of Health: Self-Help and Advice in the Late Eighteenth Century," in *Patients and Practitioners: Lay Perceptions of Medicine in Pre-Industrial Society,* ed. Roy Porter (Cambridge: Cambridge University Press, 1985), 249–282.

18. Roy Porter, "Spreading Medical Enlightenment: The Popularization of Medicine in Georgian England and its Paradoxes," in *The Popularization of Medicine 1650–1850,* ed. Roy Porter (London: Routledge, 1992), 221; hereafter cited in text.

19. Thomas Beddoes, *A Guide for Self-Preservation, and Parental Affection,* 3rd ed. (Bristol: Bulgin and Rosser, n.d. [1794?]), 8.

20. A. Hume, *Every Woman Her Own Physician; or, the lady's Medical Assistant. Containing the History and Cure of the Various Diseases Incident to Women and Children* (London: Richardson and Urquhart, 1776), vi.

21. Most pediatric works from the eighteenth century covered both the physical and mental distempers to which children were deemed subject. Many of these texts, like, for example, John Kruger's *An Essay on the Education of Children* (London: J. Dodsley, 1765) are arranged under such headings as "On forming their Bodies," "On improving their Minds," and "Concerning their Diseases."

22. Cf. Christopher W. Fox, *Psychology and Literature in the Eighteenth Century* (New York: AMS Press, 1987), 10.

23. William Buchan, *Advice to Mothers on the Subject of their own Health, Strength, and Beauty of their Offspring* (Philadelphia: John Bioren, 1804), 221; hereafter cited in text as *Advice*.

24. It is worth mentioning here that it was also common for pediatric writers of the period to attribute the onset of disease to the vicious influences of the lower orders, particularly domestic servants under whose supervision children were regularly left. This discourse of illness through inappropriate class contact was, as Mitzi Myers has noted, also utilized by pedagogical writers: "Locke,

and many later Georgian educators portray servant-child relationships in terms of disease, taint, infection" (Myers 1989, 52).

25. W. F. Bynum, "The Nervous Patient in Eighteenth- and Nineteenth-Century Britain: The Psychiatric Origins of British Neurology," in *The Anatomy of Madness: Essays in the History of Psychiatry, Vol. I, People and Ideas,* ed. W. F. Bynum, Roy Porter, and Michael Shepherd (London and New York: Tavistock Publications, 1985), 93; hereafter cited in text.

26. Bynum is describing, specifically, the opinions of Thomas Trotter, a nineteenth-century physician whom he describes as "extending . . . typical eighteenth-century assumption[s]" (93). Trotter also exemplified the psychological materialism of the eighteenth century by connecting physical ailments affecting various organs and psychological conditions: "gout, liver disease, and kidney stones were diseases of the nervous temperament as much as hysteria, hypochondria, and frank disorders of the mind" (94).

27. Buchan himself was of this opinion, remarking of cases of glandular disorders, "that cold bathing is more likely to prevent, than to remove obstruction," William Buchan, *Domestic Medicine: or, a Treatise on the Prevention and Cure of Diseases by Regimen and Simple Medicines,* 13th ed. (1769; reprint, London: T. Cadell, 1792), 636; hereafter cited in text.

28. Christian Augustus Strüve, *A Familiar View of the Domestic Education of Children During the Early Period of their Lives* (London: Murray and Highley, 1802), 305; italics his; hereafter cited in text.

29. Cited in, *Three Hundred Years of Psychiatry 1535–1860: A History Presented in Selected English Texts,* ed. Richard Alfred Hunter and Ida McAlpine (Hartsdale, N.Y.: Carlisle Pub., 1982), 380.

30. Ludmilla Jordanova remarks that the medical discourse of childhood in the late eighteenth century "sought to give a coherent account of children in naturalistic form," Ludmilla Jordanova, "Children in History: Concepts of Nature and Society," in *Children, Parents and Politics,* ed. Geoffrey Scarre (Cambridge: Cambridge University Press, 1989), 13, and further suggests that its approach was one akin to botany: "they are plants, for example, easily distorted by poor gardening" (14). While childhood approximated the state of nature, this state was extremely delicate and without proper cultivation would corrupt and degenerate.

31. James Forrester, *Dialogues on the Passions, Habits, and Affections Peculiar to Children* (London: R. Griffiths, 1748), 31; hereafter cited in text.

32. Forrester goes on to remark that the nurse's plebeian practice of frightening children with stories of "Raw-head and Bloody-bones, with all the Hobgoblins she could invent" will produce in the child "Cowardice and Timidity on the Approach of every Thing more powerful than itself . . . which is the lowest and must [sic] abject State, to which a rational Creature can be reduced" (36, 37).

33. Michael Underwood, *A Treatise on the Disorders of Childhood, and the Management of Infants from the Birth; Adapted to Domestic Use,* 3 vols. (London: J. Matthews, 1797), I:2; hereafter cited in text.

34. "Empiric," along with such terms as "mountebank" and "quack," was, in the eighteenth century, often used to describe a medical practitioner without

formal, or at least accredited, training. Underwood uses it here to refer to practices that were perceived as quite the opposite of the empirical methodologies of experimentation, careful observation, recording, and systematizing of results that were the foundation of the Enlightenment scientific revolution.

35. Promoting the larger good of society was a commonly stated goal in eighteenth-century pediatric texts. Cf., for example, James Nelson who, in his *An Essay on the Government of Children Under Three General Heads: Viz. Health, Manners and Education* (London: R. and J. Dodsley, 1753), expresses the desire that his work contribute "to the great Family of the World," (1).

36. George Armstrong, *An Essay on the Diseases Most Fatal to Infants. To Which are added Rules to be observed in the Nursing of Children; with a particular view of those who are brought up by Hand* (London: T. Caddell, 1767), 6.

37. The fact that infants and children were, by definition "simpler" creatures than adults also made the job of the medical expert easier, despite a lack of reliable verbal input from the patient. According to Moss, because infants are not yet corrupted by vice and luxury, "the diseases, and the necessary treatment of them, will, and are always found to be, more regular, uniform, and simple or plain in infancy" (9). Like the rural plebeian, the infant's lack of refinement and worldly experience makes her less susceptible to complex physical ailments.

38. William Forster, *A Treatise on the Causes of Most Diseases Incident to Human Bodies, and the Cure of them,* 2nd ed. (London: J. Clarke, 1746), 369.

39. B. C. Faush, *Catechism of Health: for the Use of Schools, and for Domestic Instruction,* trans. J. H. Basse (London: C. Dilly, 1794), 40.

40. Differentiating children from adults by way of clothing would take on a more pronounced class resonance by the nineteenth century, with, for example, the fashion of sailor suits for little boys. In its nineteenth- and twentieth-century incarnations the othering of children was coupled with an infantalization of the lower classes that their dress mimicked. Ariès traces the fashion of dressing boys in "costume inspired by military or naval uniforms" to the end of the eighteenth century, and suggests the historical class dynamics operating in this trend: "it had always been thought amusing to give children of good family a few characteristics of lower-class dress, such as the labourer's, peasant's, or convict's cap" (60).

Chapter 4

1. Christina Hardyment's *Dream Babies: Childcare from Locke to Spock* (London: Jonathan Cape, 1983) is an example of the (I believe somewhat overargued) influence of Locke and Rousseau on eighteenth-century educational and pediatric discourses: "The relationship of the medical advances to the popularization of Locke's and Rousseau's theories was reciprocal. Buchan, Nelson and other doctors referred to Locke and Rousseau when they wrote; their whole caste of thought was moulded around the twin concepts of Nature and Reason" (14). Although this oversimplifies the scope of influences, as well as the class and cultural forces at work in these discourses, it does point to the exchange of ideas between disciplines.

2. Isaac Watts, *The Improvement of the Mind; or, a Supplement to the Art of*

3. *Logick,* 5th ed. (1741; reprint, London: J. Buckland and T. Longman, 1768), II:131.

3. As well, Macaulay views the rational education of children in much the same way as Underwood or Nelson view the medical management of children—as a means of promoting the social good: "what can more conduce to the prosperity and permanent power of government, than to form in the earliest infancy the prejudices of its subject" (15).

4. It is worth comparing H———'s case to cases from medical texts such as Erasmus Darwin's description of a case of "mania mutabilis" in *Zoonomia; or, The Laws of Organic Life,* 2 vols. (London: J. Johnson, 1796): "Mrs.———, a farmer's wife, going up stairs to dress, found the curtains of her bedroom drawn, and on undrawing them, she believed she saw the corpse of her sister, who was then ill at the distance of twenty miles, and became for that time insane.... she could not be produced to counteract the insane hallucination, but she perfectly recovered in a few months" (II: 358). The stylistic similarities, from the syntax to the elision of the subject's name, are quite striking.

5. As Foucault remarks, the body is still the site of the punishment, even when mental or moral improvement are the stated objectives: "even when they use 'lenient' methods involving confinement or correction, it is always the body that is at issue—the body and its forces, their utility and their docility, their distribution and their submission" (1977, 25).

6. In "Dark Characters, Native Grounds: Wordsworth's Imagination of Imperialism," in *Romanticism, Race, and Imperial Culture, 1780–1834,* ed. Alan Richardson and Sonia Hofkosh (Bloomington and Indianapolis: Indiana University Press, 1996), 283–310, Alison Hickey recognizes the panoptic nature of Bell's proposed "hierarchy of supervision" as well, remarking that "[t]he parallel to Bentham's 'Panopticon,' explored by Foucault, is noteworthy" (295).

7. In his *Literature, Education, and Romanticism: Reading as Social Practice, 1780–1832* (Cambridge: Cambridge University Press, 1994), Alan Richardson rightly suggests that the pedagogical systems for instructing the poor proposed by Bell and Lancaster are extensions of earlier efforts to train the poor in useful industry: "the monitorial school was able to combine into a unified system the inculcation of moral behavior and the instilling of "industrious" habits which were merely juxtaposed in the combined Charity School and School of industry characteristic of the previous century" (94).

8. Andrew Bell, *An Experiment in Education, Made at the Asylum of Madras* (1797), xi; hereafter cited in text.

9. *The Dictionary of National Biography Vol. II, Beal-Browell* (London: Smith, Elder and Co., 1908), 149.

10. The British Library's copy of this pamphlet is, by some happy coincidence, bound together in a volume with Bentham's *Letter to Lord Pelham, Giving a Comparative View of the Penal Colonization of New South Wales and the Home Penitentiary System,* which contains a description of his Panopticon.

11. Foucault remarks on how this sort of hierarchization of student achievement in eighteenth-century schools serves, ultimately, to reinscribe a homogeneity among the scholars: "the marks that once indicated status, privilege and affiliation were increasingly replaced—or at least supplemented—by a whole

range of degrees of normality indicating membership of a homogeneous social body" (1977, 184). The first place student is still only first within the fixed parameters of the leveling norm of testing within the school.

12. Roy Porter has observed that instruction in English Charity Schools followed a similar logic: "[m]echanical methods of instruction and repetitive drill were taken up, partly to simulate workshop discipline and partly for economy" (*English Society in the Eighteenth Century* (1982; reprint, London: Penguin Books, 1990), 166; hereafter cited in text as *English*).

13. Sarah Fielding, *The Governess or, Little Female Academy* (1749; reprint, London and New York: Pandora Press, 1987), 8; hereafter cited in text.

14. Another example of the eldest child performing the regulatory function of parental supervision occurs in *The Child's True Friend. A series of Examples for the Proper Behaviour of Children* (London: Tabart and Co., c. 1800, n.d.). Three children reflect on the subject of disobedience, with Sophy, the eldest, remarking on the illogic of not following one's parents' commands voluntarily: "For my part . . . I think we should not only be very naughty, but very foolish; for if we were idle and disobedient, we should grow up dunces, and ill-tempered children, whom everybody would dislike" (2–3). Since obedience and industry are the established norms of behavior, contravening them would result in their own marginalization from society.

15. Richard Johnson, *Juvenile Trials, for Robbing Orchards, Telling Fibs, and Other Heinous Offences* (London: T. Carnan, 1786), xx; hereafter cited in text.

16. Johnson is clearly invoking a Lockean approach to child psychology and to child rearing. In his preface, he follows Locke in his proscription against the liberal use of physical punishment: "the rod and the cane should be very sparingly used, and only in the utmost extremity" (v). His description of how children acquire vices also mirrors that of Locke: "[c]hildren begin to think much earlier than people generally imagine; and were there [sic] inclinations and passions to be checked on their first appearance, the matter would not be difficult" (xviii).

17. Arabella Argus, *The Juvenile Spectator; Being Observations on the Tempers, Manners, and Foibles of Various Young People* (London: W. and T. Darton, 1810), 11–12; hereafter cited in text.

18. I deliberately use the term "cure" to describe the sort of self-discipline William seeks, since the sort of passion and miscarriage in behavior he is experiencing is, in Mrs. Argus's own words, "in fact, a temporary madness" (16).

19. Mary Cockle, *The Juvenile Journal; or, Tales of the Truth* (London: J. G. Ballard, 1807), 17; hereafter cited in text.

20. *The History of Young Edwin and Little Jessy* (London: E. Newbery, 1799); hereafter cited in text.

21. Dorothy Kilner, *Little Stories for Little Folks, in Easy Lessons of One, Two, and Three Syllables* (London: J. Marshall, [c. 1785, n.d]), 15; hereafter cited in text as *Little Stories*.

Chapter 5

1. *Mental Amusements* (London: G. Sael, 1797), 9.

2. Madame de [Comtesses de] Stéphanie Félicité Genlis, *La Bruyère the Less:*

or, Characters and Manners of the Children of the Present Age (London: T. N. Longman, 1800), 94; hereafter cited in text.

3. Genlis was herself a member of the French nobility—albeit one who aligned herself with many of the ideological concerns of the middle classes—who sought refuge in England during the French Revolution. It is clear that she is addressing the children of well-to-do families here; she suggests, for example, that young ladies "acquire the habit of reading in a carriage, and while our hair is combed" (93). Her intended audience would have had the means to afford personal maids and carriage transportation.

4. *The Important Pocket Book, or the Valentine's Ledger* (London: J. Newbery, c.1765, n.d.). This text includes no record of publication date, but must have been published before 1767, the year John Newbery died.

5. The ledger portion of this text is unpaginated, but it does contain entries written in a child's hand. The original owner of the text reports that he or she "was good all dinner" but "gave Master Tusler a blow;" however, these entries stop by the end of the first month, January. Perhaps the keeping of personal accounts was not sufficiently engaging to maintain the child's interest.

6. Christina Duff Stewart, *The Taylors of Ongar: an Analytical Bio-Bibliography,* 2 vols. (New York: Garland Publishing, 1975), II:814.

7. Cited in Linda David, *Children's Books Published by William Darton and his Sons* (Indiana University: Lilly Library, 1992), 40.

8. The 1797 edition of the *Pocket Book* held in the Osborne Collection was clearly owned by an older person, judging by the handwriting, the regularity of the entries, and the amounts of money the owner was transacting. This suggests that Darton and Harvey's day-timers appealed not only to the child market.

9. I am indebted to Isobel Grundy for these observations on children's economic activities and mobility in public spaces.

10. Robert Arnold, *The Arithmetical Preceptor; or, Practical Assistant* (London: R. Hindmarsh, 1791). The rules Arnold's book treats are principally those covering "Simple Interest, Commission, Insurance, Brokerage,& c." (vii).

11. [Stephen Jones], *The Natural History of Beasts,* 4 vols. (London: E. Newbery, 1798), vol. 2 hereafter cited in text. This text, originally published in three volumes in 1793 and revised and expanded to four volumes in 1798, is attributed by the Opies to Jones.

12. Lady Eleanor Fenn, *Rational Sports in Dialogues Passing Among the Children of a Family* (London: J. Marshall, c.1783, n.d.), 28–9; hereafter cited in text.

13. Isaac Kramnick's "Children's Literature and Bourgeois Ideology: Observation on Culture and Industrial Capitalism in the Later Eighteenth Century" (1983) and J. H. Plumb's "The New World of Children in Eighteenth-Century England" (1982) provide a wealth of information on this subject, the former from a Marxist historical perspective, the latter from a more traditional liberal humanist historical perspective. Mitzi Myers has also written extensively on the subject as it relates to the conditioning and education of young women.

14. Priscilla Wakefield, *Mental Improvements: or the Beauties and Wonders of Nature and Art,* 2 vols., 2nd ed. (London: Darton and Harvey, 1795), iv; hereafter cited in text.

15. John-the-Giant-Killer, *Food for the Mind: or, a New Riddle-Book* (London: T. Carnan, 1787), iii; hereafter cited in text.

16. The author of this work is given as John-the-Giant-Killer. The sort of reform and sanitization of plebeian culture for middle-class children, characteristic of the early Newbery books discussed in chapter 1, is at work here as well. The publisher of this work was Thomas Carnan, the stepson of John Newbery who took over the business on his father-in-law's death. Carnan clearly continued Newbery's marketing tactics as well.

17. *The Universal Conjuror; or, the Whole Art of Legerdemain* (London: M. Bassan, c. 1793, n.d.). Some of the tricks described in this text are quite bizarre and their explanations not what one might consider rigorously scientific. Cf., for example, "To make a Calf's Head bellow as if alive, when dressed up and served," which involves placing a frog inside the calf head just before it is served: "[t]he heat of the tongue will make the frog croak; which sound, coming from the hollow part of the head; will imitate the bellowing of a calf as if it were alive" (4–5).

18. The Friends of the Osborne & Lillian H. Smith Collections have published a useful catalog of their games and puzzles for children, *Ingenious Contrivances: Table Games and Puzzles for Children*, ed. Jill Shefrin (Toronto: Toronto Public Library, 1996); hereafter cited in text. This catalog provides color illustrations and bibliographical information on several of the games discussed below.

19. Jill Shefrin considers *A Journey Through Europe, or The Play of Geography* (1759) to be the "first surviving English juvenile table game," as it was the first to combine pedagogical objectives with board gaming (7–8).

20. This game clearly enjoyed some popularity later in the century as well, as it was republished by Laurie and Whittle of London in 1794.

21. The Wallis company continued to make instructive games well into the middle decades of the nineteenth century; cf., for example, *Wallis's Elegant and Instructive Game Exhibiting the Wonders of Nature* (1818), *Wallis's Picturesque Round Game of the Produce & Manufactures, of the Counties of England & Wales* (1841?), and *Wallis's Locomotive Game, of Railroad Adventures* (1845).

22. There are a number of similar reductions posited in the game. Some, such as the rule that "The Romance Writer at 40 shall pay two stakes & go back to the mischievous Boy at 5," suggest the pedagogical prejudices against certain literary forms in the period. That "The Tragic Author at 45" should proceed immediately "to the place of Immortal Man at 84, and win the Game" indicates which genres were most valued.

23. Maria Edgeworth, *Moral Tales for Young People*, 5 vols. (London: J. Johnson, 1801), V:23; hereafter cited in text.

24. Mme. de Rosier later takes the children to ironmonger shops, upholsterers, printers and bookbinders so that they may see "how several things were put together" (V:42).

25. Dorothy Kilner, *The Doll's Spelling Book* (London: J. Marshall, 1802), v–vi; hereafter cited in text.

26. The use of hyphens to separate syllables in books for very young children was one of Barbauld's innovations in *Lessons for Children* (as was the use of oversized typeface) that came to be widely reproduced by other authors.

27. *The Female Ægis; or, the Duties of Women from Childhood to Old Age* (London: Sampson Low, 1798), 3–4; hereafter cited in text.

28. *The Polite Academy* 4th ed. (London: R. Baldwin, 1768), v; hereafter cited in text.

29. Abbé d'Ancourt, *The Lady's Preceptor. Or, a Letter to a Young Lady of Distinction upon Politeness* (London: J. Watts, 1743), 7, italics mine; hereafter cited in text.

30. See Armstrong's *Desire and Domestic Fiction* (New York: Oxford University Press, 1987) and "The Rise of the domestic woman" in *The Ideology of Conduct: Essays on Literature and the History of Sexuality,* ed. Nancy Armstrong and Leonard Tennenhouse (New York: Methuen, 1987) for a definitive discussion of the history of conduct literature in (not only) the eighteenth century.

31. The middle class's increasing disapprobation of refined female education was reflected in such journals as *The Analytical Review*: "we have uniformly disapproved of books which contain premature instruction, and are written for the instruction of young *ladies* rather than *human beings*" (9:567, italics mine).

32. François de Salignac de la Mothe Fénelon, *Œuvres,* ed. Jacques le Brun (Paris: Editions Gallimard, 1983), 98; hereafter cited in text. All translations from the French are my own.

33. Fénelon's support of more strenuous physical and intellectual education for girls arises more out of a sense of women's spiritual equality than their social equality, as later feminist arguments on education did: "they are one half of the human race, redeemed by the blood of Jesus Christ and destined for eternal life" (93).

34. Thomas Gisborne, *An Enquiry into the Duties of the Female Sex* (London: n.p., 1797), 34.

35. Mary Wollstonecraft, *A Vindication of the Rights of Woman,* ed. and intro. Miriam Brody (1792; reprint, London: Penguin Books, 1992), 83; hereafter cited in text as *Vindication.*

36. Macaulay also employs an Orientalist trope to elucidate the degraded female manners in England: "[the] state of slavery to which female nature in that part of the world has been ever subjected, and can only suit with the notion of a positive inferiority in the intellectual powers of the mind" (49).

37. Representations of girls sewing or knitting as a form of rational play were quite common in the period. *Youthful Sports* (London: Darton & Harvey, 1801) was one of a number of books cataloging different types of children's games such as skipping rope, blind-man's-bluff, kite flying, and so on. Some games were played by both sexes, while others, such as the highly praised "Dressing the Doll," were forms of training specific to girls: "What a pleasing sight to see a little industrious girl making gowns and caps for her doll! What can be more innocent amusement for the tender youth, or what more agreeable to their future employ? For when they grow up they find they have real children to nurse; then they look back with pleasing remembrance to the time spent in imitating their present business!" (7).

38. Priscilla Wakefield, *An Introduction to Botany, in a Series of Familiar Letters* (London: E. Newbery, 1796), v; hereafter cited in text as *Introduction.*

39. Ann Shteir provides an extensive discussion of this text in *Cultivating Women, Cultivating Science: Flora's Daughters and Botany in England, 1760 to 1860* (Baltimore and London: Johns Hopkins University Press, 1996), 83–89; hereafter cited in text. She argues that Wakefield's work "is decorous science in the conduct book tradition," but that it serves the middle-class ideological ends of reform: "[i]t distances girls from the aristocratic manners that many eighteenth-century reformers railed against and emphasizes rational activities for middle-class girls instead" (86).

40. According to Shteir, Felicia learns the "plant systematics" and categories of Carl Linnaeus that were accepted by specialists of the day. Wakefield, however, "sidesteps or ignores the topic of plant sexuality" for her young female readers: "She uses Withering's bowdlerizing language of 'chives' and 'pointals' rather than 'stamens' and 'pistils' to designate the reproductive parts of plants, and, when discussing the taxonomic grouping of orchids, Gynandria, she claims ignorance of the sexualized coupling that the term denotes" (Shteir, 85). These are omissions made on the grounds of propriety rather than the author's ignorance of the proper scientific nomenclature.

41. Sarah Trimmer, *An Easy Introduction to the Knowledge of Nature, and Reading the Holy Scriptures* (London: Printed for the author, 1780), vii.

42. Priscilla Wakefield, *Domestic Recreation; or, Dialogues Illustrative of Natural and Scientific Subjects* (London: Darton and Harvey, 1805), v; hereafter cited in text as *Domestic*.

43. The microscope and the miniature world it revealed provided a particularly popular form of rational diversion for the children of the middle classes in the late eighteenth century; cf., for example, *The Wonders of the Microscope: or, an Explanation of the Creator in Objects Comparatively Minute* (c. 1804), which includes striking and well-executed plates of head lice and the mites inhabiting blue cheese to fascinate, instruct, and astonish the young reader.

44. It is worth at this point, including Terry Lovell's remarks about women's writing and middle-class ideology: "emergent bourgeois society must have contained spaces from which women were not only permitted, but actually encouraged and enjoined, to write" ("Subjective powers? Consumption, the reading public, and domestic woman in early eighteenth-century England. *The consumption of culture 1600–1800: Image, Object, Text*, ed. Ann Bermingham and John Brewer (New York: Routledge, 1997). Writing for children was just such a space in the late eighteenth century, as I have tried to demonstrate from the outset of this study, and women, like Wakefield, performed an important part in both shaping and disseminating middle-class ideology.

45. Cf. Lady Ellenore Fenn's *A Short History of Insects. Extracted from Works of Credit* (London: Stevenson and Matchett, c. 1796, n.d.), which she designed as "an epitome for the use of Ladies and Young Persons" (vii).

Conclusion

1. James Boswell, *Boswell's Life of Johnson. Together with Boswell's Journal of a Tour to the Hebrides and Johnson's Diary of a Journey into North Wales*, 6

vols., ed. George Birkbeck Hill, D. C. L. and L. F. Powell (Oxford: Clarendon Press, 1934), IV:8.n3; hereafter cited in text.

2. Johnson goes on to lampoon Anna Barbauld (and her *Lessons for Children*) as an example of the results of "early cultivation": "Too much is expected from precocity, and too little performed. Miss —— was an instance of early cultivation, but in what did it terminate? In marrying a little Presbyterian parson, who keeps an infant boarding-school, so that all her employment now is, 'To suckle fools, and chronicle small-beer.' She tells the children, 'This is a cat, and that is a dog, with four legs and a tail; see there! you are much better than a cat or a dog, for you can speak.' If I had bestowed such an education on a daughter, and had discovered that she thought of marrying such a fellow, I would have sent her to the *Congress*" (Boswell, II:408–9, see also n.3).

3. Charles Lamb, *The Life, Letters, and Writings of Charles Lamb*, 6 vols., ed. Percy Fitzgerald. (1876; reprint, Freeport, N.Y.: Books for Libraries, 1971), I:420–21.

4. William Blake, *Blake's Poetry and Design*, ed. Mary Lynn Johnson and John E. Grant (New York: W. W. Norton and Co., 1979), 1.12, 1.17; hereafter cited in text as *Blake's*.

5. Orm Mitchell, in "Blake's Subversive Illustrations to Wollstonecraft's *Stories*," *Mosaic* 17.4 (1984): 17–34 argues convincingly that Blake also subverted "what he believed to be . . . wrong-headed views" on children and education in the plates he produced for Wollstonecraft's *Original Stories from Real Life* (25). As I argue below, he does the same thing with the frontispiece to Benjamin Heath Malkin's book.

6. For a thorough discussion of the Lake poets and their support of the monitorial system's utility in colonial expansion and domestic plebeian control, see Richardson, *Literature, Education, and Romanticism*, 91–103.

7. Benjamin Heath Malkin, *A Father's Memoirs of His Child* (London: Longman, Rees, Hurst, and Orme, 1806), xxviii; hereafter cited in text.

8. William Blake, *The Letters of William Blake*, ed. Geoffrey Keynes (London: Rupert Hart-Davis, 1956), 36. It should be noted that other Romantics, including Wordsworth, held opinions about the child's divine imaginative power similar to Blake's: "Our simple childhood, sits upon a throne/ That hath more power than all the elements" (*Prelude* V.508–9).

9. See chapter 8 of Patricia Demers's and Gordon Moyles's *From Instruction to Delight: An Anthology of Children's Literature to 1850* (Toronto: Oxford University Press, 1982), "Harbingers of the Golden Age," for an overview of authors and works signaling this shift. They consider Christopher Smart's *Hymns for the Amusement of Children* (1772) to be among the earliest examples of a children's literature "that tasted more of honey than of medicine" (221).

10. Lucy Aikin, ed., *Poetry for Children* (London: R. Phillips, 1801), iv; hereafter cited in text. In *Hymns in Prose for Children* (1781; reprint, New York and London: Garland Publishing, 1977) Anna Laetitia Barbauld explained why, unlike her predecessor Isaac Watts, she opted to render her devotional writing for children in prose: "But it may well be doubted, whether poetry *ought* to be

lowered to the capacities of children, or whether they should not rather be kept from reading verse, till they are able to relish good verse: for the very essence of poetry is an elevation in thought and style above the common standard; and if it wants this character, it wants all that renders it valuable" (iv).

11. The door nonetheless still required a gate keeper, as much poetry was morally unsafe for children. Aikin performed this role as editor of the collection, selecting suitable works by Cowper, Addison, Thompson, and Dryden.

12. Dorothy Kilner, *Poems on Various Subjects, for the Amusement of Youth* (London: J. Marshall, c. 1787, n.d.); hereafter cited in text; Ann Taylor and Jane Taylor, *Original Poems, for Infant Minds. By Several Young Persons,* 2 vols. (London: Darton and Harvey, 1804); Ann Taylor and Jane Taylor, *Rhymes for the Nursery* (London: Darton and Harvey, 1806).

13. The topographical features of the Americas receive particular attention in the footnotes; for example the location of "[t]he River La Plata, in South America, on the banks of which Buenos Ayres is situated" and "Lake Huron, a large lake in the interior part of North America" are highlighted as points of interest (12). In an age of colonial expansion, such details would be of definite utility and interest.

Works Cited

Primary Sources

Aikin, John and Anna Laetitia Barbauld. *New Christmas Tales (Being the Second Part of Evenings at Home)*. London: n.p., c. 1790, n.d..

Aikin, Lucy, ed. *Poetry for Children*. London: R. Phillips, 1801.

The Analytical Review; or, History of Literature, Domestic and Foreign, on an Enlarged Plan. 28 vols. London: J. Johnson, 1788–1798.

Ancourt, Abbé d'. *The Lady's Preceptor. Or, a Letter to a Young Lady of Distinction upon Politeness*. London: J. Watts, 1743.

Argus, Arabella [pseud.]. *The Juvenile Spectator; Being Observations on Tempers, Manners, and Foibles of Various Young People*. London: W. and T. Darton, 1810.

Armstrong, George. *An Essay on the Diseases Most Fatal to Infants. To Which are added Rules to be observed in the Nursing of Children; with a particular view of those who are brought up by Hand*. London: T. Caddell, 1767.

Arnold, Robert. *The Arithmetical Preceptor; or, Practical Assistant*. London: R. Hindmarsh, 1791.

Barbauld, Anna Laetitia. *Hymns in Prose for Children*. 1781. Reprint, New York & London: Garland Publishing, 1977.

———. *Lessons for Children*. 3 vols. 1778. London: J. Johnson, 1794.

———. *The Works of Anna Laetitia Barbauld*. 2 vols. London: Longman, Hurst, et al., 1825.

Beddoes, Thomas. *A Guide for Self-Preservation, and Parental Affection.* 3rd ed. Bristol: Bulgin and Rosser, n.d. [1794?].

Bell, Andew. *An Experiment in Education, Made at the Asylum of Madras.* London: Caddell and Davies, 1797.

Bisset, James. *The Orphan Boy.* London: E. Newbery, 1800.

Blake, William. *Blake's Poetry and Design.* Edited by Mary Lynn Johnson and John E. Grant. New York: W. W. Norton & Co., 1979.

_____. *The Letters of William Blake.* Edited by Geoffrey Keynes. London: Rupert Hart-Davis, 1956.

Boswell, James. *Boswell's Life of Johnson. Together with Boswell's Journal of a Tour to the Hebrides and Johnson's Diary of a Journey into North Wales.* 6 vols. Edited by George Birkbeck Hill, D. C. L. Powell, and L. F. Powell. Oxford: Clarendon Press, 1934.

Brand, John. *Observations on the Popular antiquities of Great Britain: Chiefly Illustrating the Origin of our Vulgar and Provincial Customs, Ceremonies, and Superstitions.* 3 vols. Edited by Sir Henry Ellis. 1848–49. Reprint, New York: AMS Press, 1970.

Brouzet, Pierre. *An Essay on the Medicinal Education of Children, and the Treatment of their Diseases.* London: Thomas Field, 1755.

Buchan, William. *Advice to Mothers on the Subject of their own Health, Strength, and Beauty of their Offspring.* Philadelphia: John Bioren, 1804.

_____. *Domestic Medicine: or, a Treatise on the Prevention and Cure of Diseases by Regimen and Simple Medicines.* 1769. 13th ed. London: T. Cadell, 1792.

Cadogan, William. *An Essay upon Nursing, and the Management of Children, from their Birth to Three Years of Age.* 1748. 6th ed. London: J. Roberts, 1753.

The Child's True Friend. A Series of Examples for the Proper Behaviour of Children. London: Tabart and Co., c. 1800, n.d.

Cockle, Mary. *The Juvenile Journal; or, Tales of the Truth.* London: J. G. Barnard, 1807.

Collier, Mary. *The Woman's Labour.* Edited by E. P. Thompson and Marian Snyder. 1739. Reprint, London: Merlin Press, 1989.

Cooper, Mary. *The Child's New Plaything: being a spellingbook intended to make the learning to read a diversion instead of a task.* 1742. 2d ed. London: Printed for the author, 1743.

The Cottager's Saturday Night. London: J. Evans, c. 1794, n.d.

The Cries of London; or Child's Moral Instructor. London: E. Ryland, c. 1765, n.d.

Darwin, Erasmus. *Zoonomia; or, The Laws of Organic Life.* 2 vols. London: J. Johnson, 1796.

Day, Thomas. *The History of Little Jack.* London: John Stockdale, 1788.

———. *The History of Sanford and Merton; A Work Intended for the Use of Children.* 3 vols. London: John Stockdale, 1783–89.

Dease, William. *Observations in Midwifery, Particularly on the Different Methods of Assisting Women in Tedious and Difficult Labours; to which are Added Observations on the Principal Disorders incident to Women and Children.* Dublin: J. Williams, 1783.

Despiau, M. L. *Select Amusements in Philosophy and Mathematics; Proper for Agreeably Exercising the Minds of Youth.* London: G. Kearsley, 1801.

Edgeworth, Maria. *Moral Tales for Young People.* 5 vols. London: J. Johnson, 1801.

———. *The Parent's Assistant.* 2 vols. 1800. Reprint, New York: Garland Publishing, 1974.

Edgeworth, Maria, and Richard Lovell Edgeworth. *Practical Education.* 2 vols. 1798. Reprint, New York: Garland Publishing, 1974.

The Entertaining and Instructive History of John Trueman. Gainsborough: Henry Mozley, c. 1800, n.d.

Falconer, William. *A Dissertation on the Influence of the Passions Upon Disorders of The Body.* London: C. Dilly, 1788.

Father Gander's Tales, or, Youth's Moral Companion. 2 vols. London: H. Roberts, c. 1800, n.d.

Faust, B. C. *Catechism of Health: for the Use of Schools, and for Domestic Instruction.* Translated by J. H. Basse London: C. Dilly, 1794.

The Female Ægis; or, the Duties of Women from Childhood to Old Age. London: Sampson Low, 1798.

Fénelon, François de Salignac de la Mothe. *Œuvres.* Edited by Jacques le Brun. Paris: Editions Gallimard, 1983.

Fenn, Lady Eleanor. *The Art of Teaching in Sport.* London: J. Marshall, 1785.

_____. *Cobwebs to Catch Flies; or, Dialogues in Short Sentences, Adapted to Children from the Age of Three to Eight Years.* 2 vols. 1783. London: J. Marshall, 1800.

_____. *Rational Sports in Dialogues Among the Children of a Family.* London: J. Marshall, c. 1783, n.d.

[Fenn, Lady Eleanor]. *A Short History of Insects. Extracted from Works of Credit.* London: Stevenson and Matchett, c. 1796, n.d.

Fielding, Henry, *Joseph Andrews,* 1742. Reprint, Peterborough. Ontario: Broadview Press, 2001.

Fielding, Sarah. *The Governess or, Little Female Academy.* 1749. Reprint, London & New York: Pandora Press, 1987.

Forrester, James. *Dialogues on the Passions, Habits, and Affections Peculiar to Children.* London: R. Griffiths, 1748.

Forster, William. *A Treatise on the Causes of Most Diseases Incident to Human Bodies, and the Cure of them.* 2d ed. London: J. Clarke, 1746.

Franklin, Benjamin. *Franklin's Way to Wealth; or, Poor Richard Improved.* London: W. Darton, 1814.

The Friends; or, the History of Billy Freeman and Tommy Truelove. London: J. Marshall, c. 1790, n.d.

Genlis, Stéphanie Félicité, Madame de (Comtesses de). *La Bruyère the Less: or, Characters and Manners of the Children of the Present Age.* London: T. N. Longman, 1800.

Gisborne, Thomas. *An Enquiry into the Duties of the Female Sex.* London: n.p., 1797.

Godwin, William. *The Enquirer; Reflections on Education, Manners, and Literature.* London: G. G. and J. Robinson, 1797.

Hamilton, Alexander. *A Treatise of Midwifery, Comprehending the Management of Female Complaints and the Treatment of Children in Early Infancy.* London: J. Murray, 1781.

The History of Jack and the Giants, The First Part. N.p.: J. Eddoes, n.d.

The History of Little Goody Two-Shoes, Otherwise Called Mrs. Margery Two-Shoes. London: J. Newbery, 1766.

The History of Master Billy Friendly, and his Sister, Miss Polly Friendly. London: J. Marshall, c. 1787, n.d.

The History of Tommy Sugar Plumb, and his Golden Book. Gloucester: John Pytt, c. 1773, n.d.

The History of Young Edwin and Little Jessy. London: E. Newbery, 1799.

The Horse's Levee, or the Court of Pegasus. London: J. Harris, 1808.

Hume, A. *Every Woman Her Own Physician; or, the lady's Medical Assistant. Containing the History and Cure of the Various Diseases Incident to Women and Children.* London: Richardson and Urquhart, 1776.

The Important Pocket Book, or the Valentine's Ledger. London: J. Newbery, c.1765, n.d.

Johnson, Richard. *The Adventures of a Silver Penny. Including many Secret Anecdotes of Little Misses and Masters both Good and Naughty.* London: E. Newbery, c. 1787, n.d.

————. [Michael Angelo]. *Juvenile Sports and Pastimes. To which are Prefixed, Memoirs of the Author: Including a New Mode of Infant Education.* London: T. Carnan, 1780.

————. *Juvenile Trials, for Robbing Orchards, Telling Fibs, and Other Heinous Offences.* London: T. Carnan, 1786.

————. *The Toy-Shop; or, Sentimental Preceptor; Containing some Choice Trifles, for the Amusement of Every Little Miss and Master.* London: E. Newbery, c. 1787, n.d.

John-the-Giant-Killer. *Food for the Mind: or, a New Riddle-Book.* London: T. Carnan, 1787.

[Jones, Stephen]. *The Natural History of Beasts.* 4 vols. London: E. Newbery, 1798.

The Juvenile Cabinet of Amusements; Consisting of Pleasing Fairy Tales. Gainsborough: Mozley and Co., 1795.

Juvenile Dialogues; or, Entertaining Conversations Designed for the Improvement of Youth. London: J. Marshall, c. 1799, n.d.

Kilner, Dorothy. *The Doll's Spelling Book.* London: J. Marshall, 1802.

_____. *The Good Child's Delight; or, the Road to Knowledge in Short Entertaining Lessons of One or Two Syllables.* London: J. Marshall, [1785?].

_____. *Little Stories for Little Folks, in Easy Lessons of One, Two, and Three Syllables.* London: J. Marshall, c. 1785, n.d.

_____. *Poems on Various Subjects, for the Amusement of Youth.* London: J. Marshall, c. 1787, n.d.

_____. *The Rational Brutes; or, Talking Animals.* London: J. Harris, 1803.

_____. *The Village School; or, a Collection of Entertaining Histories, for the Instruction and Amusement of all Good Children.* 2 vols. London: J. Marshall, c. 1795, n.d.

Kilner, Mary Ann. *The Adventures of a Pin-Cushion, Designed Chiefly for the Use of Young Ladies.* 2 vols. London: J. Marshall, c. 1780, n.d.

_____. *Memoirs of a Peg-Top.* London: J. Marshall, c. 1790, n.d.

Kruger, John Gottlob [Johann Gottlieb Krueger]. *An Essay on the Education of Children.* London: J. Dodsley, 1765.

Lamb, Charles. *The Life, Letters, and Writings of Charles Lamb.* 6 vols. Edited by Percy Fitzgerald. 1876. Reprint, Freeport, N.Y.: Books for Libraries, 1971.

Lancaster, Joseph. *Improvements in Education, as it respects the industrious classes of the community.* London: n.p., 1803.

Leake, John. *A Lecture Introductory to the Theory and Practice of Midwifery.* 1773. 3rd ed. London: R. Baldwin, 1776.

_____. *Syllabus or General Head of a Course of Lectures on the Theory and Practice of Midwifery: Including the Nature and Treatment of Diseases Incident to Women and Children.* London: J. Murray, 1787.

The Life and Death of Robin Hood, the Renowned Outlaw. And the Famous Exploits Performed by Him and Little John. Glasgow: n.p., n.d.

A Little Pretty Pocket Book. London: J. Newbery, 1744.

Locke, John. *Some Thoughts Concerning Education.* Edited by John W. and Jean S. Yolton. 1693. Reprint, Oxford: Clarendon Press, 1989.

_____. *Two Treatises of Government.* Edited by Peter Laslett. 1960. Reprint, Cambridge: Cambridge University Press, 1990.

[Long, James?]. *An Enquiry into the Origins of the Human Appetites and Affections, Shewing how each Arises from Association, with an Account of the Entrance of Moral Evil into the World. Four Early Works on Motivation.* Edited by Paul McReynolds. 1757. Reprint, Gainsville, Fla.: Scholars Facsimile and Reprints, 1969.

Macaulay, Catharine. *Letters on Education; With Observations on Religious and Metaphysical Subjects.* 1790. Reprint, London & New York: Garland Publishing, 1974.

Malkin, Benjamin Heath. *A Father's Memoirs of His Child.* London: Longman, Rees, Hurst, and Orme, 1806.

Memoirs of Dick the Little Pony. London: J. Walker, 1800.

Mental Amusements. London: G. Sael, 1797.

The Minor's Pocket Book for the Year 1791. London: W. Darton, [1790?].

Moore, J. Hamilton, ed. *The Young Gentlemen and Ladies Monitor.* London: J. H. Moore, c. 1772, n.d.

Moss, William. *An Essay on the Management, Nursing, and Disease of Children, From the Birth: and on the Treatment and Diseases of Pregnant and Lying in Women: with Remarks on the Domestic Practice of Medicine.* 3rd ed. Egham: C. Boult, 1800.

Mother Chit-Chat's Curious Tales and Puzzles; or, Master and Miss's Entertaining Companion. 8th ed. Newcastle: S. Hodgson, 1798.

Mother Shipton's Legacy. York: Wilson, Spence and Mawman, 1797.

Nelson, James. *An Essay on the Government of Children Under Three General Heads: Viz. Health, Manners and Education.* London: R. and J. Dodsley, 1753.

Nurse Dandlem's Little Repository of Great Instruction for all who Would be Good and Noble. London: J. Marshall, c. 1784, n.d.

Percival, Thomas. *A Father's Instructions to His Children.* London: n.p., 1775.

Pilkington, Mary. *Tales of the Cottage; or, Stories, Moral and Amusing, for Young Persons.* London: Vernor and Hood, 1799.

Pole, Thomas. *A Syllabus of a Course of Lectures on the Theory and Practice of Midwifery, Including the Diseases of Women and Children.* London: Stephen Couchman, 1797.

The Polite Academy. 4th ed. London: R. Baldwin, 1768.

Priestley, Joseph. *An Appeal to the Public, on the Subject of the Riots in Birmingham.* Birmingham: n.p., 1791.

_____. *An Essay on the First Principles of Government; and the Nature of Political, Civil, and Religious Liberty.* London: J. Johnson, 1768.

_____. *Hartley's Theory of the Human Mind, On the Principle of the Association of Ideas.* London: J. Johnson, 1775.

_____. *Miscellaneous Observations Relating to Education.* London: R. Crutwell, 1778.

Rousseau, Jean-Jacques. *Emile; or, On Education.* Translated with an introduction by Alan Bloom. 1762. Reprint, New York: Basic Books, 1979.

Salzmann, C. G. *Elements of Morality, for the Use of Children, with, an Introductory Address to Parents.* Translated by Mary Wollstonecraft. In *The Works of Mary Wollstonecraft Vol. 2.* Edited by Janet Todd and Marilyn Butler. London: William Pickering, 1989.

Scenes for Children. London: J. Marshall, c. 1790, n.d.

[Smythies, Miss]. *The History of a Pin.* London: E. Newbery, 1798.

Strüve, Christian Augustus. *A Familiar View of the Domestic Education of Children During the Early Period of their Lives.* London: Murray and Highley, 1802.

Taylor, Ann, and Jane Taylor. *Original Poems, for Infant Minds. By Several Young Persons.* 2 vols. London: Darton and Harvey, 1804.

_____. *Rhymes for the Nursery.* London: Darton and Harvey, 1806.

Trimmer, Sarah. *The Charity School Spelling Book, Part I.* 11th ed. London: F. C. and J. Rivington, 1808.

_____. *An Easy Introduction to the Knowledge of Nature, and Reading the Holy Scriptures.* London: printed for the author, 1780.

_____. *The Œconomy of Charity; or, an Address to Ladies Concerning Sunday-Schools; the Establishment of Schools of Industry Under Female Inspection.* London: J. Johnson, 1787.

_____. *Fabulous Histories; Designed for the Instruction of Children, Respecting their Treatment of Animals.* 1786. Reprint, New York: Garland Publishing, 1977.

————. *A Selection from Mrs. Trimmer's Instructive Tales.* London: F. C. and J. Rivington, 1815.

Trimmer, Sarah, ed. *The Guardian of Education.* 5 vols. London: J. Johnson, 1801–1805.

[Trimmer, Sarah?]. *The Silver Thimble.* London: E. Newbery, c. 1800, n.d.

The Twelfth Day-Gift: or, the Grand Exhibition, 2nd ed. London: Carnan and Newbery, 1770.

Underwood, Michael. *A Treatise on the Disorders of Childhood, and the Management of Infants from the Birth; Adapted to Domestic Use.* 3 vols. London: J. Matthews, 1797.

The Universal Conjuror; or, the Whole Art of Legerdemain. London: M. Bassan, c. 1793, n.d.

Wakefield, Priscilla. *Domestic Recreation; or, Dialogues Illustrative of Natural and Scientific Subjects.* London: Darton and Harvey, 1805.

————. *An Introduction to Botany, in a Series of Familiar Letters.* London: E. Newbery, 1796.

————. *Juvenile Anecdotes, Founded on Facts.* London: Darton and Harvey, 1798.

————. *Mental Improvements: or the Beauties and Wonders of Nature and Art.* 2 vols. 2nd ed. London: Darton and Harvey, 1795.

————. *Reflections on the Present Condition of the Female Sex; with Suggestions for its Improvement.* London: J. Johnson, 1798.

Watts, Isaac. *The Improvement of the Mind; or, A Supplement to the Art of Logick.* 1741. 5th ed. London: J. Buckland and T. Longman, 1768.

Williams, David. *Lectures on Education.* 4 vols. London: J. Bell, 1789.

The Wisdom of Crop the Conjuror. London: J. Marshall, c. 1785, n.d.

Wiseman, Mary. *A Letter from a Lady to her Daughter, on the Manner of Passing Sunday Rationally and Agreeably.* London: J. Marshall, 1788.

Wollstonecraft, Mary. *Original Stories from Real Life.* 1791. *The Works of Mary Wollstonecraft Vol. 4.* Edited by Janet Todd and Marilyn Butler. London: William Pickering, 1989.

_____. *Thoughts on the Education of Daughters*. 1787. *The Works of Mary Wollstonecraft Vol. 4*. Edited by Janet Todd and Marilyn Butler. London: William Pickering, 1989.

_____. *A Vindication of the Rights of Woman*. Edited with an introduction by Miriam Brody. 1792. Reprint, London: Penguin Books, 1992.

Wordsworth, William. *Wordsworth: Poetical Works*. Edited by Thomas Hutchinson. Oxford: Oxford University Press, 1969.

Youthful Sports. London: Darton & Harvey, 1801.

Secondary Sources

Althusser, Louis. *Lenin and Philosophy and Other Essays*. Translated by Ben Brewster. London: New Left Books, 1971.

Ariès, Philippe. *Centuries of Childhood: A Social History of Family Life*. Translated by Robert Baltick. New York: Vintage Books, 1962.

Armstrong, Nancy. "The Rise of the Domestic Woman." In *The Ideology of Conduct: Essays on Literature and the History of Sexuality*. Edited by Nancy Armstrong and Leonard Tennenhouse. New York: Methuen, 1987.

Avery, Gillian. *Childhood's Pattern: A Study of the Heroes and Heroines of Children's Fiction: 1770–1950*. London: Hodder and Stoughton, 1975.

Becker, Marvin B. *The Emergence of Civil Society in the Eighteenth Century*. Bloomington and Indianapolis: Indiana University Press, 1994.

Belcham, John. *Industrialization and the Working Class: The English Experience, 1750–1900*. Brookfield, Vt: Gower Pub., 1990.

Blumenberg, Hans. *Work on Myth*. Translated by Robert M. Wallace. Cambridge, Mass: MIT Press, 1985.

Briggs, Asa. *The Collected Essays of Asa Briggs, Vol. 1: Words, Numbers, Places, People*. Brighton: Harvester Press, 1985.

_____. *A Social History of England*. 1983. Reprint, Penguin Books, 1987.

Brown, Richard, ed. *A History of Accounting and Accountants*. 1905. *Reprints of Economic Classics*. New York: Augusta M. Kelley, 1971.

Bynum, W. F. "The Nervous Patient in Eighteenth- and Nineteenth-Century Britain: The Psychiatric Origins of British Neurology." In *The Anatomy of Madness:*

Essays in the History of Psychiatry, Vol. I, People and Ideas. Edited by W. F. Bynum, Roy Porter, and Michael Shepherd. London and New York: Tavistock Publications, 1985. 89–102.

Clark, J. C. D. *English Society, 1688–1832: Ideology, Social Structure, and Political Practices During the Ancien Regime.* Cambridge: Cambridge University Press, 1985.

Coveney, Peter. *The Image of Childhood: The Individual in Society; a Study of the Theme in English Literature.* Baltimore: Penguin Books, 1967.

David, Linda. *Children's Books Published by William Darton and his Sons.* Indiana University: Lilly Library, 1992.

Davidoff, Leonore, and Catherine Hall. *Family Fortunes: Men and Women of the English Middle Class, 1780–1850.* London: Hutchinson, 1987.

DeMause, Lloyd, ed. *The History of Childhood.* New York: Psychohistory Press, 1974.

Demers, Patricia. *Heaven Upon Earth: the Form of Moral Children's Literature to 1850.* Knoxville Tenn.: University of Tennessee Press, 1993.

Demers, Patricia, and Gordon Moyles. *From Instruction to Delight: an Anthology of Children's Literature to 1850.* Toronto: Oxford University Press, 1982.

The Dictionary of National Biography Vol. II, Beal-Browell. London: Smith, Elder and Co., 1908.

Eagleton, Terry. *Ideology: An Introduction.* London: Verso, 1991.

Earle, Peter. *The Making of the English Middle Class: Business, Society and Family Life in London, 1660–1730.* Berkeley and Los Angeles: University of California Press, 1989.

Feather, John. *The Provincial Book Trade in Eighteenth-Century England.* Cambridge: Cambridge University Press, 1985.

Foucault, Michel. *The Archaeology of Knowledge.* 1969. Translated by A. M. Sheridan Smith. London and New York: Tavistock Publications, 1972.

———. *The Birth of the Clinic: An Archaeology of Medical Perception.* 1973. Translated by A. M. Sheridan Smith. New York: Vintage Books, 1994.

———. *Discipline and Punish: The Birth of the Prison.* Translated by Alan Sheridan. New York: Pantheon Books, 1977.

_____. *The Order of Things: An Archaeology of the Human Sciences.* 1966. Edited and translated by R. D. Laing. New York: Vintage Books, 1970.

_____. "The Politics of Health in the Eighteenth Century." *Power/Knowledge: Selected Interviews and Other Writings.* Edited and translated by Colin Gordon. New York: Pantheon Books, 1980.

Fox, Christopher W. *Psychology and Literature in the Eighteenth Century.* New York: AMS Press, 1987.

Golby, J. M. and A. W. Purdue. *The Civilization of the Crowd. Popular Culture in England 1750–1900.* London: Batsford, 1984.

Hardyment, Christina. *Dream Babies: Child Care from Locke to Spock.* London: Jonathan Cape, 1983.

Harley, David. "Honour and Propriety: the Structure of Professional Disputes in Eighteenth-Century Medicine." In *The Medical Enlightenment of the Eighteenth Century.* Edited by Andrew Cunningham and Roger French. Cambridge: Cambridge University Press, 1990. 138–164.

Hay, Douglas, and Nicholas Rogers. *Eighteenth-Century English Society.* Oxford: Oxford University Press, 1997.

Hickey, Alison. "Dark Characters, Native Grounds: Wordsworth's Imagination of Imperialism." In *Romanticism, Race, and Imperial Culture, 1780–1834.* Edited by Alan Richardson and Sonia Hofkosh. Bloomington and Indianapolis: Indiana University Press, 1996. 283–310.

Hill, Bridget. *Servants: English Domestics in the Eighteenth Century.* Oxford: Clarendon Press, 1996.

Hunter, Richard Alfred, and Ida MacAlpine, eds. *Three Hundred Years of Psychiatry 1535–1860: A History Presented in Selected English Texts.* Hartsdale, N.Y.: Carlisle Pub., 1982.

Jackson, Mary V. *Engines of Instruction, Mischief, and Magic: Children's Literature in England from its Beginnings to 1839.* Lincoln: University of Nebraska Press, 1989.

Jordanova, Ludmilla. "Children in History: Concepts of Nature and Society." In *Children, Parents and Politics.* Edited by Geoffrey Scarre. Cambridge: Cambridge University Press, 1989. 3–24.

_____. "Conceptualizing Childhood in the Eighteenth Century: The Problem of Child Labour," *British Journal of Eighteenth-Century Studies* 10 (1987a): 189–99.

————. "New Worlds for Children in the Eighteenth Century: Problems of Historical Interpretation," *History of the Human Sciences* 3.1 (1990): 69–83.

————. "The Popularization of Medicine: Tissot on Onanism." *Textual Practices* 1.1 (1987b): 68–79.

Kelly, Gary. "Class, Gender, Nation, and Empire: Money and Merit in the Writing of the Edgeworths." *The Wordsworth Circle* 25.2 (1994): 89–93.

————. "Revolution, Reaction, and the Expropriation of Popular Culture: Hannah More's *Cheap Repository.*" *Man and Nature/L' Homme et la Nature* 6 (1987): 147–59.

Kramnick, Isaac. *The Age of Ideology: Political Thought, 1750 to the Present.* 1964. New Jersey: Prentice Hall, 1979.

————. "Children's Literature and Bourgeois Ideology: Observations on Culture and Industrial Capitalism in the Later Eighteenth-Century." *Studies in Eighteenth-Century Culture* 12 (1983): 11–44.

————. *Republican & Bourgeois Radicalism: Political Ideology in Late Eighteenth-Century England and America.* Ithaca: Cornell University Press, 1990.

Lovell, Terry. "Subjective power? Consumption, the reading public, and domestic woman in early eighteenth-century England." In *The Consumption of Culture 1600–1800: Image, Object, Text.* Edited by Ann Bermingham and J. Brewer. New York: Routledge, 1997. 23–41.

Mitchell, Orm. "Blake's Subversive Illustrations for Wollstonecraft's *Stories.*" *Mosaic* 17.4 (1984): 17–34.

Muir, Percy. *English Children's Books 1600–1900.* London: B. T. Batsford, 1954.

Myers, Mitzi. "Reform or Ruin: 'A Revolution in Female Manners.' " *Studies in Eighteenth-Century Culture* 11 (1982): 199–216.

————. "'Servants as They are Now Educated': Women Writers and Georgian Pedagogy." *Essays in Literature* 16.1 (1989): 51–69.

Neuberg, Victor E. *The Penny Histories: A Study of Chapbooks for Young Readers Over Two Centuries.* Oxford: Oxford University Press, 1968.

Pederson, Susan. "Hannah More Meets Simple Simon: Tracts, Chapbooks, and Popular Culture in Late Eighteenth-Century England." *Journal of British Studies* 25.1 (1986): 84–113.

Pickering, Samuel F. Jr. *Moral Instruction and Fiction for Children, 1749–1820.* Athens: University of Georgia Press, 1993.

_____. *John Locke and Children's Books in Eighteenth Century England.* Knoxville, Tenn.: University of Tennessee Press, 1981.

Plumb, J. H. "The New World of Children in Eighteenth-Century England." In *The Birth of a Consumer Society: The Commercialization of Eighteenth-Century England.* Edited by J. Brewer, N. McKendrick, and J. H. Plumb. London: Europa Pub., 1982. 286–315.

Porter, Dorothy, and Roy Porter. *Patient's Progress: Doctors and Doctoring in Eighteenth-Century England.* Cambridge: Polity Press, 1989.

Porter, Roy. *English Society in the Eighteenth Century.* 1982. London: Penguin Books, 1990.

_____. *Health for Sale: Quackery in England 1660–1850.* Mancheter University Press, 1989.

_____. "Spreading Medical Enlightenment: The Popularization of Medicine in Georgian England and its Paradoxes." In *The Popularization of Medicine 1650–1850.* Edited by Roy Porter. London: Routledge, 1992. 215–31.

Postman, Neil. *The Disappearance of Childhood.* New York: Delacorte Press, 1982.

Richardson, Alan. *Literature, Education, and Romanticism: Reading as Social Practice, 1780–1832.* Cambridge: Cambridge University Press, 1994.

_____. "Mary Wollstonecraft on Education." In *The Cambridge Companion to Mary Wollstonecraft.* Edited by Claudia Johnson. Cambridge: Cambridge University Press, 2002. 24–41.

_____. "Wordsworth, Fairy Tales, and the Politics of Children's Reading." In *Romanticism and Children's Literature in Nineteenth-Century England.* Edited by James Holt McGovern. Athens: University of Georgia Press, 1991. 34–55.

Roscoe, S. *John Newbery and His Successors: A Bibliography,* Wormley: Five Owls Press, 1973.

Shefrin, Jill, ed. *Ingenious Contrivances: Table Games and Puzzles for Children.* Toronto: Toronto Public Library, 1996.

Shteir, Ann B. *Cultivating Women, Cultivating Science: Flora's Daughters and Botany in England, 1760 to 1860.* Baltimore and London: Johns Hopkins University Press, 1996.

Smith, Ginnie. "Prescribing the Rules of Health: Self-Help and Advice in the Late Eighteenth Century." In *Patients and Practitioners: Lay Perceptions of Medicine in Pre-Industrial Society.* Edited by Roy Porter. Cambridge: Cambridge University Press, 1985. 249–82.

Solecki, Sam. "Ideology." In *Encyclopedia of Contemporary Literary Theory: Approaches, Scholars, Terms.* Edited by Irena R. Makaryk. Toronto: University of Toronto Press, 1993. 558–60.

Stewart, Christina Duff. *The Taylors of Ongar: an Analytical Bio-Bibliography.* 2 vols. New York: Garland Publishing, 1975.

Summerfield, Geoffrey. *Fantasy and Reason: Children's Literature in the Eighteenth Century.* London: Methuen, 1984.

Tarr, Laszlo. *The History of the Carriage.* Translated by Elisabeth Hoch. London: Vision Press, 1969.

Thompson, E. P. "Eighteenth-Century English Society: Class Struggle Without Class?" *Social History* 3.2 (1978): 133–65.

Townsend, John Rowe. *John Newbery and his Books: Trade and Plumb-Cakes For Ever, Huzza!* Metuchen, N.J.: Scarecrow Press, 1994.

Watt, Ian. *The Rise of the Novel: Studies in Defoe, Richardson, and Fielding.* Berkeley and Los Angeles: University of California Press, 1957.

Weiss, Harry B. *A Book about Chapbooks: the People's Literature of Bygone Times.* 1942. Hatboro, Penn.: Folklore Associates, 1969.

Williams, Raymond. *Keywords: A Vocabulary of Culture and Society.* 1976. London: Fontana Press, 1988.

———. *Marxism and Literature.* Oxford: Oxford University Press, 1977.

———. *Problems in Materialism and Culture.* London: Verso Editions, 1980.

Yolton, John W. *Thinking Matter: Materialism in Eighteenth-Century Britain.* Minneapolis: University of Minnesota Press, 1983.

Board Games

The Game of Chance, or Harlequin Takes All. London: Laurie and Whittle, 1794.

The New Game of Human Life. London: E. Newbery and John Wallis, 1790.

The Royal Genealogical Pastime of the Sovereigns of England. London: E. Newbery and John Wallis, 1791.

The Royal Passtime of Cupid, or the New and Most Pleasant Game of the Snake. London: W. Dicey, c. 1750, n.d.

Wallis's Tour Through England and Wales, a New Geographical Pastime. London: John Wallis, 1794.

Index

Children's Literature and Culture
Jack Zipes, *Series Editor*

WAYS OF BEING MALE
Representing Masculinities in Children's Literature and Film
by John Stephens

PINOCCHIO GOES POSTMODERN
Perils of a Puppet in the United States
by Richard Wunderlich and Thomas J. Morrissey

THE PRESENCE OF THE PAST
Memory, Heritage, and Childhood in Postwar Britain
by Valerie Krips

THE FEMININE SUBJECT IN CHILDREN'S LITERATURE
by Christine Wilkie-Stibbs

RECYCLING RED RIDING HOOD
by Sandra Beckett

THE POETICS OF CHILDHOOD
by Roni Natov

REIMAGINING SHAKESPEARE FOR CHILDREN AND YOUNG ADULTS
edited by Naomi J. Miller

REPRESENTING THE HOLOCAUST IN YOUTH LITERATURE
by Lydia Kokkola

BEATRIX POTTER
Writing in Code
by M. Daphne Kutzer

UTOPIAN AND DYSTOPIAN WRITING FOR CHILDREN AND YOUNG ADULTS
edited by Carrie Hintz and Elaine Ostry

THE MAKING OF THE MODERN CHILD
Children's Literature and Childhood in the Late Eighteenth Century
by Andrew O'Malley